Morris as Elvis

Morris as Elvis:
The Fifties

Morris as **E**lvis

Take a Chance on Life

by

Morris Bates

The World's Greatest Elvis Impersonator

and

Jim Brown

F O X
M U S I C
B O O K S

Dedicated to:
Phyllis Bates
Brittany Lee Bates
&
Alma Cunningham

ISBN-10 1-894997-15-8
ISBN-13 978-1-894997-15-7

Edited by Bob Hilderley.
Design and type by Laura Brady based on a concept of Gord Robertson.
Front cover Native totem and Vegas sign concept by Dennis Compo.
Back cover native power board painting by Stephen Gibbons-Barrett.
Printed and bound in China by Everbest Printing Co. Ltd.

Published by Fox Music Books, a division of Quarry Press Inc, PO Box 1061,
Kingston, Ontario K7L 4Y5 Canada www.quarrypress.com.

Contents

Morris as Elvis: The Sixties

Foreword

Elvis Presley inspired a lot of young people. I was one of them. I grew up on the Sugar Cane Reservation at Williams Lake in British Columbia, and when I was in high school I watched the *NBC-TV Comeback Special* that Elvis made in 1968. There was a resemblance — I did look quite a bit like Elvis.

At the time, I was a bass player in a teenage band and resolved to make music my life. I worked and worked at it — and I studied Elvis. In 1970, I watched *Elvis: That's the Way It Is*, the movie he made about putting his band together. I studied how he rehearsed his band and created the celebrated show that people flocked to night after night in the big showroom at the Hilton International in Las Vegas. Little did I know at the time that I would play the Vegas casino circuit for 10 years with my *Morris as Elvis* show after the King died.

I worked really hard at becoming an entertainer, not just a singer and a bass player. I put together my first stage show and began performing a graffiti music set, which was a tribute to fifties rock and roll. People liked the fifties music, but they went wild when I did Elvis songs, so I designed a show called "The Graffiti Band of Gold Presents a Tribute to Elvis," and I kept on performing it all over western Canada.

After Elvis died, I was asked to come to Las Vegas to do

my tribute. People in Vegas liked it and paid me a lot of money to do my Elvis Presley Story show. I also paid tribute to the King in faraway places, taking my show to Taiwan, Hong Kong, Singapore, Indonesia, Malaysia, Thailand, Japan, Brazil, and South Africa. I performed my Elvis tribute show for 15 years — 10 years in Vegas.

There is nothing you can't do if you put your mind to it, and you work really, really hard.

I had some really good bands in those days, and some of the musicians were with me on and off through everything that went down. We were all just young kids, and we believed we could do anything. We had a dream.

I never knew we could go all the way to Honolulu, Tokyo, and Las Vegas, but we got it done.

Elvis unleashed female sexuality. He was unique. He was the greatest. He had perfect pitch, he had magnetism, he had power, and he knew it — he knew he was one of the most popular men in the entire world. When he made his comeback TV special after starring in all those popcorn movies, all of a sudden he had this rawness, this raunchiness — this sex appeal …whatever you want to call it — charisma. When he went back to Vegas and began touring again, he performed so well and handled everything so gracefully. Toward the end, he would go on stage and sing *An American Trilogy* like he was representing the United States to the whole world. He became a very special performer. Everything fit together like a jigsaw puzzle. It was like a play … and he played his part perfectly.

Elvis had a dream. He took a chance on life. He was just a poor truck driver in Memphis when he recorded some songs for his mother and got on the radio with his first hits. Then he performed on the Dorsey Brothers, Milton Berle, and Ed Sullivan shows. Soon, everybody on the planet knew who he was. His music took him all the way to Hollywood, where he starred in 33 movies. Elvis became the King, and he inspired many poor boys, like me, to believe that we could do more than anyone imagined.

I was inspired by Elvis to take a chance on life. And once I got going, I never looked back. I just kept going and going. Now that my performing career has drawn to a close, I have tried to bring the same energy and commitment to my work as a native youth counselor on the streets of downtown eastside Vancouver, and I have put this book and a companion film together because I want to inspire young people today to do the same. There are a lot of kids out there who might think they can't be stars or do something with their talent that will lead to something great.

There is nothing you can't do if you put your mind to it, and you work really, really hard. Believe me, you can do it. You can do great things, but you won't get anywhere or do anything, if you don't get started now, and, like Elvis, take a chance on life.

— MORRIS BATES

Morris as Elvis:
The Seventies

The King Is Dead ...
Long Live the King!

Showtime

The house lights dim. All we can see on the showroom stage is an ebony Gibson Dove sitting there on a guitar stand in a pool of soft blue light. The band begins a furious fanfare, bright strobe lights flash, and a spotlight searches the set looking for the star of the show to emerge from the wings — there he is, starting to sing *That's All Right (Mama)*. He looks like a young Elvis — explosive energy, dark charisma and a sexual sneer that drove teenagers and their parents crazy back in the fifties, though for opposing reasons.

This can't be the King, though. It's the summer of 1980 and Elvis passed away at Graceland three years ago in August 1977, but this young entertainer has got the groove and he's making all the right moves. He's dressed in a pink jacket, black shirt, black pants, and white shoes. He's pumped.

"Welcome ladies and gentlemen to the first show," he intones in the King's sultry voice. "We're going to get things started with the very first song that Elvis Presley recorded for RCA Victor, January 10th, 1956..."

"Well, since my baby left me..."

His rendition of *Heartbreak Hotel* sends shivers up and down the spine. He tells us a little Elvis history, narrating

11

above a throbbing *Don't Be Cruel* bass line, and then he's off at a breakneck clip singing *Hound Dog*.

As he relaxes into the haunting strains of *I Want You, I Need You, I Love You*, the horn players come out front, dressed like the Jordanaires in plaid jackets, to add the familiar vocal harmonies the Jordanaires sang on the King's hit records. He sings *Love Me Tender* that has all the women in the crowd swooning. While the band plays on, he ventures into the audience and stops at tables here and there during this traditional Vegas "walkabout," but nevertheless manages to regain the stage right on cue to sing a final verse and chorus.

> All 780 of us packed into the Empire Showroom at the Landmark casino collectively suspend our disbelief, and, to all of us, for the moment, this is the King – even though the casino marquee reads "Morris as Elvis."

All 780 of us packed into the Empire Showroom at the Landmark casino collectively suspend our disbelief, and, to all of us, for the moment, this is the King – even though the casino marquee reads "Morris as Elvis." Yes, this is, after all, Morris Bates performing, not Elvis Presley.

Still, it's a great show, superbly paced, a production that Nevada critics have reported to be the best Elvis tribute act to play the Strip, since Presley's death. Morris appears to be exceedingly comfortable paying tribute to the King of Rock & Roll. He's been at it for seven years now and has packed showrooms in Canada, Japan, Hong Kong, Indonesia, South Africa, and Hawaii. He was held over for a three-week stint at "Le Boom Boom Club" in Honolulu, and has recently completed a two-year engagement here in Vegas at the Silver Slipper Casino.

Before moving to the bigger, more prestigious Empire Room at the Landmark, across the Strip and a patch of desert from the Hilton International where Elvis performed more than 800 shows, Morris acquired Presley's band arrangements for his musicians. So even though the rhythm section of his 15-piece band is not James Burton, Jerry Scheff, and Ronnie Tutt, they sound a lot like the King's TCB band.

Bandleader, lead guitarist and master of ceremonies, David Maitland, delivers Scotty Moore's signature guitar licks and

Burton's trademark solos with effortless grace. Drummer Nardo Lee and bass player Kenny Nelsen look so much like Tutt and Scheff that people are whispering to each other that Morris must be using the King's band tonight. They are indeed a tight unit behind their "young Elvis," as he ends the fifties segment of his show with *(Now and Then There's) A Fool Such As I* and *Jailhouse Rock*.

As Morris leaves the stage, David Maitland begins to introduce band members and backup singers, amusing us with a line of patter while his mates deliver classy instrumental solos played to a pulsing jazz rhythm.

All the lights go out and Morris reappears, his slicked-back pompadour combed into a relaxed, sixties style. The spotlight widens, and as he launches into *Trouble*, we can see that he's dressed in black leather and looking like the Elvis we all remember from the King's 1968 *NBC-TV Comeback Special*. He's happy now, big smiles on his face, and the hits keep coming — *Love Me, A Big Hunk O' Love, Are You Lonesome Tonight*, a rollicking *Lawdy Miss Clawdy*, and a raunchy *One Night*. The band is incredibly tight, punctuating Morris's gyrations, his dramatic pauses and flourishes, as he drag-phrases his way through trademark arrangements to classic endings, and the sixties section of the show closes with Morris singing *If I Can Dream*.

When the curtain is raised again, the band begins the fanfare theme from *2001: A Space Odyssey* and we have the full production of Elvis Presley's seventies show. Our Vegas Elvis appears dressed in the familiar white, high-collared, rhinestone-studded American eagle suit. His chest bared, he comes straight at us from the top of a white staircase, and, as he descends, the interactive stairs light up, each one pulsing with a newly assigned color. Morris belts out *C.C. Rider* before slowing things down with *In The Ghetto* and revs up the tempo again with Tony Joe White's *Polk Salad Annie*. *The Wonder Of You* is followed by a driving rock & roll medley: *Johnny B. Goode, Long Tall Sally, Whole Lotta Shakin' Goin' On*,

The spotlight widens, and as he launches into *Trouble*, we can see that he's dressed in black leather and looking like the Elvis we all remember from the King's 1968 *NBC-TV Comeback Special*.

and *Proud Mary* with Morris recreating Presley's TCB arrangements and running through the key changes as his band is "rollin' on the river . . ." Morris strikes the same martial-arts inspired poses that the King used in his Vegas shows. For 25 more glorious minutes, Morris *is* Elvis.

The show goes on — *Suspicious Minds, My Way, Viva Las Vegas*, and *An American Trilogy*. Preparations for the move from the Slipper to the Landmark are rumored to have cost Morris more than $50,000. The set with interactive white stairs completes an illusion that is as much a theater production as a rock & roll show. Fog machines provide the illusion that Morris is emerging from the clouds as he spreads his cape and displays the full image of the American eagle, and the audience gasps in appreciation of this spectacle.

As the house lights come up, we are saddened and yet strangely, illusively, buoyant — the King is dead — long live the King!

We are in the home stretch now as Morris croons *Can't Help Falling In Love* and "scarves" his audience, smiling serenely as women and young girls rush the stage and reach out, hoping for a souvenir scarf or perhaps even a brief kiss on the lips. As the house lights come up, we are saddened and yet strangely, illusively, buoyant — the King is dead — long live the King!

Morris has legions of fans that come to Vegas and to his show every night during their weeklong holidays, and they'll likely be back next year eager to bask in his presence again. That's why they've been paying this Shuswap Indian from Williams Lake, British Columbia, as much as $40,000 a week here at the Landmark. After all, Morris Bates is the number one Elvis impersonator of all time.

Elvis Lives

By the time most of us learned that Elvis Presley had passed away on August 16, 1977, singers performing Elvis tributes were already in high demand. Las Vegas booking agents were making frantic calls trying to locate Elvis look-a-likes to fill the void that his sudden departure had created, but Morris Bates, the first and the best of the professional Elvis tribute artists, was not available.

Bates, a 27-year-old Canadian, was definitely the most qualified to perform a complete tribute show. He had been paying tribute to the King for four years and was already much in demand before Elvis died. On that day in August 1977, Morris and his 15-piece band were in Los Angeles playing the Playgirl Club. Bates' manager, Richard Cheung, received a call from Silver Slipper Casino manager Bill Friedman who wanted to book Morris immediately; however, Richard had to decline their generous offer because the promoters holding an open-ended contract for Morris to perform for six months in the Orient had already called in their option. Thus Morris Bates' arrival at the Silver Slipper Casino was delayed for seven months — he would perform before hundreds of thousands of international fans before he stepped for the first time on a stage in Nevada.

On that day in August 1977, Morris and his 15-piece band were in Los Angeles playing the Playgirl Club.

On August 17, the day after Presley's death, Las Vegas casino managers faced a dilemma. They needed a "live" Elvis, but there were few qualified tribute artists who were not heavily booked, especially overseas where Elvis had never performed during his 23-year career as a recording artist for Sun Records and RCA. So for a short-term fix, promoters were sticking any kid who resembled the King on stage to take advantage of the situation. Before his tragic early death at age 42, Elvis had become a legend in the entertainment capital of the world. And while thousands of mourners gathered outside his Graceland mansion in Memphis, his image loomed over the Las Vegas Strip, like a neon ghost that rose nightly from the glitter of flashing marquees. Tourists came to Vegas to revel in the King's presence — his infamous after-hours parties, his rumored romances with beauty queens, Hollywood starlets, and long-legged chorus line dancers, and the steady stream of celebrities who paid homage in his penthouse suite.

Elvis was so popular that it has been said that management crammed up to 4,000 people into a showroom that usually sat a little over 2,300 for each of his record 850-plus sold-out shows.

The King's passing created a black hole in the entertainment business, into which hundreds of lookalike wannabes were sacrificed in the years that followed his demise.

Maitre d's were said to have palmed tips amounting to thousands of dollars in return for ushering incoming ticket holders to front row seats. The King's passing created a black hole in the entertainment business, into which hundreds of lookalike wannabes were sacrificed in the years that followed his demise.

Morris Bates was devastated. "I'm in shock," he told a reporter who phoned him in Los Angeles from the *Vancouver Sun* daily newspaper offices in Canada. "I still can't believe it. He was the greatest show biz phenomenon ever. When he was alive you could giggle at 'Elvis the Pelvis'. You can laugh about a lot of things when a person is still alive. But it'll be different now. You see, people come to see my act that couldn't get to see the real thing. Now, people will be coming to see what Presley was really like. They are going to want to see Presley, not me doing Presley. The act is going to be pretty heavy."

Many years later Morris told a Las Vegas journalist that "at times I am besieged by women, and I don't understand why. I'm always amazed at the madness. Elvis fans, then and now, are like a cult. They know everything there is to know about Elvis; they watched for his every whisper and hung on every breath that he took. I'm walking in some mighty big footsteps."

"I'm not trying to be Elvis," Morris insisted, and reported that "I can still put on my cutoffs and walk through the shopping mall without people stopping me. But when I'm in costume or when I leave the showroom after a show, people act very differently. They're awestruck. And sometimes they do some crazy things. One man came barging into my dressing room one night demanding a scarf for his wife. It took four guys to get him calmed down. When things like that happen, I just wonder what all Elvis had to go through. I feel that I have the best of both worlds. I can be Elvis for a while and I can go back to being Morris Bates. But Elvis had no choices. He had to hide out in order to get any peace at all."

Morris wasn't the first Elvis tribute artist to play Vegas, but he *was* one of the first, if not the very first, entertainer on the planet to dress up in costume and perform an Elvis tribute, long before the legions of tribute artists and impersonators began multiplying exponentially. His Landmark show was filmed by a BBC-TV crew and used prominently in the director's final cut of the documentary *Elvis Lives* as an example of just how good some tribute shows can be.

> . . . at times I am besieged by women, and I don't understand why. I'm always amazed at the madness. . . I'm walking in some mighty big footsteps.

As the 1980 BBC-TV documentary begins, Morris is featured singing *Trouble*. Later on he is seen again, finishing the song with a flourish, a performance that is followed by an interview clip where Morris tells the BBC-TV audience that "I heard Elvis on the *'68 NBC Special* and I could understand why this man was so powerful. He done it like they were going to take it away from him tomorrow. And it was his comeback and all those years that he'd been makin' movies, and he just done it. He was like a cat in that black leather suit."

Later on in the documentary *Elvis Lives*, Morris explains that he had already begun to make good use of the new technology that was available in 1980 in order to study the King's performances in detail. "I can sit in front of my five-foot TV with a Betamax and I can study it and watch him," he confided. "I can run a thing back and catch a movement. Took me a little trick to get that cape (movement) that he does, when I do a thing when I turn around. So I just run it 15 times till I get the move and practice it. Then I practice it to the point it becomes natural and a part of me so I'm not stumbling on stage. The big TV really helps. I can sit there and watch him blink his eye at a particular moment and the people that are really Elvis fans will know that I studied it. Even to the way he walked. He walked a little pigeon-toed sometimes."

> I can be Elvis for a while and I can go back to being Morris Bates. But Elvis had no choices. He had to hide out in order to get any peace at all.

The documentary continues with Morris now in his eagle suit coming down the white staircase and belting out *C.C. Rider* and several more songs before moving on to more trivia about Elvis fans and fan clubs. As this 1980 film and other documentaries

As this 1980 film and other documentaries spread the gospel according to Elvis, Elvis sightings became second only to UFO sightings, and Colonel Tom Parker's Elvis conventions became a big hit in Vegas.

spread the gospel according to Elvis, Elvis sightings became second only to UFO sightings, and Colonel Tom Parker's Elvis conventions became a big hit in Vegas. A recent BBC-TV documentary film suggests that there are 85,000 Elvis impersonators and no sign of their numbers decreasing in the near future. Former Japanese Prime Minister Junichiro Koizumi is an Elvis impersonator. There is still a market for Beatlemania tributes, ABBA tributes, Hank Williams tributes, and even Patsy Cline tributes, but there aren't thousands of Hank or Patsy or John, Paul, George and Ringo impersonators roaming the planet. Elvis was bigger than life. As long-time Vegas headliner Wayne Newton recently told veteran Vancouver radio and TV personality Red Robinson, "Elvis was the one guy that I've ever seen walk on stage, and when he walked on stage, it was the peak of his act. Not that his act went down from there, but the audience was just so blown away when he walked on stage that it was phenomenal to watch."

Wayne Newton has performed more than 31,000 shows in Vegas, so many that he has become known as "Mr. Las Vegas." Wayne began by playing lounges in Nevada but couldn't break into the showrooms until Jack Benny took a fancy to him when Benny saw a show that he did in Sydney, Australia. After he opened for Benny in Vegas, Newton soon became a headliner. For many years, he built his show around Elvis songs, and, ironically, Elvis had fun at Newton's expense as well. As Morris recalls, "When I saw Elvis live in Spokane, he introduced himself by saying, 'Hi, my name is Wayne Newton.' I didn't understand this joke until several years later when I played Vegas."

Wayne Newton was performing the same Vegas shtick that had worked so well for all of the best entertainers, from Louis Prima, Jack Benny, Frank Sinatra, and Dean Martin on down to Bobby Darin, Paul Anka, and Tom Jones. Elvis had taken that approach to the next level, eclipsing all of his predecessors.

The Press

After completing his tour of the Orient and Hawaii, Morris played the Cave nightclub in Vancouver and Lucifer's in Calgary and Edmonton before flying to Nevada: Seven hundred adoring female fans were at Vancouver International Airport to greet Morris when his flight from Hawaii touched down. His arrival was covered by all of the local TV news shows. Morris signed as many autographs as he could before being whisked away in a limousine, which took him to his West End apartment overlooking Lost Lagoon. Morris had packed the Cave week after week for months at a time before breaking out of Canada and moving on to LA and the world at large, but he would continue to return there whenever his obligations in Vegas and overseas permitted. He was as much a hometown hero in Vancouver as he was in Williams Lake, where he had first played dances on the Sugar Cane Reserve.

This time the press was out in force on opening night. "On stage, Morris does bear an uncanny resemblance to the King," *Vancouver Province* critic Jeannie Read wrote in January 1978, "but it is a resemblance based more on attitude and manner than physical or vocal attributes."

"What sells this show more than anything else," Morris told Jeannie Read, "is the characterization. It's the whole presentation, and how you carry yourself. If you listen to me on tape, I'm not that close. But it does look a lot like Elvis. That first glance at me walking on stage in the fifties section — I've seen some people freak out."

"Nobody has exactly freaked out at the Cave," Read reported, "but crowds of women tend to rush to the lip of the stage during Morris's Elvis-in-Vegas routine, and squeal with excitement if he offers a scarf or a kiss — a pretty impressive testimonial to how convincing the illusion really is."

Other critics have been moved to write their own descriptions

On stage, Morris does bear an uncanny resemblance to the King, but it is a resemblance based more on attitude and manner than physical or vocal attributes.

of Morris as Elvis, few as graphic as Lee Bachus in the *Vancouver Sun*: "He has the looks. The obligatory lip curl. The sleek, black hair that glistens with tiny dewdrops of sweat. The tangled rug of chest hair, those sleepy, puppy-dog eyes, and, of course, the copulatory pelvic thrusts, which, to no one's surprise, evoked loud sighs from the many young ladies in the audience. Close your eyes during *Love Me Tender* and one could imagine the King, his voice deep and tremulous pouring out just one last ballad through your pocket radio."

This is not just another Elvis imitator, Morris has captured all of the excitement and charisma of the late King of Rock & Roll.

Morris Bates' bared chest was subsequently banned by civic censors from his performances at the Cave nightclub in Canada, but when he arrived at the Silver Slipper in the spring of 1978 his "tangled rug of chest hair" was prominently displayed in Nevada, and his "Morris as Elvis" tribute show packed the Gaiety Theater at the Silver Slipper for three shows nightly, just like he had back in Canada and everywhere else he had been since he had begun performing his three-segment tribute in Alberta nightclubs in the mid-seventies. Morris got rave reviews from Nevada journalists, and the word spread rapidly that there was something special about his presentation of the Elvis story. One of his biggest supporters was Silver Slipper president, Bill Friedman. "This is not just another Elvis imitator," Friedman told a *Las Vegas Mirror* reporter. "Morris has captured all of the excitement and charisma of the late King of Rock & Roll."

"Morris is so steeped in the Presley presence," the reporter told his readers, "that he could teach a course on the subject: How to drop the right hand at the wrist. How many fingers to hold the mike with. When to raise the lip and drop the eyelid . . ."

"You've got to sell it in the first part," Morris confided to Jeannie Read. "Elvis is a very dear presence to a lot of people. When I start the show, it's very important that I give the people what they want to remember and hear, and how they want me to look. After that, the people have already decided that if they like me, anything I do is going to be okay by them."

Morris kept a lot of people's memories of the King alive. In fact, aspiring Elvis impersonators often studied his shows to learn what being Elvis was all about.

By October 1979, the first wave of Elvis impersonators had subsided, and for a brief moment, Morris was the only Elvis tribute artist on the Strip. As Lynn Beck described the "Morris as Elvis" show in *The Las Vegas Mirror*, "He *looks* like Elvis Presley. He *is* Morris Bates, and he is bringing his Elvis Presley Story into the showroom of the Slipper. He was one of the first entertainers to capitalize on his dark, good looks and his husky voice long before Presley died in Memphis. And now, two years later, he is also the last."

"To do this," Morris told Lynn Beck, "you have to be a professional — and there were only a few guys who could survive. But for a while there, every time I'd turn around, there'd be somebody in the audience sitting there with sunglasses and taking notes. One guy came in completely decked out in the Elvis suit and he'd sit through three straight shows. I mean, any kid who knew five Elvis songs, had sideburns, dark glasses, and black hair, they'd stick him on the stage and have him do Elvis. Elvis, to me, was a very special man with a very special talent, and he had a very special way to entertain people. So when I do his show, I always try to maintain the class, try to keep the memory intact. It isn't just getting up there and wriggling around and throwing scarves."

You only stay in Vegas for one reason and that's to put people in chairs. If you can't do that, you don't stay here.

Asked why, after all of the other Elvis impersonators who had come and gone, he was still employed at the Slipper, Morris said simply, "You only stay in Vegas for one reason and that's to put people in chairs. If you can't do that, you don't stay here."

Morris Bates played Las Vegas for 10 years and made his own fame and fortune paying tribute to the King at the Slipper, the Landmark, Vegas World, the Union Plaza, and the Nevada Palace. There are said to be tens of thousands of Elvis impersonators, but none as successful as Morris Bates in celebrating the spirit of the King and in putting people in chairs.

Elvis Lives

Viva Las Vegas

C.C. Rider

Roots

Fairy Tale

In the summer of 1949, a strikingly beautiful young Shuswap Indian girl named Lillian from the Sugar Cane Reserve met a handsome Haida man while she was working in a salmon cannery in Port Edward, 15 miles south of Prince Rupert, British Columbia. Their bittersweet summer romance must have had its spiritually uplifting moments because together they conceived a very special human being. However, the union did not lead to marriage, and their son, Morris Bates, was born "out of wedlock" on April 12, 1950 in Vancouver General Hospital.

After giving birth to Morris, Lillian returned to Williams Lake with her baby boy, but she was young and restless and not at all prepared for the responsibilities that the life of a single mother entailed. Infant Morris would soon be taken under wing by his uncle, Pascal Bates, and Pascal's wife, Phyllis. As Morris relates, "during the Williams Lake Stampede in the summer of 1950, my mom went down to the Ranch Hotel and left me outside in my baby carriage. She went in the bar and left me there. Many hours later I was 'up to my neck in shit' and Phyllis and Pascal came out of the bar and found me and took me to their home."

Pascal and Phyllis didn't have any children of their own yet, and for many years, Morris knew them as his only parents. "It was the best thing that could have happened to me," Morris says. "One minute I was a little, helpless, abandoned baby, and the next I had been taken home by the best parents in the whole world. Pascal always looked out for me. He became my dad and Phyllis became my mom. She is just a little bit of a thing, but she has a big, big heart. She is 83 years old now and she's still as smart as a whip. Them finding me and taking me home was the first lucky break that I got."

One minute I was a little, helpless, abandoned baby, and the next I had been taken home by the best parents in the whole world.

Morris would not learn his birth father's identity until many years later when he spent time with his birth mother before Lillian passed away. As he recalls, "I didn't know who my dad was until I was 45 or 46 years old. When my birth mother, Lily, was very sick, before she died, she said, 'I should have told you a long time ago.' My father is Arthur Adams, a Haida First Nations' advocate."

This revelation explained something that Morris had often wondered about. "I am an unusually tall Shuswap Indian," he explains. "I am five foot eleven and a half. My mom is four foot eleven and my dad was five foot five. I am tall for a Shuswap Indian, but Haida *are* tall; and it has been said that they were originally from Hawaii."

His Haida heritage was confirmed when Morris received a check from the executors of his grandfather's estate. As Morris recalls, "My Haida grandfather, Henry Alexander, died and they discovered that he had $20,000 or $30,000 dollars hidden away in a tin can under his bed. When they were settling Henry Alexander's estate, they sorted out the documents and I was sent $500. That was my inheritance."

No doubt, baby Morris had already suffered some trauma before being taken in and provided a home. His mom later told him that he never said a word until he was four or five years old. Morris would have to overcome a severe stutter before he was able to realize his dreams of becoming a star entertainer, and there would be plenty of struggles on his way. But the love and nurturing he received from his new mom and dad ensured that his sunny disposition would prevail.

Younger brother BJ Bates remembers a family story that has been told and retold many times. "When Morris was really little," BJ recalls, "he said he was going to run away from home. So Pascal packed his bags and pushed him out the front door. Morris started crying his eyes out and he ran around to the back, and finally Pascal let him back in. That was the end of that."

Morris doesn't remember that incident, but he does cherish some fond memories of his early years. "I had a collie and a cat and a wagon and a tricycle, and I used to tie the wagon to the tricycle, tie the dog to the wagon, tie the dog to the cat . . . and all of us went on 'escapades'. I remember when I was just a little boy I got the nickname of 'Spud'. They couldn't drive in or out of our place during the springtime, so a plane would come by and they dropped us food and mail. When the potato sacks hit the ground, the spuds would be all over the place. I would run around and pick up all the potatoes, and that's how I got to be called 'Spud'."

Large cattle ranches abound in the Cariboo region, north of Kamloops and south of Prince George, and Pascal frequently worked as a ranch hand. Morris's first home was a small rural cabin on remote ranchland near Horsefly Lake, where his earliest memories are rooted.

Morris's first home was a small rural cabin on remote ranchland near Horsefly Lake, where his earliest memories are rooted.

As he recalls, he learned to work with horses long before he began attending elementary school. "We fed a lot of cattle in the winter. My dad would fill up the wagon with hay. He would bundle me up so I was warm and he would put the reins in my hands. The horses were fine as long as someone was holding the reins. We would go around in circles. My dad would take the reins and turn the team around. I would sit there and hold them. I was really young. I don't think we had our own vehicle. In the summer when the roads were good, I think they came and got us. But we didn't go to town very much because there was a lot of cattle that we were looking after."

By the time Morris had turned six, Pascal and Phyllis had moved back to the Sugar Cane Reserve and were living in a house that his uncle Bill Sellars had built. Morris attended grades one and two at a small school on the reservation. When Pascal left the Sugar Cane Reserve and took a job as a ranch hand at 150-Mile House, Morris was able to attend grades three and four at a regular public school.

Morris remembers that when he was eight or nine and living with his grandmother on the reserve for the summer, an Indian Affairs Department school bus pulled up one day and everybody was loaded onboard. They were taken 500 miles to strawberry fields near Chilliwack where they were employed picking strawberries. They were paid according to how many strawberries they picked, and for the first week that he was there Morris didn't earn very much money because he ate all of the large, juicy berries he picked. His granny had warned him not to eat too many berries because he would get sick — and he did. To this day, he still doesn't care for strawberries. He also recalls going to the mudflats near White Rock, where he and the others dug in the sand and harvested buckets and buckets of clams. "For a week after that," he says, "we ate clam chowder."

Ranch Days

In the late fifties, the predatory behavior of some priests, teachers, and administrators at "Indian" residential schools was well known by the aboriginal community and carefully avoided, if possible. Unfortunately, this was not always possible, and young residents were often subjected to physical and sexual abuse. Decades later, class-action suits were successfully brought against these pedophiles, but it was too late to truly compensate the thousands of native children who had been violated. These residential schools had been created, not to provide equal education to aboriginal children, but to speed up the process of assimilation of First Nations people. English language and culture was substituted for their native names, language, and heritage. Children were forbidden to speak their native tongue and given English names. Strictly enforced by law, this was nothing

... the predatory behavior of some priests, teachers, and administrators at "Indian" residential schools was well known ...

less than a white supremacist doctrine scarcely more humane than the apartheid politics practiced in South Africa. Reservation children could not attend public schools in nearby towns, and, if they were not sent to the residential schools, they would be scooped up by police officers and taken there by force.

Half a century later, in June 2008, the Prime Minister of Canada and leaders of the opposition parties publicly apologized for the federal government's policy of forcibly removing native children from their parents' homes and putting them in residential schools. The apologies included acknowledgement that this policy had tried to "kill the Indian in the child" and erase their cultural heritage. There was no mention of sexual abuse that day, but there was mention of brutal beatings and many people, both white and aboriginal, used the words "past atrocities."

The apologies included acknowledgement that this policy had tried to "kill the Indian in the child" and erase their cultural heritage.

In his response to Prime Minister Harper, Chief Phil Fontaine said that "this day testifies to nothing less than the achievement of the impossible." Standing on the floor of the House of Parliament in Ottawa, he referred to the pain of generations of children taken from their families' guidance and declared that it was time to "put that pain behind us. ... I reach out to all Canadians today in this spirit of reconciliation."

The schools are closed now, but back in the late fifties in Williams Lake, Pascal Bates decided to avoid sending his sons to a residential school by literally moving out of the country.

St. Joseph's Mission had begun to strictly enforce a policy where all Indian children had to attend residential schools. Pascal was able to protect his sons by securing a position as a ranch hand in Loomis, Washington, where the RCMP, who enforced the Indian Act, and the Indian Affairs Department had no jurisdiction. Phyllis was also able to secure employment as a housekeeper. Morris and his brother Bernie were enrolled in a school in Loomis. Their younger brother, BJ, was only one year old at the time.

As Morris later commented when testifying before a Senate committee hearing on urban aboriginal youth, "My dad would not let them put me in a residential school. My dad packed up my two brothers and me and took us to the States to school so they could not touch us down there. I got an education; I was one of the first natives from my town of Williams Lake to graduate." Life in Williams Lake had been tough — when Morris first arrived in Loomis, he sported two black eyes from a rock fight on the reserve.

I got an education; I was one of the first natives from my town of Williams Lake to graduate.

Pascal's employer, Ross Woodard, owned three ranches in the Tonasket-Oroville area. Ross looked after one, his son after another, and Pascal after the third. It was a large spread with 5,000 head of cattle, and they also raised quarter horses. There were extensive hayfields and cornfields.

The move from their home on the reserve to the ranch house in Loomis brought many changes, not the least of which was the luxury of indoor plumbing. The first year, they lived in a small house just like the rest of the ranch hands' families. When Pascal proved his ability to manage the spread, they moved to a larger house. "We ended up living in John Woodard's original family home, which was a gorgeous house overlooking the valley," Morris recalls. "It was so big it was like a mansion to us. It had a big fireplace and two bathrooms. Me and Bernie and little BJ had a bathroom and my mom and dad had a bathroom in their bedroom. That was pretty exciting."

As family life settled into a more comfortable groove, Pascal was strict but fair to his boys, and they remember him as their prime inspiration. "Pascal was tough," BJ says, "he was smart, and he pushed us — he pushed us to do our best at anything we set our minds to do. That was what I admired the most about him."

Morris helped out on the ranch, with calving in the spring and baling hay in the summer. He remembers fondly the many hours he worked with Pascal. "Every spring," he says, proudly, "Pascal and I calved five hundred heifers. You shouldn't breed 'em until they are three but you breed 'em with Angus bulls when they are two and you get smaller calves and you get an extra year out of them. When you do that, when you breed 'em when they are two, you have to pull the heifer calves out. You don't have to do that with three-year-old cows, but the heifers need help. We pulled 500 every spring and we would only lose about 25 of them. So we had 475 extra calves that were going to make it to market."

One summer his 'auntie Lily' came to visit and Morris heard her sing and play the guitar for the first time. "I never spent much time with her," he says, "and I didn't learn that she was my birth mother until I was in my mid-teens. But I remember that in those days nobody had record players and radio stations went off the air at midnight. So people who could sing and play the guitar were the life of the party when folks got together.

"For a while when we were living in the States we forgot that we were Indians. Being an Indian in Canada in those days was like being a black person in Mississippi, which I learned about when I was doing shows years later in the Deep South. But my dad was really inspirational. He inspired me to believe that I could do anything I set my mind to doing."

Hoop Dreams

While attending junior high in nearby Tonasket, Washington, Morris developed a passion for playing basketball. His mother, Phyllis, remembers that he would have to make his own way 17 miles home on foot after school because the school bus would leave while he was at basketball practices. "I used to run three telephone poles and then walk one," Morris recalls, "and then run three more and walk one . . . And my mom would put my supper in the oven to keep it warm until I got home and did my chores. Sometimes, I would get a lift home, but mostly I ran."

In order to practice when he wasn't doing chores, Morris built an indoor practice facility, where he could shoot hoops even in the winter months. As he recalls, "I built a basketball hoop and backboard in the garage where the two big trucks would be parked when they were not being used. It had hinges on it so that I could put it up out of the way of the trucks."

The basketball camp was in Snoqualmie Pass in Washington State. I was going to be a professional basketball player!

Pascal surprised Morris that summer with news that was every teenage athlete's dream in those days. "My dad sent me to basketball camp after I had worked all summer on the ranch," he explains. "The basketball camp was in Snoqualmie Pass in Washington State. I was going to be a professional basketball player!"

In grade eight, Morris made the basketball team and his athletic abilities and natural good looks attracted attention from many of the young girls, including his father's boss's daughter. "I liked her, and she liked me," Morris admits, "but my daddy was a ranch hand and the ranch owners were powerful Republicans. I used to ride on the school bus with her, and she would come around when I was working for my father."

When Pascal saw what was going on, he warned Morris not to become involved with the girl. As Morris recalls, "He said, 'Morris if you have anything to do with this girl, I will lose my job. They will fire me. I don't care what she does or says you stay yourself away from her.' Because of that, it was instilled in me not to mess with white girls."

Not long after that one of the trucks came into the garage and my basketball setup was down and they drove right through it and smashed it all up.

One late winter afternoon during Morris's fourteenth year, the boss's daughter came down to where he was working with one of the jeeps they had on the property.

"I was working with my cousin, Marvin," Morris explains, "putting penicillin pills inside calves that had Scours disease, a form of diarrhea. Marvin would drive the jeep and I would be standing in the jeep and roping the calves. We would rope them and stick these big penicillin tablets down their throats with these long forceps.

"We were driving this jeep over this frozen cow shit and it was tricky getting around at that time of year; and she came down there and told me that she wanted to take the jeep for a ride. I said, 'You can't take the jeep for a ride; you can't drive.' And she said, 'If you don't give me the keys to that jeep, I'm going to tell my daddy that you touched me . . .'"

Morris felt a sinking feeling in his stomach. He knew that whatever he decided to do, nothing good was going to come out of this. "Pascal had talked to me before this about this exact situation," he relates. "She took the jeep for a little ride through the fields and came back, but I never did touch her, nothing like that."

Whatever the girl did or didn't say to her father, the incident foreshadowed the end of the time that the Bates family would spend in Loomis, Washington. "It was kind of ironic," Morris says, "that not long after that one of the trucks came into the garage and my basketball setup was down and they drove right through it and smashed it all up."

My father and my uncle passed away, along with so many family members, but still there is no treaty that honors the land.

Fifteen years after the jeep incident, Morris met up with the boss's daughter one last time. As he recalls, "When I was doing shows at the Landmark Hotel casino in Vegas the boss's daughter came in. She was married to a Senator at that time. And she came into the Landmark showroom and she met my mom. I visited with her, too, between shows, but I remembered what had happened when we were kids and I just didn't have any warmth for her."

Pascal secured a job working for another rancher in nearby Oroville, and Morris again starred on the Oroville high-school basketball squad. However, as the spring of 1965 rolled around, the family received a letter in the mail that would change their lives.

"We got a letter from Canada reminding us that we had been down there in Washington for five years and we had to be back at the reservation in Williams Lake to be head-counted for a treaty negotiation. This was in 1964 and 45 years later in 2009 still nothing has happened – there is no treaty. My grandmother died. My father brought us back home and built us a house, which later burned down, and I helped build another one for my mother. My father and my uncle passed away, along with so many family members, but still there is no treaty that honors the land."

Return to the Reserve

"In the spring of 1965," Morris explains, "the Canadian government wanted all the Indians back on the reserves so that they could start negotiations, a treaty process that would allow us to claim our land. Pascal said, 'I don't have anything to give you kids other than my heritage. So I am going to have to take you home.' He piled all of us and all of our belongings into his Buick and a U-Haul trailer, and we drove back to Williams Lake. He got a job out in Black Creek near Horsefly Lake. We lived in a shack, but my mom cleaned it up and made it look like a home, and I worked on the green chain at the sawmill, which was owned by the Gunderson family."

We lived in a shack, but my mom cleaned it up and made it look like a home.

In September 1965, Morris was 15, fully-grown to his adult height of five feet, eleven and a half inches. He weighed 155 pounds and had excelled in sports, playing football and basketball in the American schools he had attended. He was put back a grade by Canadian school administrators because he lacked required credits in French and Algebra. Enrolled in classes at Columneetza Senior Secondary School in Williams Lake — and living in a dormitory because Pascal was still working in Black Creek — Morris immediately became a starting player on his high-school rep teams. He played basketball, soccer, football, and rugby with boys who were much older than he was.

Living away from his family for the first time in his life was tough. When he wasn't practicing or playing sports, he spent his spare time at local hangouts, pool parlors and cafes. Williams Lake was a pretty rough town, but he could pretty much look after himself no matter what situations arose.

One afternoon, Morris beat a notorious bully at a game of pool. The bully asked him to step out the back. Morris thought that he was going to pay what he owed him, but the pool shark bully sucker punched Morris and laid a beating on him. To put a stop to this, Morris went to the only person he knew that could stand up to the bully. "Shorty Moore was about five-ten and two hundred and twenty pounds in grade twelve," Morris recalls. "He was a powerhouse and he was a good friend of mine. I told him what had happened to me out back of the pool hall. He could see that I got beat up pretty bad. We were both still in high school at the time, and he went down there and had a few words with that bully and I was never ever bothered again. It wasn't that I couldn't defend myself, but I got suckered punched by someone that was bigger and older and meaner than I was." It was a lesson that would stand Morris in good stead later in life when he needed to hire bodyguards to protect him in Las Vegas and when he was on tour.

Williams Lake was a pretty rough town, but he could pretty much look after himself no matter what situations arose.

In September 1966, Pascal enrolled Morris in classes at Prince George College, a Senior Secondary Catholic residential school, where they had an excellent basketball program. Right away he was on the starting five along with the older boys. "Gene Buein was an excellent high school basketball coach," Morris recalls. "He was from the University of Utah and he became my mentor. He could have been a professional basketball player, but his Mormon faith did not embrace playing in the NBA."

That year, Morris became a local legend playing basketball. Younger brother BJ remembers that when Morris and the PG College team came to play at the local invitational tournament the Williams Lake School made up a banner that read: "Welcome MORRIS BATES and P.G. College." By the end of the season, Morris had begun to believe that he might one day play in the NBA.

Spring Break

Morris Bates' friendship with Gordon Sebastian deepened during spring break in 1967. "I had no place to go on spring break," Morris recalls, "and he invited me to come home with him. He said, 'Come to Hazelton with me.' We had no money, so we got out on the road and we started hitchhiking. We got a ride with a bunch of crazy Indians. They were drinking, but none of them had a driver's license. I had got one when I had turned sixteen. So they put me behind the wheel and I drove all the way to Hazelton. We stayed overnight in Hazelton on the Hagwilget Reserve and in the morning Gordon's mom, Elsie Sebastian, made us breakfast, and Gordie got to visit with all his family and everything. But we were pretty restless young guys, and we decided that we were going to hitchhike to Prince Rupert to see some people there — Gordie had an auntie there and we had some friends living there, too.

It was so cold that we went into a laundromat where you could put ten cents in one of the dryers and open the door and the heat would come out.

"We got into Terrace really late, and it was so cold that we went into a laundromat where you could put ten cents in one of the dryers and open the door and the heat would come out. We pulled up benches next to the dryer and lay there. Then we got back on the road to Prince Rupert.

"I was pretty new to that area, and I was just getting to see everything for the first time. I remember the road goes right alongside the Skeena River, and at some points you could literally step out of your car and pee into the river. For me it was really scary.

"Some more crazy Indians came along, and we got a ride to Prince Rupert. It was raining — all it does is rain there. They let us off in the downtown area and we climbed up all of these flights of wet, slippery wooden stairs and sidewalks to where his auntie lived. We were so tired and wet and burnt out from being on the road hitchhiking that all we wanted was to sleep on the floor. But when we got to his auntie's house, she was entertaining sailors. We told her we just wanted to dry off and sleep on the floor, but she kicked us out."

The two hapless youths climbed back down the slippery wooden staircases and sought refuge inside a car in a used car lot. At eight o'clock in the morning they were wakened up by the car lot employees and back on the street again."We had enough money to buy rice and gravy from a Chinese takeout place on the main street," Morris recalls. "I think we had fifty cents between us, not very much, so we got two big bowls of gravy and rice. We had a friend that lived there, Lorgen Bob. We went to school with his brother, Dempsey Bob, who is a world-renowned carver now. Lorgen lived with his sister, Betty Bob. We didn't know where they lived so we just started asking people, 'Do you know where we can find Lorgen or Betty?' And they said, 'Oh, up the hill and over that way there is an apartment.' So we climbed up the hill and searched and we found them. We were cold and shivering and we just wanted to get warm and sleep. They put us up in the bathroom. Gordon slept on the floor. I slept in the bathtub."

Their friendship has lasted throughout their lifetimes. "The way it was then is exactly the way it is today," Morris says. "If I had a dime, both of us had two nickels."

> The way it was then is exactly the way it is today. If I had a dime, both of us had two nickels.

Learning to Play Bass

After basketball season ended, Morris found himself to be merely a poor resident student in a residential school in Prince George, where richer students and day students, in particular, enjoyed many privileges.

Morris was one of the unfortunate kids who didn't have money for snacks that could be purchased in the cafeteria after dinner and before bedtime. So he and some of the teenagers who were in the same boat conspired to get some of the food that was stored in the cookhouse for themselves without paying for it. They got away with that. Emboldened, they got into all sorts of shenanigans. And when they finally got into trouble with the school authorities, Morris was singled out and blamed for the most of it, punished by being isolated for the rest of the school year. Instead of sulking or becoming depressed, the young teenager taught himself how to play the bass guitar. In retrospect, it was a fortunate turn of events. Today, he will jokingly say, "there's the culprit," and point to a photo of his lifelong pal, Gordon Sebastian.

> Today, he will jokingly say, "there's the culprit," and point to a photo of his lifelong pal, Gordon Sebastian.

"We've been friends since we were 16 years old," Morris explains. "I was best man at his wedding. But what happened was that we had no money and we were growing young guys and we ate a lot. We got breakfast and lunch and supper, but after that we didn't get anything. We convinced this really nice girl to help us out. She could help us because she had access to the pantry downstairs that we didn't. We had nothing to eat at night and all the kids that had money could go down to the cafeteria and buy snacks. So, I set it up and three or four of us went down to the cookhouse where someone had left a basement window open for us. And we got armloads of snack food, but we had nowhere to store it. So we decided we would store it on top of the roof. It was nice and cold up there. It was like a refrigerator. We had cookies and candy bars — we had everything!"

After the raid on the cookhouse, life was good, until a schoolhouse prank went wrong. "It was a fashion statement for teenage girls to have hickeys in those days," Morris explains. "If they were wearing a scarf or a turtleneck sweater it implied that they had one. All the girls wanted to have hickeys, but the boys didn't want to kiss all of the girls. Then me and Gordie Sebastian came up with a solution, we learned how to pinch their necks and twist, and their skin would be bruised and it would look like they had hickeys. So for a while a lot of girls were wearing scarves and turtlenecks. Anyway, one of the girls went and told her mother, and blamed me and Gordie, and I took the rap. I was blamed for being the instigator; I didn't even know what the word meant. I don't think they found the food, but I was busted down from Hostel 9, where my buddies were at, to Hostel 8. Nobody was allowed to talk to me. My marks were good, but I was being punished. They announced every morning over the school intercom that no one was allowed to talk to Morris Bates. And as soon as I was out of classes, I was escorted back to Hostel 8. Fortunately, there was a bass guitar in there."

They announced every morning over the school intercom that no one was allowed to talk to Morris Bates.

There was no amplifier for the electric, solid-body bass guitar, but Morris was a resourceful teenager. "If you take a bass guitar," he explains, "and put it upright on a wooden desk or table, you don't need an amplifier. The wood resonates. And that's how I learned how to play bass. I went and got a book, *Play Bass with Mel Bay*, and it gave me the scales and formations. And that's how I learned how to play music."

Local Hero

At the Williams Lake Stampede, Morris got a summer job playing bass with Ray Benson & the Chiefs, a band from Yakima, Washington that was playing the rodeo circuit. "I played with Ray all summer," he recalls. "We played in northern California and Oregon, and we ended up in Tacoma at the Washington State Fair. Ray brought in his cousin to play bass and put me on rhythm guitar, which we really needed on all of those Ventures' instrumentals we were playing."

Morris recalls that a benevolent older man gave him a gold-colored Gibson Les Paul guitar, and by the time that he hitch-hiked home, it was early October. He'd been told not to come back to Prince George College, so he enrolled in classes at Prince George Senior Secondary School, where he played for the best high school basketball team in the area, the Polars. The Department of Indian Affairs paid his tuition and living expenses.

I could beat anybody on the small pool tables they had in the bars. Pascal taught me a lot of trick shots, and we got run out of some places for hustling.

"The Polars went all the way to the provincial high school championships," Morris recalls, proudly, "and we came in fifth at the tournament that we played at UBC."

That following spring Gordon Sebastian's father, Joe Sebastian, was walking down Two-Mile-Hill on the highway near Hazelton and he was clipped by a truck and killed. Morris was unable to be there when Gordon and his brothers buried their father, but when school was out in June the two friends set out hitchhiking once again, this time in search of summer jobs. They found employment north of Burns Lake at a sawmill.

"We had taken a summer job in Lake Babine," Morris recalls,

"pulling lumber off the green chain. Me and Gordon and my cousin, Morris Sellers, but we didn't have any money yet. So we hitchhiked over to Telkwa. I said the only way we're going to get any money is if I shoot some pool. In those days, I played snooker on the big tables. I could beat anybody on the small pool tables they had in the bars. Pascal taught me a lot of trick shots, and we got run out of some places for hustling. So I was going to raise some money shooting pool, but Gordie decided to go to Smithers to this car bingo. Another guy paid five dollars for Gordie to get in, just for companionship, and Gordie won the car. It was a brand new, red 1967 Chevelle.

"I was playing pool in the bar in Telkwa, and here comes Gordie in this new car with about eight Indians. So me and Gordie and my cousin Morris Sellers got in the car and went back to Hazelton. There was a big dance going on. There was a lot of animosity toward Gordon's family at that time, and there was this big bully at the dance. Gordie is tough but not that tough. Morris Sellers pulled the two-by-fours and two-by-sixes off the green chain. Gordon pulled the two-by-tens. And I pulled the two-by-twelves. I pulled two-by-twelves, 24 feet long, all day long. *I* was tough. And this 250-pound bully went after Gordon and I stepped in. There was, like, 800 people outside this dance hall watching me fight this guy. I fought him for half an hour. All I could hear was people hollering 'Morris don't let him grab you, don't let him grab you!' I had already had boxing lessons, and I was fighting for Gordon and his family. I got him down and I beat him and he went into a coma.

"We went back to Babine Lake and the word was out that if he died they were going to kill me. We just stayed out in the bush, pulling lumber off the green chain, and after about two weeks he came out of the coma and he lived. I had to go back there, to Hazelton. It was a fair fight and I won, and 'if anybody wants to f—- with me, c'mon down, Charlie.' I went there and I went out on the reserve. I went to Hazelton and New Hazelton and South Hazelton and Moricetown, and all over the place. So, if he wanted at me, I was right there. And nobody ever touched me.

Nobody ever talked to me about it. It was just something that was done."

Morris would have graduated from the high school in Prince George in the spring of 1968, but he lacked the necessary credits in French and Algebra. That summer he got a very good job because he had taken typing classes. As Morris recalls, "I worked for the PGE, the Pacific Great Eastern Railway. I got a fulltime job with the PGE because I could type. None of the guys that I worked with could type. So they put me to work as a train clerk typing the lists of all the boxcars that came in. I was making $150 a week — that was the same money that a married man with a wife and five children was making."

In January, Morris enrolled in the two classes he needed to pass to complete his high school graduation credits at Williams Lake Columneetza Senior Secondary School, where he starred in high school basketball games for the Columneetza Cougars. He also continued to work for the railroad. As he recalls, "The guys at the PGE were really good to me because I was a high-school basketball star. I was the only high-school player in those days who scored more than 50 points in one game. My teammates fed me like crazy and I just kept popping 'em in."

This sunny, positive attitude was one of his best qualities, and it would continue to be a valuable asset throughout his adult life. The only cloud on the horizon was the fact that Morris had celebrated his eighteenth birthday, but he had not grown to fully six feet tall. Still, he dared to dream. "I was five foot eleven and a half. Gail Goodrich was six-foot-one and he made the NBA. And I thought, 'that's me!'"

Goodrich, picked tenth overall in the 1965 NBA draft by the LA Lakers, was nicknamed "stumpy" by his teammates because of his relatively short stature, but went on to star alongside Jerry West, Wilt Chamberlain, and Kareem Abdul-Jabbar on the championship Lakers teams of the seventies. Of course, for many aspiring teenage basketball players in the sixties, Gail was an inspiration to believe that they, too, could make it in the NBA

I was making $150 a week — that was the same money that a married man with a wife and five children was making.

even if they were not six-foot-nine, sky-hook, high-scoring centers who had changed their names from Ferdinand Alcindor Jr. to Kareem Abdul-Jabbar. Typical of teenage athletes, Morris was steeped in the NBA lore that chronicled the careers of big league stars and was developing some moves of his own.

"I had really big hands," Morris reminisces, "and I had a trick play that the referees couldn't figure out." His trick play worked for him all season long until he came under heavy scrutiny during the Columneetza Cougars' Annual Invitational Basketball Tournament. "I would palm the ball as I was still dribbling, and literally walk around you, then release it and go on dribbling," he explains. "They couldn't figure it out. They would look but they couldn't figure it out because I did it so fast and didn't put both hands on the ball — it wasn't a traveling violation. Then in the tournament one of the coaches for the other teams complained. And the refs blew their whistle every time I got the ball and we lost the crucial game, but I was named MVP of the tournament. It was a battle. It was brutal — I had a bloody nose and ended up with five stitches. You can see it in the picture they took after the game with me with my trophy."

> I was named MVP of the tournament. It was a battle. It was brutal — I had a bloody nose and ended up with five stitches.

Morris Bates' basketball exploits had made him into a local hero, and a lot of people believed that some day he really would be playing in the NBA. As BJ recalls, "I was real young when Morris was playing basketball. Steve Nash is good today in the NBA, but back in the sixties Morris had some moves, and I heard rumors that some pro-ball guys were scouting him."

Long before women began rushing to the stage to get a scarf or a kiss from Morris during his tribute to Elvis shows, his athleticism and healthy, handsome features had attracted hordes of adoring teenage girls. "The girls were all after him," BJ confirms. High-school classmate Norma Byard remembers Morris as being "a gentle person, soft-spoken and well-liked by those who knew him."

Despite Morris Bates' high-school basketball heroics, there were no five-foot-eleven-and-a-half-inch prospects making it onto the rosters of NBA teams. Even though he had not grown an inch since he was 14, Morris's spirits were not diminished. He had received such an encouraging upbringing from his family that he had discovered he had an almost inexhaustible resource of nervous energy. When he counted his blessings, there were many. He had a very good job with the railroad. He had continued on with his guitar and electric bass playing. And when he was not working, attending classes, practicing or playing basketball games, he and his friends had a teenage band that played local dances.

"There was an area beside the garage where we practiced," Morris remembers, "and my mother never complained about how much noise we were making. I asked her about that and she said, 'At least I knew where you were when you were playing music with your band.' I played dances on the Sugar Cane Rez — from eleven o'clock at night till eight in the morning. Then they'd ring the church bell and walk around the dance hall and go to church."

That winter, Morris saw Elvis Presley's *NBC-TV Special* and was inspired to envision another career. Many years later, Morris would tell a young South African journalist by the name of Cilla Duff that "when I saw Elvis in this *NBC-TV Special* in '68, he was just killer, man. I figured, 'Where's he been all my life?' I recognized the similarities between us, and I thought, 'Hey, this is my ticket through the door, this is how I make it!'"

Such oversimplifications, told to journalists in the heat of the moment during brief backstage interviews, rarely tell the whole story. Nevertheless, there is little doubt that, right from that moment in December 1968 when Morris Bates saw Elvis performing live on TV, the teenage basketball star was intrigued. BJ remembers that "in those days, Morris would walk five miles to see an Elvis movie."

In June 1969, Morris graduated from high school, and for his graduation present Pascal bought him his first wheels, a red and white, two-door, 1957 Ford Fairlane hardtop convertible.

> I played dances on the Sugar Cane Rez — from eleven o'clock at night till eight in the morning. Then they'd ring the church bell and walk around the dance hall and go to church.

> In those days, Morris would walk five miles to see an Elvis movie.

"I was still working for the PGE," Morris recalls, "and thoughts of working there the rest of my life kept gnawing at me. This is it? This is my life? It was the July 1st weekend – the Williams' Lake Stampede. I'd been bumped from working as a train clerk, a relatively easy job, to laborer, because of my lack of seniority. I was now grinding railway tracks, breathing in all the black metal soot, or unloading boxcars in the sweltering heat. It just so happened that the boss wanted all these boxcars emptied over the long, Stampede Weekend, and because I was lowest man on the totem pole, it became my job. I worked the long weekend and he came in to see how I was doing. I thought, everyone is having a good time at the Rodeo and I'm emptying boxcars and not even playing any music during the big annual event of the year. I told him the boxcars were empty and to send my check to Prince Rupert, General Delivery.

"That weekend I saw a great band playing at the Elk's Hall in William's Lake. They were from Vancouver and called Mock Duck."

Morris was totally entranced by the Mock Duck's fusion of jazz rhythms and rock instrumentation. In particular, he was impressed by guitarist and vocalist Joe Mock, and inspired by the rock star to continue on his musical path.

"Mock Duck were so much ahead of their time," Morris enthuses. "They were like Yes was later; their music wasn't like anything you had ever heard before."

Morris's job working for the railroad was over, but a new career as an entertainer, which had begun the previous summer when he had hit the road with Ray Benson & the Chiefs, would soon become an overriding passion.

> Morris's job working for the railroad was over, but a new career as an entertainer would soon become an overriding passion.

Stamp on Life

Reflecting back on his roots, Morris says, "My dad's name was Pascal, but most called him 'Pasco'. He had a great sense of humor and we endured a lot of Pasco-isms while we were growing up. My brothers, Bernie and BJ, both became commercial artists and present a cartoonish sense of humor in their work. Bernie once painted a sign that advertised for a barbershop that offered '$6.00 Haircuts,' then went across the street to a competing hair salon and painted a sign that said, 'We Fix $6.00 Haircuts.' BJ is equally talented, managing to capture the time and essence of the moment in his work, and is more commercially oriented.

'A man's ambition is very small to write his name on a shit-house wall.'

"For youngsters growing up in northern BC, many homes didn't have the luxury of indoor plumbing. Ours was one of them. Someone had written someone's name on the wall of the outhouse. My dad got us all together and all he said was, 'A man's ambition is very small to write his name on a shit-house wall.'

"We all managed to put our stamp on life in our own little way. I chose the marquees of the world and a red, neon sign that simply read 'Morris...' My brothers, our families, and friends all enjoyed the notoriety. Bernie even went to the length of being married to his wife Janet by an Elvis Impersonator in Las Vegas. My mom says it was the 'Love Me Tender' package."

Top left: Aunt Lily (a.k.a. Morris's birth mother).
Top right: Morris with his mother, Phyllis Bates.
Bottom left: Morris, age 3. Bottom right: Morris's
first communion

Top left: Calf with two heads and two tails: Morris's brother BJ, uncle Louis, brother Bernie, and father Pascal check out this freak of nature. Photographed by Morris. Top right: Pascal, Morris, Bernie, Phyllis, and BJ (front). Bottom left: Morris (left) with his brothers at Christmas in Loomis, Washington. Bottom right: Morris with his dog Scottie

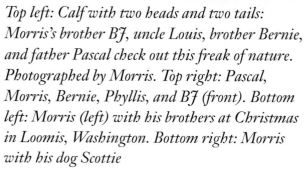

Top left: Morris as a Rocky Mountain Ranger, age 16. Top right: Bonnie Forsythe, Gord Sebastian, and cousin Morris Sellers. Bottom: Morris as high-school basketball MVP .

MOST VALUABLE PLAYER of the Cougar Invitational Basketball Tournament during the
was Morris Bates (right) of the Columneetza Cougars. He was chosen for his shotmak
playmaking abilities. Good sportsmanship was also a reason for the judges decision. Pr
the trophy is Rick Nelson.

Above: Dempsey Bob, Gordon Sebastian, and Anton (Tony) Madam. Bottom: Morris's brother Bernie and Janet were married in Las Vegas by an unknown Elvis impersonator

Jailhouse Rock

Paying Gigs

Ho-Ho Thunderbird Room

Soon after leaving Williams Lake, Morris got another job as a professional musician, filling in for a guy who had become drunk and was unable to continue playing. "In 1969, I graduated from high school and I got a job that summer in a sawmill in Prince Rupert," Morris tells the story. "They had a little club there called the Ho-Ho Thunderbird Room. They had a band in there and a young girl singer who was singing Tammy Wynette songs. Prince Rupert is a drinking town, and in the afternoons the fishermen come in and the action heats up. One night the guitar player got to drinkin' before the band went on, and when he went up there, he fell off the stage. Gary Gust was the bass player, and he could play guitar, too, so they asked over the PA if anybody in the club could play bass guitar because the guitar player was out cold. Gary was up there with a guitar and a drummer and this young singer."

Morris was at the nightclub that night with some friends, and his buddies encouraged him to go ahead and go up and play. "They said, 'go on, go ahead, go on up there and tell them that you play bass,'" he recalls. "I didn't have that good an ear, but I knew the formation of the chords. So, I went up there and backed up the girl who was singing Tammy Wynette songs, playing electric bass. The club owner was

51

I didn't have that good an ear, but I knew the formation of the chords. So, I went up there and backed up the girl who was singing Tammy Wynette songs.

really pissed off at the guy who fell off the stage, and I was offered a job as a bass player. The band had something like a six-month contract to play the Thunderbird Room — ten at night till about two o'clock in the morning. So I started at about seven-thirty in the morning at the mill, worked there until three or four, and I would go and sleep until about nine o'clock. Then I'd boot it down to the club, play until two o'clock, walk home, go back to sleep, and do it all over again."

This relentless routine went on through the summer, and Morris got to be pretty good friends with Gary Gust. He also met some of the musicians who were playing in local rock bands. "Although I was only nineteen at the time," Morris explains, "I could pass for twenty-one, plus I was playing in the band that was playing in the Ho-Ho Thunderbird Room. We played country standards to please the adult clientele. There were a lot of very good musicians who played in the rock bands that played local dances. Tom Rysstad played guitar and just about anything else that made a sound or a note. He had a unique voice and was a good songwriter. We became good friends and he's played in many versions of my bands over the years. Tom also developed a niche as a one-man band, playing all over Canada, the USA, and Mexico and on Cruise ships."

Bachelor's Three

When their gig at the Thunderbird Room came to an end, Gary Gust returned to Vancouver, and Morris returned to Williams Lake, where he was offered a two-month contract to play the brand-new Chilcotin Inn Cabaret. Morris had played dances on the Sugar Cane Reserve with high-school bandmates, and filled in as a bass player for Gust, but he knew he would have to put together a more professional lineup in order to entertain adults in a cabaret. He phoned the musicians union hall in Vancouver and told them he needed a hot-shot guitar player and vocalist. They sent him Joe Mock. He couldn't believe his good fortune.

He had been standing there gawking at Joe in the summer at the Stampede grandstand show and now he was going to be playing in a band with him.

When Mock arrived, there was plenty of rehearsal to be done. "It was totally bizarre to go up there," Joe recalls, "meet a couple of guys, and put a band together on the spot, build a repertoire, and play the gig. Mock Duck was a hippie band. And after that to go and play in a hotel cabaret — not very many people had long hair in those days; so we had to try and be a club band not an avant-garde band and play music that the locals would like. They were a rhythm section and they needed a front-man, a guy with a repertoire that could just walk in and they could tag on to."

According to the reviews printed in the local newspaper, they did pretty well when they opened the new cabaret at the Chilcotin Inn on New Year's Eve 1969. Along with drummer Rick Wilkinson, Morris and Joe called themselves the Bachelor's Three.

Mock was a university graduate with a degree in psychology, and had ten years experience as a folk artist and as leader of a rock band. With his mixed Chinese and Hungarian parentage, he fit right into the Williams Lake scene. Joe had toured as a folk duo in the early sixties with Stephen Gibbons-Barrett before forming Mock Duck with Stephen's younger brother, Ross, a sax and keyboard player. Mock Duck had played shows with the Doors and Country Joe & the Fish and were very popular throughout BC before breaking up in the fall of 1969.

Joe taught Morris the "number system" that professional musicians use to enable them to play in any key by counting up four notes from the root and then five notes from the root to find the three basic chords for each key. "Joe Mock sat me down and taught how to play with anybody. He showed me the alphabet of 'G' and told me that if I learned the alphabet of 'G' and could count up one, two, three, four, I could play anything."

"It's just one, four, five," Morris says enthusiastically.

It was totally bizarre to go up there, meet a couple of guys, and put a band together on the spot, build a repertoire, and play the gig.

He showed me the alphabet of 'G' and told me that if I learned the alphabet of 'G' and could count up one, two, three, four, I could play anything.

"And sometimes you throw in a second. It's right there. It's right there in front of you, but you have to have someone experienced point it out to you for the first time. I have to give real credit to Joe Mock. He showed me more about music theory and structure that made sense to me than anyone had before. The music was getting more complex as were the arrangements. He sat down with me at a piano and showed me quite a lot about music."

"We had to pull together and learn how to play together," Joe explains, "and for Morris to develop and learn a little more about music and all that kind of stuff. We sat down and spent time doing that — explaining some of the rules about music and how to make things sound good." Joe respected Morris for the effort. "Morris was enthusiastic and open minded," Joe recalls, "and we had a pretty interesting time together."

The drummer was a bizarre guy. He would get a *Playboy* magazine and try and phone the girl.

Mock thoroughly enjoyed the time he spent in Williams Lake and also remembers fondly times spent with Morris Bates' family "His dad, Pascal, was a really affable guy. He was a real character. We went out on the lake on the ice with him. He was the kind of guy that was fun to hang out with."

Still, it was difficult for Joe to comprehend what a mystery the world outside the northern Cariboo region represented to his young band mates, who had never been to either Regina, where Joe was born, or Vancouver, where he had been raised. "The drummer was a bizarre guy," Joe remembers. "He would get a *Playboy* magazine and try and phone the girl. He would be calling Hollywood or wherever trying to talk to her. He was a bizarre guy." Morris's determination to make it as an entertainer in Las Vegas must have seemed equally fanciful.

When their two-month booking at the cabaret was done, Joe returned to Vancouver, where he soon joined Rick Scott and Shari Ulrich to form Pied Pumkin, a rocking folk trio. After Mock left town, Morris played guitar, Stanley Stump played bass, and Rick Wilkinson played drums for a few events before Morris also made his way to Vancouver.

"I'd sold my car," he recalls, "and I decided I was going to come to Vancouver. I loaded up my bass amp on the plane and flew to Vancouver and got a room with a kitchenette at Seventh and Oak."

The Big City

Morris Bates' first Vancouver gig was playing bass for legendary West Coast country star Evan Kemp. "I worked for Evan Kemp, $10 a night, up at the Arlington Club," he recalls. "They had a polka band downstairs and Evan Kemp upstairs."

I worked for Evan Kemp, $10 a night, up at the Arlington Club.

Evan Kemp & His Trail Riders were booked into the Arlington Ballroom on West Broadway throughout the sixties and early seventies. As Marilyn Bentley recalls, "when I was about 19, I was a featured singer known as Marilyn Hart, Vancouver's Queen of Hearts, with Evan Kemp & His Trail Riders. We played the Arlington Ballroom every Friday and Saturday night." Kemp was a recording artist with singles and albums released on the RCA Victor and Aragon Records labels, and a definite step up from the raggedy band that had been booked into the Thunderbird Room in Prince Rupert and the Bachelor's Three group in Williams Lake.

This fourth job as a paid professional continued Morris Bates' journeyman education in the music business. It was pretty basic stuff, as Marilyn Bentley explains. "Back then we played a lot of different music — country, rock and standards. I didn't have a car and I remember getting on the bus in my long, sparkly gown to go perform at the Arlington."

Morris recalls that "they had a lot of European people who didn't speak a lot of English that used to go there, and they had a polka band downstairs for them, a lonely heart's club upstairs, and a marquee with a big heart that had an arrow through it. I also played at the Gulf Club, and a lot of places on Hastings Street and Granville Street. I played a lot of these gigs, and then we played in the Penthouse."

The Penthouse nightclub on Seymour Street was a legendary venue where club owner Joe Filippone entertained late night celebrity guests as famous as Frank Sinatra, Errol Flynn, and Gary Cooper — and where Sammy Davis Jr., Nat King Cole, and George Burns had entertained. The walls of the club were plastered with signed black and white 8x10 photos of these famous Hollywood celebrities, but by the early seventies the club mostly featured striptease dancers who performed nightly sets to the accompaniment of live music from the house band. Morris Bates' pal, Gary Gust, was the bandleader. "I just played bass and sang a couple of songs during the sets," Morris recalls.

The Penthouse nightclub on Seymour Street was a legendary venue where club owner Joe Filippone entertained late night celebrity guests as famous as Frank Sinatra, Errol Flynn, and Gary Cooper.

Working as a musician in bar bands in Vancouver in the early seventies, Morris quickly learned that there were limited opportunities in the big city. Along with some band-mates, he set off for greener pastures, touring through British Columbia and across the Prairie provinces, where, it was rumored, there were bigger clubs and bands were paid better. Changing liquor laws throughout western Canada benefited musicians because before this time bands had not been allowed to play in lounges and beer parlors.

Alberta Bound

Dennis Compo, a young musician who would soon play a major role in Morris Bates' career, remembers that, "in 1963 I was playing bass guitar in Edmonton with Jayson Hoover. We were the first band to play at a licensed entertainment venue in Alberta, at Billy Warwick's club in Edmonton. We were so young we couldn't stay in the club after we finished playing. Not long after that, Jayson moved to Vancouver and joined the Epics. I followed a year later and got into the talent agency business."

With the Alberta economy fueled by the rapidly expanding oil industry and the largest cattle ranches in Canada, it wasn't long before large Texas-style country music nightclubs, like Ranchman's in Calgary and Tumbleweeds in Edmonton, were paying top dollar for bands. Rock musicians were booked into big venues like the Mayfield Inn and Lucifer's nightclubs. Bar bands were working six nights a week all over the province. Morris immediately recognized the commercial potential of playing there.

Once again, it was Gary Gust who got him the gig. "Gary Gust gave me a call and said, 'do you want to go to Alberta?' I said, 'Well, I'm just gigging around. I'll be there in a couple of hours.'"

After this brief introduction to the Alberta scene, Morris decided to take charge of his career. "I broke away," he recalls, "and got a gig playing bass in a house band in The Blue Room Cabaret in the Plaza Hotel in Kamloops. The band was called Country Soul, and when the band decided to go on the road into Alberta, our drummer was unable to travel." Morris made a call to Joe Mock in Vancouver, asking Mock to recommend a dependable replacement who was willing to come out on the road. Plenty of paying gigs had already been booked.

Joe recommended Stephen Gibbons-Barrett, a painter and former folk singer who had also played drums in bar bands in downtown eastside nightclubs. Gibbons-Barrett joined Morris and the Country Soul band in Kamloops. "We wore blue shirts with pearl buttons and string ties," Stephen recalls, "and we played cowboy music in the big clubs in Alberta."

After this brief introduction to the Alberta scene, Morris decided to take charge of his career.

"Stephen put the *soul* in Country Soul," Morris explains. "Before that we had a country drummer that played every song in polka time. Every song sounded the same. Stephen didn't play like that. Stephen played cut time and laid down the beat for everybody else. If you listen to early Elvis records, DJ Fontana, Scotty Moore, and Bill Black play three time signatures against each other."

"It came natural," Stephen adds, "from playing the clubs in the East End in Vancouver. We were playing rhythm and blues all the time."

"We had a pedal steel player," Morris recalls, "named Ray Morrison. He had a prosthetic leg. He was on his motorcycle and somebody drove out with a forklift and cut it right off. I remem-

If you listen to early Elvis records, DJ Fontana, Scotty Moore, and Bill Black play three time signatures against each other.

ber we would go over to this friend's place in North Kamloops and this guy had a pit bull. Ray would open up the gate and stick his wooden leg in there, and the dog would jump on his leg and sink his teeth into it. Ray had a really weird sense of humor."

"We were booked into The Blue Room for all summer and fall," Morris continues. "But it was just a small cabaret, and I was starting to get pretty ambitious. I wanted to get out of BC. Alberta was the place to go. Everything was bopping in Alberta. Stephen came along with this 49-passenger Bluebird school bus and no heater. It was the middle of the wintertime and I damn near froze to death."

"It was a big bus," Stephen acknowledges, "it had chairs and seats and a sleeping room."

"And no heat," Morris says, again. "We headed to Alberta to play at the Riviera Hotel, which was one of the top venues in Edmonton. We didn't realize it at the time, but the Country Soul band had a very unique sound, crossing traditional country with rock. We had a rock guitar player by the name of Jimmy Mann, a pedal steel player by the name of Ray Morrison, and the smooth country vocals of Al Earl. Our sound became the crossover sound of the Eagles, the Flying Burrito Brothers, and many other Southern California groups. I remember singing *I'm A Man* by Stevie Winwood to the sound of a pedal steel. I think Ray even hooked up a wah-wah pedal and a fuzz-tone to his steel guitar; it made for some weird sounds – psychedelic country."

This new foray into the prairies precipitated a change in direction for Morris. As he explains, "In Alberta, in those days, they had laws that they had to have live entertainment in order to have a liquor license. But when we first started playing there in the early seventies, a lot of the venues didn't have dance floors, so audiences sat there and listened to you. In order to fill those rooms, you had to become an entertainer."

Morris had to learn to speak on the microphone as well as sing into it. Singing came naturally to him, but speaking didn't. "I used to stutter badly," he admits, "and they took me to a therapist. The doctor said, 'Your mind is going way too fast for your mouth to keep up to. If you can slow your mind down for your mouth to catch up, you won't stutter any more.' It was quite a process for me."

One of his vocal coaches was Al Earl. "Al could really sing Marty Robbins songs, he could sing Elvis — he could sing anything. Al was a vocal gymnast. We worked together a lot and he really helped me out. "

One night Morris told an off-color joke during their show and nearly got the band fired. "It seemed funny at the time,' he recalls," but they took my microphone away from me. We could still play there, as long as I didn't tell any more jokes.

Singing came naturally to him, but speaking didn't. "I used to stutter badly," he admits.

Top left: Early band members Gary Gust (left) and Tom Rystaad. Bottom: The Mock Duck featuring Joe Mock

Above: Stanley Stump, Danny Case, and Morris. Bottom: Drummer Stephen Gibbons-Barrett and Joe Mock.

Country Soul: Stephen Gibbons-Barrett, Ray Morrison,
Morris, and Tyi Parkinson (kneeling)

Travelin' Band: Morris, Al Earle, Jimmy Mann, and Stephen Gibbons-Barrett

Don't Be Cruel

Becoming Elvis

Finding His Voice

As Country Soul toured Alberta, Morris was making big strides in his bass playing and his singing was improving, but some of the older men in the band were not getting along all that well. Some nights Jimmy Mann and Al Earl couldn't get along with each other at all. Ray Morrison hankered to return to BC, and by the time they were playing the Airport Inn in Edmonton, Ray received an offer he could not refuse. As Morris recalls, "The day I turned 21 years old, my life changed — I was about to discover my full vocal range.

"I never considered myself a lead singer. I was always the second or third singer in the group. I would do a song so the other singers could rest their voices. I was always the youngest in the group and not even allowed to play in the clubs legally. The songs I learned were rock songs using the high register of my vocal range, screaming out songs by CCR and Deep Purple, not thinking about tone and texture. That Sunday when I turned 21, the liquor laws had changed. They dropped the legal age to be allowed in the bars in Alberta to 19 years old. That same weekend, Ray Morrison told me he was leaving the Country Soul group to become a house musician for Wally Zayonce in his club in Kelowna. Jimmy Mann said that if Ray was leaving he was quitting, too, and going home to Medicine Hat. Al Earl said he had offers to do some single work. And Stephen said if everybody else was quitting the band, he was going back to Vancouver.

"For the first time since I hit the road, I was alone with no band and a long way from home with no transportation, a limited repertoire of rock songs, and not a whole lot of money. I promised myself I would never be in that situation again. I had met a girl named Verna Anne Moore that weekend. She was a medical student and she'd just got back from skiing in Switzerland. Verna Anne told me that I could hang out with her until I figured out what I was going to do. I kept in touch with Al Earl and we worked as a duo we called 'The Mr. & Mrs.' I had really long hair and Al had a crew cut. We were kind of like Cheech & Chong before Cheech & Chong. We were both native and we did a lot of racially-charged humor.

"Even though Al was a great singer, he encouraged me to share the vocal load for the act. He used a lot of one-liners and I had a knack for story jokes, and we used a lot of props and gimmicks. That is where we worked up the satirical comedy routine 'Elvis the Pelvis and his brother Enis'.

"Al got a job at a Coca-Cola plant, and Verna Anne and I got a little studio apartment. I picked up casual gigs playing in bands and doing the duo with Al. I was also trying to learn enough material to support myself doing a single with just me and my guitar; that way I wouldn't have to depend on anyone but myself. One morning after Verna Anne left the apartment to go to classes, I was messing around with my guitar, learning Rod Stewart's *Maggie May* from his new album. I had also picked up a 45 of Elvis's *Wonder Of You*, which was just beginning to climb the charts. I was trying to find a key to sing the song in so as to not get kicked out of the apartment for singing too loud. I put on the Elvis record and began fumbling with the chords. Then I started to sing, 'When no one else can understand me . . .' the words and notes came out rich and deep. I was stunned. I had never sung like that in my life. It was deep and rich and effortless.

The day I turned 21 years old, my life changed — I was about to discover my full vocal range.

We were kind of like Cheech & Chong before Cheech & Chong. We were both native and we did a lot of racially-charged humor.

I remember sitting there smiling and looking out the window, not believing what I had just done. I sat for a couple minutes and tried it again, and out it came, again. I had found my voice!

"After that I worked up enough songs for three sets of music. To do a single booking, I needed four sets. So I thought I'd repeat the first set for my last set. Then I landed a job in the lounge of a dingy hotel for $25 per night, playing Thursday, Friday and Saturday. I was so nervous I could hardly eat. I'd practiced the three sets over and over, and I thought if anything would save me, it would be my guitar playing.

"While I was putting my lounge sets together, I discovered an interesting way to structure keys of songs to modulate from one song to another, which would help me in later years structuring my shows. The opening song of my sets was always up-tempo, and, if it was in the key of G. the next song would be in the key of A, and the next song after that in the key of C. Then I would slow the tempo to a ballad in the key of D, always modulating the next song to a higher key and giving the audience a sense of acceleration or an uplifting feeling.

"As I set up my gear in the lounge and was about to start singing, I noticed there were only three people in the room – an elderly lady, the bartender, and me. After I had finished my first set, the elderly lady summoned me over to her table and asked if she could buy me a drink. Then she said, 'Son, you've got a beautiful voice, but you gotta work on your guitar playing . . .'

> I had never sung like that in my life. It was deep and rich and effortless. I had found my voice!

Going Solo

"I continued to get more solo gigs and I kept on learning more tunes. So I decided to audition for Ida Banks, a local booking agent whose husband was local legend, Tommy Banks, an actor and piano player who had his own CBC TV talk show. I showed up at Ida's office and she had me sing a couple of songs. One of them was *The Wonder of You*, which I sang with my very best newly acquired Elvis voice. Ida said that I sounded fine and asked if I would be available for a job at the Sheraton Lounge Pub for three weeks at Christmas. Inside, I was jumping for joy, barely able to contain my excitement, but she was still speaking, saying, 'learn more Feliciano and James Taylor material, you aren't going to get anywhere playing that Elvis stuff . . .'

"I was so happy to be working, playing every night of the week in an uptown Edmonton hotel that was only about 10 blocks from my apartment. I had money for Christmas. I was living high! The three weeks flew by, but then one night the bartender asked if I knew Tom Jones' *Delilah*. He said it was his favorite. As I was finishing the night the bartender asked if I was booked for January. I said I wasn't, and he said he was the booking agent for the acts in the lounge and he would tell Ida he wanted me for the month of January. I said, 'Yes! Yes! For sure.' He asked me to sing *Delilah* again. I finished the night, packed up my guitar, and, as I stepped out into the night, I could see giant snowflakes falling in the light from the lampposts. I skipped all the way home in the ankle deep snow feeling I was the luckiest man ever."

I had money for Christmas. I was living high!

During the time that Morris worked as a solo act in Edmonton, he saw Elvis Presley's documentary film *That's The Way It Is* for the first time. The documentary tells the story of how the King put his band and Vegas show together for his opening in Nevada. Morris realized that this movie was a blueprint for success. When he learned that *Elvis: That's The Way It Is* had come back to one of the cheap theaters in Edmonton, he watched it day after day, studying and learning how Elvis had done it. As BJ Bates recalls, "When we were in Edmonton there was this all-day and all-night theater on Jasper Avenue and I went there with Morris and we watched these four *Planet of the Apes* movies because the Elvis movie was the last one. We were all sleeping, but Morris was still wide-awake waiting for the Elvis movie." "Going to that Elvis movie at that theater," Morris quips, "was the best twenty-five cents I ever spent."

Meanwhile, Morris was developing his entertainment skills on the lounge circuit, but there was a limit to how much money he could make as a single act." "My solo act was getting popular in the local lounge circuit," he recalls, "and I was making better money and was seldom out of work. Verna Anne was in second year at the University of Alberta in Edmonton, studying to be a doctor. When we first met she had been fooling around with some folk guitar chords and now in her spare time she was messing with my bass. I taught her some basic finger exercises, and she had a good ear. I was always working on my material, and she would thump along on the bass the best she could. When we'd get on each other's nerves, she would go into the bedroom and practice. One evening, she brought this girl home she'd met at U of A who had grade 10 classical piano training. Her name was Barbara Bates (no relation). The three of us started jamming and put an ad in the university paper advertising for a drummer. This young guy named Jerry answered the ad and the girls thought he was cute so we hired him for our little group, which we called BATESESSION — and, as they say in showbiz, the rest is history."

At first, playing with the college students in BATESESSION was sort of a hobby band for Morris. He was still making his bread and butter playing in the duo with Al Earl and as a solo act in Edmonton area lounges. But after Verna Anne finished her classes at the University of Alberta, Morris and Verna Anne hit the road and picked up professional guitarists and drummers like Billy Ray Houston and Jeff Hogg to play with them in BATESESSION.

"When we hit the road," Morris recalls, "we played all kinds of music. It was like a musical jukebox. Whatever was number one on the chart, we went out, got it, and learned it. You had to keep on top of it. We played all kinds of things. Deep Purple came out then and John Fogerty. Creedence Clearwater was big — *Down On The Corner*— we played all sorts of things."

However, Morris wanted to do more than merely repeat this pattern, week after week, venue after venue. "I was looking for something that would set me apart from just being another bar

> Going to that Elvis movie at that theater, was the best twenty-five cents I ever spent.

> When we hit the road, we played all kinds of music. It was like a musical jukebox.

band," he explains. "Because the bar bands out there in Alberta were just like they were in Vancouver. Whoever got the gig got to be the bandleader — you'd see the same four musicians every week, but different names on the marquee. Bar musicians played all the same music — *In The Midnight Hour, Smoke On The Water, Mustang Sally* . . . that type of stuff. Everybody would do the same 20 songs."

Along with personnel changes, the band's name would change, as well, and quite a few of Morris Bates' longtime musical pals, like Cree drummer Peter Hamlin, Prince Rupert guitarist Tom Rysstad, and Stephen Gibbons-Barrett, would join him on the road. As guitar slinger Billy Ray Houston recalls, "Morris Bates, a full-blooded Shuswap Indian from Williams Lake, hired me to play guitar for BATESESSION. We changed the name shortly afterward to Injun Joe's Medicine Show and spent the better part of the summer of 1973 in a hotel cabaret in Nelson, BC."

"I fell in love with Nelson," Morris admits. "There was this really nice hotel owner there, a Scandinavian gentleman who had this large hotel with a nice cabaret, and he asked me to stay there and take over the cabaret. I was too young to do that and handle all of the issues involved, including hiring staff, waitresses, cashiers, and all of that. But I spent the best part of a year in Nelson. We had real good rooms in the hotel, and the gig was relaxed, providing me time to increase my repertoire as a vocalist."

> My room on the third floor of the hotel looked out at the famous Kokanee Glacier. It is the same view that you see when looking at a bottle of Kokanee beer, which meant that I got to see a lot of that glacier both day and night.

"My room on the third floor of the hotel looked out at the famous Kokanee Glacier," Billy Ray recalls. "It is the same view that you see when looking at a bottle of *Kokanee* beer, which meant that I got to see a lot of that glacier both day and night."

Injun Joe's Medicine Show was a band name that was a take-off on Dr. Hook's Medicine Show. Morris utilized the time spent in Nelson to learn more and more Elvis songs. He still had long hair and wasn't making any attempt to dress up in costumes that made him look more like Presley, but every night when he performed his Elvis medley with Injun Joe's Medicine show he noticed that the audience response was getting better and better. Nelson is a mere 168 miles north of Spokane, Washington, and when Morris learned that Elvis was coming to Spokane, he didn't miss this golden opportunity to see the King live.

"It was while I was still at the Hume Hotel in Nelson," he recalls, "that I saw Elvis do a show in Spokane." He attended Presley's evening show in Spokane on April 28, 1973 and one of two shows the King performed in Seattle the following day and night. "I paid ten dollars a ticket," he says, "and everybody bought fifty dollars worth of memorabilia, including myself."

Elvis, the '68 Comeback Special had first aired on December 3, 1968, and had marked the first time the King had appeared before a live audience since his last concert in Pearl Harbor, Hawaii on March 25, 1961. While watching that TV special, Morris noticed for the first time that he looked a lot like Elvis. It was more than merely the King's handsome facial features, which some people attributed to Presley's Cherokee heritage. Morris was almost the same height, a mere half-inch shorter than Elvis, and both men were fit and trim and graceful on their feet. Morris had been inspired by the TV special and had studied Elvis's moves in the documentary movie, but seeing the King perform live was the impetus he needed to concentrate on his Elvis medley and make it the focus of the next new band he formed, which he would call the Graffiti Band of Gold.

Nuts over You

Personnel changes and a change in direction were factors in the change of the band's name from BATESESSION to Injun Joe's Medicine Show, but the creation of Morris Bates' Graffiti Band of Gold, where he really began to focus on paying tribute to Elvis was not far off. As he recalls, "during the transition from BATE-SESSION to Injun Joe's Medicine Show and on to the Graffiti Band of Gold, I used a variety of booking agents, but mostly myself to arrange work for the group. To keep working you had to be everything to everybody. I met a guy named Robert Cloutier. Robert was a rock promoter and was booking arenas and other rock venues in Western Canada with Rush and a few other acts. We decided to start my own booking agency, calling it West Talent Management. Basically, it was only me and a mess of various musicians in different ensembles. The band Injun Joe was a hard act to book because of its name. Sometimes we would show up to play a gig and we were booked as the Wranglers. Nobody was going to buy Injun Joe's band doing a tribute to Elvis, even if you *were* Elvis. The creation of the Graffiti Band of Gold was the nostalgia band designed to market the tribute to Elvis show, and it worked."

It was also during this time that Morris got some good advice from Heart's Ann Wilson. The occasion was a hockey arena show in Cranbrook, BC, featuring Injun Joe's Medicine Show, Heart, and Randy Bachman. "I played a show with Heart and Randy Bachman's Brave Belt," he recalls. "I was wearing a black acetate suit and I went out on stage and did five Elvis songs. I was still doing Injun Joe's Medicine Show and using a cover of Redbone's *Maggie* as the set opener, then the medley of Elvis songs, and we closed with Deep Purple's *Flight of the Rat*. After the show, Ann Wilson came up to me and she said, 'Morris, you know, if you take that Elvis stuff and go to the United States they are going to go flat-ass nuts over you.'

> Morris, you know, if you take that Elvis stuff and go to the United States they are going to go flat-ass nuts over you.

"Heart was scheduled to play Ming's Restaurant in Regina the next night, and I was scheduled to play in Regina, too, in a country rock club. We finished the show in Cranbrook on a Sunday night and drove straight through to Regina and opened up there on a Monday night. We just got off stage, put our stuff in the van, and drove all night. We got there about an hour before we were scheduled to go on. We were just burnt to a crisp.

"Heart was Roger 'the dodger' Fischer, his brother Mike, and the two sisters, Ann and Nancy Wilson. They were from Seattle. Roger was the lead guitar player and Mike was doing sound and managing the band a bit. Roger was a *hot* guitar player. In those days, he used to do that Deep Purple stuff. Heart was one of the hottest rock bands in western Canada, and they came over to my Saturday afternoon jam and played with us. Annie brought her flute and played a great solo. The crowd went wild. I think that's the reason I later used a flute intro to Eddie Arnold's *Welcome To My World* in my Elvis tribute show."

Not long after this, Heart signed with Mushroom Records in Vancouver and recorded their breakout hits *Crazy On You* and *Magic Man*, and their million-selling debut album *Dreamboat Annie*. Morris took Ann Wilson's advice seriously. "That was the first time that I thought I should seriously pursue this," he admits. "Heart was just another bar band in those days, but they were dynamite. They had a great sound. And I really respected Annie and what she told me. It sure meant something to me. She just looked me in the eye and said, 'You're gonna make a fortune if you take this stuff to the states. They are going to eat you alive!'"

With Ann Wilson's words of encouragement added to the better wages he was making, Morris realized he really was onto something good. "I realized that there was an incredible market," he says, "and after that, it just took off!"

> I realized that there was an incredible market, and after that, it just took off!

Graffiti Band

When Billy Ray Houston, aka Bruce Hillstead, left Injun Joe's Medicine Show, guitar player Bob Stewart replaced him, but Bob was not cut out for the road and soon gave Morris his notice. Bob wanted to return to his girlfriend in Nelson. Morris made some calls and Gary Gust suggested that his brother, Wayne Gust, would be an excellent lead guitar player for Injun Joe's Medicine Show. Wayne had been in the Devilles, a teenage band, with Gary, and had moved to Toronto to become a supporting musician for a Canadian production of the popular sixties musical, *Hair*. After playing in the Schmaltz Band in Ontario, Wayne had drifted westward and was playing country music with Laura Vinson's band Red Wyng in Edmonton. When Morris learned that Wayne wanted to come back to his home province, he made the guitarist an offer.

"We were on our way to play Francie's, a club in Williams Lake," Morris recalls, "and I got a call from Wayne. He told me he wanted me to buy him a plane ticket so that he could fly to Vancouver before joining us in Williams Lake. So I did that. Then we heard that Wayne had been arrested on an outstanding warrant in Vancouver and he needed me to bail him out. I arranged that, I posted bond, and we were told that Wayne and his brother Eddy were driving up to Williams Lake in Eddy's new T-Bird. Injun Joe's Medicine Show was supposed to play Francie's, and in those days we played from 9:30 until 2:30."

Morris and the other band members arrived and set up their equipment, but at 9:30 there was still no sign of Wayne Gust or the blue Thunderbird Wayne's brother was driving up the Cariboo Highway from Vancouver. During their first set, Wayne did show up but was too bent him out of shape to play because someone had given him some pills to keep him awake. "I can't feel my hands, I can't feel my hands" is all Morris remembers that Wayne said before he went back outside and crashed in the back seat of his brother's car. Bass player Verna-Anne was not impressed — especially when she learned that the hotshot guitar player from the big city had shown up without an amp or a guitar.

"I had an ES-335 Gibson guitar, like BB King's original 'Lucille' guitar," Morris relates, "and I had a Gibson acoustic that was fully electric. And about 12:30, Wayne comes sauntering in, got up on stage with the red Gibson, and blew me away. The first song that he played with us was Chuck Berry's *School Days*, and he nailed it. That went so well that we kept him — he was in the band. He was a good guitar player. He could play the sound that I wanted to hear, and he could sing, too."

It was the beginning of a musical camaraderie that lasted a goodly long time and led to a friendship that

About 12:30, Wayne comes sauntering in, got up on stage with the red Gibson, and blew me away. The first song that he played with us was Chuck Berry's *School Days*, and he nailed it.

continues to this day. Wayne Gust would be in and out of Morris Bates' bands for the next three decades.

Many people have wondered why Wayne Gust was in and out of Morris Bates' bands so many times throughout the years. Dennis Compo provides a valuable insight that illuminates some of the reasons. "Wayne and Morris have a sort of love-hate relationship," Dennis explains, "and it's ongoing — it's never been any different . . . it's been that way from day one. Wayne wrote original material and he was more into a country-R&B flavor, and Morris was nothing like that. So you're going to have conflict there, for sure. Wayne has pretty good ears. He knows what he wants to hear. And there was probably some conflict going on all the time, but Morris wanted what Morris wanted, and if you were playing in his band, that's how you played it. Nine times out of ten, Morris was 100 percent right — some players loved working with him because they knew where they stood, and other players just wanted to play what they wanted to play and Morris wasn't the band for them. But he had no problem replacing good talent. He had a lot of really good talent that wanted to play for him."

Nine times out of ten, Morris was 100 percent right — some players loved working with him because they knew where they stood.

Wayne Gust's experience performing fifties material spurred Morris on to eventually form a nostalgia band, and whenever Wayne was in the band the two musicians were as thick as thieves. "Some Elvis songs, like *Money Honey*, I never heard the original, but Wayne taught me how to play and sing them," Morris relates. "We were in a hotel room in Slave Lake, Alberta, and he said I should learn some more Elvis stuff. So he wrote it down and we went over it and I learned it from him. By the time I had a chance to hear Elvis sing *Money Honey*, I already had my interpretation. My version wasn't exactly the same, but it was pretty close.

"From a musical point of view, it was a weird relationship working with Wayne. He was playing music of the fifties in the fifties, and therefore missed the sixties, and I was playing music of the seventies and I had missed the fifties."

Morris remembers that another American artist who had

encouraged him to take his Elvis show to the US during this same time frame was Donnie Sneed of the Sneed Family Band, an act that was popular whenever they toured in Alberta. Morris would meet up with Donnie Sneed again, when he and his brother, pedal steel legend Danny Sneed, were booked into a club in Las Vegas. "The Sneed Family Band was a real show band," Morris recalls. "When they were just young kids, they appeared on *The Ed Sullivan Show*."

I just kept working on the show. Learning how to put a band together. Learning how to keep the audience's attention.

With these encouraging comments from American artists, Morris refined his act even further. "I just kept working on the show. Learning how to put a band together. Learning how to keep the audience's attention. I was one of the first guys to have a follow spot to really center me right out. Donnie Sneed had a big band, but they were all featured in every song — the sax player, the pedal steel, they were a band — I wasn't a band. I packed eighty per cent of the vocals doing my shows. I just kept pushing the envelope."

Williams Lake Rock Festival

When the summer of 1974 rolled around, Morris was back in his hometown for the July first weekend and the Williams Lake Stampede. "It was a big deal in those days," he recalls. "It was bigger than the Pendleton Rodeo in Oregon, second only to the Calgary Stampede. Up to 100,000 people would show up in my hometown that weekend and attend rodeo events. It was wide open, spontaneous, but there were nowhere near that many hotel rooms or rodeo grounds campsites. So I decided to have a rock festival on my dad's land and sell tickets that would include camping space."

I decided to have a rock festival on my dad's land and sell tickets that would include camping space.

Camping space on the rodeo grounds was now at a premium. The commercial success of the Williams Lake Stampede prompted local businessmen to develop the rodeo grounds, which is on reservation land, for their own use and to charge people for a limited number of official camping sites.

"Prior to that," Morris explains, "all of the Indians were allowed into the rodeo free and they camped on the site for free. The Chilcotin, the Carrier, all the Shuswaps, everybody, came there each year. It was a big powwow . . . That was originally, and, as far as I know, still is Indian land. It was a perfect little bowl and people could sit up on the hills and watch the rodeo. And it has been gradually taken away from the Williams Lake Indian Band."

Before the days when most families had cars and trucks and RVs, people traveled in wagons to the rodeo and pitched their tents. They spent their time attending or participating in rodeo events during the daytime and visiting, playing music, and gambling around their campfires at night. And before they returned to their rural homes they stocked up on supplies and memories that would last them until the next annual rodeo.

Morris Bates' father and uncles were all Cariboo cowboys and ranch hands, and they often participated in the rodeo. "My Uncle Louie," Morris recalls, "fought in WWII. He got shot several times. But when the Williams Lake Stampede resumed after the war, Louie was back in the saddle again. He was all-around cowboy twice and he won the suicide race twice. He's in the British Columbia Cowboy Hall of Fame alongside Williams Lake's most well known saddle bronc rider, Jack Palmantier. Jack won Saddle Bronc Champion at the International Finals Rodeo in '76, and he was always a favorite at the Williams Lake Stampede. Jack Palmantier, 'Man in Motion' Rick Hansen, and Montreal Canadiens goalie Carey Price are three of Williams Lake's most famous sons.

> My Uncle Louie was all-around cowboy twice and he won the suicide race twice. He's in the British Columbia Cowboy Hall of Fame.

"One year, Pascal won the steer-decorating competition. He won $750, which was a lot of money in those days. You had to jump off the horse and put two ribbons on the horns of the steer. One steer flipped and he almost lost an eye. I think he got a broken rib as well. He won a lot of money and he took us to Radium Hot Springs and into Alberta for a vacation. My dad's rib was broken, he was in a lot of pain, and I did most of the driving. It was our first real vacation.

"I tried my luck in the sport of rodeo. Growing up on cattle ranches and on the reservation, our weekend entertainment was 'off to the rodeo'. I started out riding sheep. Next was falling off calves — then cow-riding — then bulls. I don't remember ever winning anything, but I do remember Teepee Creek, Alberta. I was on a bull and in the process of being bucked off when I got hung up. By the time the bull got done with me, and the rodeo clowns got me back to the chutes, my arm had already started to swell up like Popeye the Sailor. I had pulled all the ligaments in my arm and I was a hurting puppy.

"Pascal really wanted all of his sons to rodeo, but it just wasn't in the cards for me. I went to him and told him my rodeo days were over. I explained that I didn't see the percentage spending my hard-earned money on the back of an animal that didn't want me there, then after bucking me off comes looking for me. My brothers Bernie and BJ fared a bit better, but not much. My guitar was not near as dangerous."

For his rock festival during Stampede week, Morris picked a festival site on the reservation at the opposite end of the lake and offered free camping. He booked musicians, printed posters ... and soon discovered that there was a lot more work involved than he had at first anticipated. But his family and friends were more than willing to pitch in to help make his vision a reality. As he recalls, "I woke up one morning and heard all this hammering and banging and went outside and there was my dad, Pascal, building me this big new stage next to the barn. We cut a hole in the wall of the barn and used the tack rooms for dressing rooms. We charged people five dollars for the festival and camping space, and 5,000 people showed up and camped on Pascal's land. I made more money that weekend than I had ever made before. The City of Williams Lake tried to stop me, but they had no right to say what we did on the reserve. I ran the security and we had a whole mess of people that weekend."

Joe Mock, Stephen Gibbons-Barrett, Smilin' Jack Smith, Danny Mack, Dan "Tapper" Tapanila, and some other Vancouver

> I didn't see the percentage spending my hard-earned money on the back of an animal that didn't want me there, then after bucking me off comes looking for me.

musicians came up to Williams Lake to play at the rock festival, along with local heroes Tim Williams and Morris Bates.

"Morris and his family were real down to earth people," Joe Mock recalls. "I was raised a city boy and the chance to hang out with guys like that who were into horses and the farm and all that kind of stuff was a real nice experience for me. I remember me and 'Tapper' and Pascal sitting in the stands drinking wine and watching the rodeo."

Morris will never forget that Joe saved Verna-Anne's life one night when she stepped out on a wet stage and plugged in her bass guitar. "Her hair was sticking out in all directions," Stephen remembers, "and I thought, 'What an act!' And then Joe went over and whacked her, and knocked her off the stage. We thought that it was real neat, her hair sticking out like that — we thought that it was part of the show, but Joe saw what was really happening . . ."

"Verna Anne had this long black hair down to her ass," BJ recalls, "and when the shock went through her, her hair stood up on end and sparks were coming off her fingertips and coming out her mouth . . ."

"It wasn't pretty," Morris admits, "she fell off the stage and onto the stairs. She was real shaken up, but she survived. She was being electrocuted because in those days they didn't have all the wires and equipment grounded."

"I just remember seeing her standing there on stage in shock, and running over and knocking her off without even thinking," Joe explains, humbly. "It was a spontaneous reaction. Something alerted me. I think she screamed. It was so fast that I can't remember exactly what it was, but it wasn't normal. I wouldn't be knocking somebody off the stage for nothing. I didn't even realize that was what I was doing — knocking her off the stage. I just wanted to break the connection."

Morris remembers rescuing a young man trapped beneath a

We charged people five dollars for the festival and camping space, and 5,000 people showed up and camped on Pascal's land. I made more money that weekend than I had ever made before.

Verna Anne had this long black hair down to her ass, and when the shock went through her, her hair stood up on end and sparks were coming off her fingertips and coming out her mouth . . .

car that had driven into a meadow and became hung-up on the bumpy terrain, but all in all it was a wonderful weekend for everybody who showed up at Morris Bates' first rock festival.

The same could not be said about some of the other events that were going on that weekend. Joe Mock recalls being totally puzzled by going to an outdoor dance hall on the rodeo grounds that the locals called "Squaw Hall," where there was broken glass on the dance floor.

"They had big dances in the Civic Centre and the hockey rinks, but they didn't want Indians up there," Morris explains. "Rather than have the Indians uptown on their streets, they built this outdoor dancehall on the rodeo grounds and they called it Squaw Hall. They put wire mesh around the top and built a small bandstand. There was only one way in and one way out, and they had bleachers. The Thompson Valley Boys was the band that always played there. They played covers of Buck Owens songs and stuff like that. And when they stopped serving liquor in the bars and beer parlors and at the dances, white people came down to Squaw Hall in droves."

The incidences of violence inside and outside the open-air dancehall escalated when these overflow crowds mingled with people coming in and out of Squaw Hall. As Morris recalls, "They wouldn't let the Indians come uptown, but *they* would come down to Squaw Hall and there were always fights going on. There were some really tough Indians that came to the Stampede. And people that were outside that couldn't get in would throw beer bottles over the wire mesh fence and there would be broken glass all over the dance floor."

BJ became friends with Stephen and his girlfriend Barb during the rock festival, and when he moved to Vancouver, he lived with them in their house in east Vancouver. "I helped Stephen build the racks in his mobile eight-track tape exchange trailer," BJ recalls. "When Stephen would sell a painting, he would take Barb and me out for a nice dinner."

Morris held a second rock festival the following summer and

They wouldn't let the Indians come uptown, but they would come down to Squaw Hall and there were always fights going on.

nearly twice as many people came to camp and attend the shows. BJ remembers proudly that both festivals were held on his dad's land, Pascal's ranch near the lake, and that for the second event, called The Strawberry Hill Rock Festival, Sweeney Todd was the headliner and they played their big hit *Roxy Roller*. "I wanted BTO to headline," Morris recalls, "but Randy Bachman wanted his 5000 bucks up front. For the second festival, I moved the site closer to the lake and I rented two 40-foot trailers for the stage. We rented port-a-toilets and generators. I was to headline with Sweeney Todd, but there were so many gatecrashers that I spent most of the time riding my stallion up and down the fence and roping guys that were getting in without paying. I would pull them across the cactus for a few feet and then set them free, and they would settle for running over to the ticket booth and paying the admission charge."

The Elvis Thing

"I learned early on that people want to hear what they know, and they hear with their eyes," Morris explains. He wanted to put on a show that would pack venues and create a buzz, and he needed to find an angle that would make his show dramatically different than his competition. He chose fifties revival music partly because, like many young people in the early seventies, he had been inspired by watching Sha Na Na perform *At The Hop* during the *Woodstock* movie, but also because he glimpsed a new market that would soon be opening up.

"Sha Na Na had come out," he recalls, "and I got hooked on them and nobody else was doing that type of material. They were not so much a musical influence as a realization that, 'Wow, this is marketable!' These people are in their thirties and forties and they want to go out and have a beer, and they love fifties music. It was just sitting there — it was just waiting to be tapped — it was an opportunity."

Morris Bates had already come a long way from the Sugar Cane Reserve by taking some chances and stepping out. He was quick to realize when an opportunity came his way. This time, his instinct that fifties revival music might become popular turned out to be one his most savvy realizations.

"I started looking at it and I thought, 'this is interesting!'" he enthuses. "So I put together a set of graffiti music, you know, *Rock Around The Clock* and Buddy Holly songs, and I stuck some Elvis songs in. I mixed in three or four classics like *Heartbreak Hotel* and *Blue Suede Shoes*."

During a week off from touring, Morris holed up in a northern British Columbia hotel with his new band and rehearsed the new show. When they got back on the road, the result was immediately evident.

"People just loved the graffiti set," he says, proudly, "and when I did the Elvis thing, it really took off.

"I grew up in a really small town in the north part of British Columbia, where we lived in some sort of time warp. We heard old rock & roll — that's what I grew up with and when I got into bands I started doing stuff I could understand — fifties music. I was always a showman. I got a lot of attention on the basketball court and I guess I really dug the attention. The entertainment thing, you know, can kind of feed your ego, so I decided to get into entertaining to make a living. When you're young, it all looks so glamorous. But when I would do Elvis songs, I would always get a good response, so I always kept Elvis material in my repertoire.

> I guess you could say that I got into this by accident because I never planned to be an Elvis Presley impersonator. There was no such thing in those days.

"I guess you could say that I got into this by accident because I never planned to be an Elvis Presley impersonator. There was no such thing in those days. I never imagined I'd be playing Vegas and touring all over the world doing it.

"I had really long hair and I just sang Elvis and the people loved it. When I first started doing Elvis, it was a comedy routine. It didn't start out as a tribute. In those days it was a satire thing. You sort of mocked the artist in a satirical way. But the one thing that I was really lucky about was that I always took the music seriously. I stayed structured to the original versions of the songs, the original licks that were done on the original records. Whatever the song was, we copied the essence of the hit record. So, we might have mocked the artist when we were performing the song, but the music was dead on. That's what really separated us from other acts at that time. We didn't have, say, Jimi Hendrix jumping out in the middle of *Johnny B. Goode*. We played *Johnny B. Goode* exactly like Chuck Berry played it. We didn't jerk around with the songs."

Morris Bates' hunch that working up a fifties' revival show might be a good idea had paid off and he was able to book himself into better venues. The big surprise, though, was the audience response to his performance of Elvis songs. "When I noticed the response to the 'Elvis thing', I was overwhelmed," he admits. "I just couldn't believe it. Every time I did it, people would clap like crazy and we'd pack these bars! I went from making $500 a week to making $3,500 a week, which was a lot of money back then. It was just because we packed the rooms."

I went from making $500 a week to making $3,500 a week, which was a lot of money back then. It was just because we packed the rooms.

With more money to work with, Morris added production to their shows. In those days, bands worked with a minimum of stage lighting and battered sound equipment that was bandaged with duct tape. One of the band members would adjust volume levels from time to time. There was no budget for a sound technician, let alone someone to run a light show. In many venues, there wasn't anywhere to hang lights even if you had them in your band bus or Econoline van.

"The best investment I ever made," Morris recalls, "was a follow spot. When I realized how well the Elvis material was going over with audiences, I 'woodsheded' 10 or 12 Elvis songs, the ones I thought I could really lay on. I cut my hair so I could get it into a pompadour. I went down to the secondhand store and bought one of those wool plaid jackets and a black shirt and black pants, and a pair of white buck shoes. I combed my hair up and I was so nervous I couldn't believe it — I was gonna pretend that I was Elvis Presley!

"When you are on stage in a bar, everything is lit up. It's hard to get a focus on one person. Doesn't matter how good you are. And you've got guys in your band who have no concept of a show — you've got one guy over there pretending he's Jimi Hendrix, and another guy over there pretending something else. There are just a lot of distractions as you are trying to present the show. Putting myself in that spotlight really solved a lot of problems and brought real focus to my show."

The new setup, with the spotlight focused on Morris, increased the impact of his dramatic renditions of ballads like *Love Me Tender* and brought a sharp focus to what had been an undisciplined band whose wardrobe and body language distracted audiences when he performed up tempo numbers like *Suspicious Minds*. "I isolated myself from the band," he explains, "and we turned down the house lights so that they had to look at me perform the set."

Adding more and more Elvis songs proved to be astute, especially after George Lucas' trend-setting movie American Graffiti was released and fifties revival music became fashionable overnight.

Adding more and more Elvis songs proved to be astute, especially after George Lucas' trend-setting movie *American Graffiti* was released and fifties revival music became fashionable overnight. The film is remembered today as the movie that launched the careers of Harrison Ford, Richard Dreyfuss, and Cindy Williams — and led to the creation of the popular TV shows *Happy Days* and *Laverne & Shirley*. Soon, Sha Na Na had a TV show. The *American Graffiti* soundtrack album, with 40 classic fifties songs, sold than three million vinyl copies. Morris would later tell a Las Vegas reporter "there was nothing in that movie about Elvis Presley at all. They never mentioned him once. Maybe they couldn't get the rights from the Colonel to release any of his material, not while Elvis was in the midst of his comeback and still a vibrant driving force in the music industry."

Step by step, Morris developed his first Elvis tribute set. "I did the graffiti set first. It was like a warm-up set. Then I went and changed into my fifties Elvis wardrobe. We only had a four-piece band so we would play a tape of *2001: A Space Odyssey* on the sound system. We'd cut the tape machine and the thundering drums for *That's All Right (Mama)* would come roaring in. I'd hit the stage, and the place would just go nuts."

"Morris was good at singing Elvis," Stephen Gibbons-Barrett recalls. "He really looked like Elvis. We went over the top with that Elvis show. We had our own lights. I had a huge drum kit — two bass drums, a forest of cymbals, congas, bongos, and tympani."

No doubt, those early seventies bar audiences were mystified by the sound of the fanfare music from Stanley Kubrick's movie. Morris knew that "Space Odyssey" music was used to open shows in Vegas. Fifteen-piece show bands played the exotic classical music arrangements. Wayne Newton used it. Elvis used it. Morris Bates was proving himself to be a most resourceful fellow, creating a "big production" out of whatever was at hand. As the production developed, girlfriends were conscripted to run the follow spot and sew Elvis-style scarves, and, eventually stage costumes.

As the production developed, girlfriends were conscripted to run the follow spot and sew Elvis-style scarves, and, eventually stage costumes.

"That's basically where the show started back in those days," Morris recalls with a rueful grin. "And as we got better, it turned into an act we called the Graffiti Band of Gold presents a fifties tribute to Elvis."

"We did young Elvis, sixties Elvis, Vegas Elvis," Stephen recalls, "and we had seen a TV documentary of Elvis in Hawaii, and we did that, too. Morris was really good at impersonating Elvis, and he had all these costumes. By the time we swung back into Edmonton, we were billed as 'The Graffiti Band of Gold featuring Morris Bates as Elvis.' When we did the Elvis segment, you couldn't get a seat in the house."

"The shows were just packed!" Morris exclaims. "We played the big bar at the Mayfield Inn in Edmonton, and I think that's where we really opened it up. I just did the Elvis show. I'd get up to leave, and they would yell, "Play *Return To Sender*, play *Treat Me Nice*. At first, I didn't know all the songs. I didn't start out singing Elvis. I was singing Hank Williams and Creedence Clearwater Revival. I didn't really hear Elvis much until '68 when he did the NBC Special. Before that I had only seen him perform in the popcorn movies."

Ringo Starr's cover version of Johnny Burnette's *You're Sixteen* had rocketed to the top of the *Billboard* chart in '74, confirming that Morris was definitely on the right track. "Ringo's version wasn't spectacular," Morris notes, "but people just wanted that type of music. I had learned how to put a show set together, and it wasn't as good as I did later on down the road in Vegas, but I put the graffiti set together with a little Elvis mixed in and people loved it."

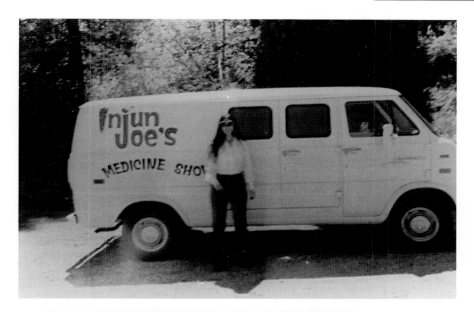

Above: Injun Joe's Medicine Show van with Verna Anne Moore.

Below: Verna Anne Moore and Morris

Top left: BATESESSION: *Billy Ray Houston,
Peter Hamlin, and Morris. Top right: Heart:
Ann and Nancy Wilson. Bottom: Wayne Gust
& Morris*

Top left: Morris's old stompin' grounds. Top right: Dan Tapanila and Danny Mack at Rohan's Rockhouse. Bottom: Morris's uncle Louis, decorated World War II veteran and member of the BC Cowboy Hall of Fame.

Trouble

Live at the Cave

The next bold move that Morris made was deciding to put a full, three-part tribute to Elvis together, a 90-minute show that he would often perform two or three times a night in some venues, leaving opening sets and sometimes even late-night closing sets to his band to take care of. With a bigger budget, Morris would add a horn section and eventually female backup singers.

"I changed the name of the act to Canada's Tribute To Elvis," Morris relates. "It just kept getting bigger and bigger. I didn't put my name on it at all. Because I wasn't really sure yet — once you stick your name on something, that's about it. If it falls to the floor, you are stuck with it. I just kept going with Canada's Tribute To Elvis, still playing good rooms, starting to move into the cabaret rooms all over western Canada. And the money kept getting better, too."

Success followed success. When 5,000 fans showed up at the Keystone Centre in Brandon, Manitoba, they showed their appreciation by storming the stage. "That show was a gas," Morris recalls. "It was the first time that I had played an arena. The show that followed me was the Ice Capades. It was the biggest show that I had done. I was really scared.

"All these young girls rushed to the front of the stage when the show started. I didn't want to get too close to the audience because I wasn't sure what they might do. When I

I changed the name of the act to Canada's Tribute To Elvis. It just kept getting bigger and bigger.

reached out my hands and some of the women reached out to touch me, someone stole my pinky ring. I finished the song and said, 'Somebody out there has got my ring and would they please return it to me.' A young girl put her hand up with my ring on her finger and gave it back to me. After that I taped my ring fingers in concert.

"Near the end I started giving out scarves, but the girls were really going crazy and I thought that somebody was going to get hurt. I turned to Wayne and said, 'Don't give me any more scarves, somebody might get killed.' And Wayne said, 'If somebody gets really hurt, then it's going on the front page.' Lacking better judgment, I asked Wayne to give me more scarves." Nobody was badly hurt, though four women *were* taken to hospital to have minor cuts and scratches attended to.

Near the end I started giving out scarves, but the girls were really going crazy and I thought that somebody was going to get hurt.

With his tribute to Elvis gaining momentum on the Canadian prairies, Morris Bates was already contemplating a Las Vegas engagement, where he might possibly be performing at the same time the King was doing his show at the Las Vegas Hilton International. However, there were many hurdles to be overcome before that possibility would become a reality. One was his agent. "I was working with an agent by the name of Chris Siller," Morris recalls, "but he was based in Regina."

The Cave

Before breaking out of Canada, Morris would change the act's name again, from Canada's Tribute to Elvis to A World Tribute to Elvis. "It was getting bigger," he says, "so we changed the name, but there were still some nuts to crack. Every city had a room that paid $10,000 a week, but because we were seen as locals, as Canadians, we couldn't get into them. You had to be from someplace else. I had an apartment in the West End in Vancouver, but I had never played Vancouver. If you lived in Vancouver, you were considered a local. If I played any of the small Vancouver clubs, I was likely to get pigeonholed. I needed to play the Cave."

The Cave, Isy's, Baceda's, and Oil Can Harry's were the crème de la crème of the large downtown Vancouver nightclubs. They featured imported acts from New York, Nashville, Memphis, and Hollywood, leaving local acts to play the seedy bars and small nightclubs in Vancouver's downtown eastside skid row district. Since the Cave opened in 1937, Ella Fitzgerald had recorded a live album there, and Patti Page, Peggy Lee, Johnny Cash, the Righteous Brothers, Ike & Tina Turner, and the Supremes had performed there on a regular basis.

In Morris Bates' mind, playing the Cave would be the first step to playing Las Vegas. He definitely had Las Vegas in mind — perhaps a booking at the Frontier Hotel, where Elvis had made his Vegas Strip debut in 1956. The hotel's Venus Room was a good venue for debuts. Liberace had debuted there in the forties. Judy Garland had debuted there, too. But it hadn't worked out all that well for Elvis the first time around. Colonel Tom Parker had booked Elvis into the Frontier for two weeks in April 1956. Elvis, Scotty Moore, Bill Black, and drummer DJ Fontana were part of an entertainment package that included comedian Shecky Greene, Freddy Martin and his orchestra, and a bevy of Vegas showgirls. Elvis was billed as "The Atomic Powered Singer," a designation Parker hoped would link his protégé to the nearby Nevada nuclear bomb test sites. But the show miscalculated the audience. Elvis had been drawing thousands of young people to bigger and bigger arenas and stadiums, whereas the Las Vegas audiences were much older, many of them parents who were alarmed by Elvis's outrageous behavior on stage — parents who blamed Elvis for inciting rebellion.

A critic for *The Las Vegas Sun* panned Presley's opening night show, calling Elvis an "uncouth bore" singing "nonsensical lyrics." Drummer DJ Fontana later said, "I don't think the people there were ready for Elvis. He was mostly for teenagers, kids. We tried everything we knew. Usually Elvis would get them on his side. It didn't work that time. The Colonel did a show for teenagers on Saturday and it was just jam-packed with everyone screaming and hollering."

By the time Elvis died in 1977, most people were too young to have seen the rockabilly Elvis from the fifties, their image of the King being his triumphant return to the Strip wearing rhinestone-studded jumpsuits and capes. From the beginning, Morris told the whole Elvis Presley story, from his rockabilly debut to being crowned the monarch in the entertainment capital of the world.

> From the beginning, Morris told the whole Elvis Presley story, from his rockabilly debut to being crowned the monarch in the entertainment capital of the world.

During a Las Vegas interview, Morris would later say, "I don't know why people have such a 'thing' about Elvis. Maybe it was the fact that he was merchandised as the first genuine sex symbol in this country. He was the polite, All-American boy who also performed sexy gyrations and hip movements. The crowds went wild over that, young and old. Plus, he was as pretty a man as can reasonably be, while he was still the ultimate masculine figure. Tom Jones came on the scene and performed similar movements, but it wasn't quite the same. I think that Tom Jones' presence was the reason Elvis went back to performing live shows. And that is where he shone the most." Morris has always shown surprising insight into Elvis's career. He has always been respectful of the King, always paying tribute, telling interviewers that, "I'm not trying to be Elvis."

The Hustle

To play the Cave, Morris had to convince owner Stan Grozina that he could fill the house. Grozina wasn't about to give a local act a break. Morris had played the Penthouse as a bass player and he went back there to visit manager Joe Filippone. "When I went to see him," Morris recalls, "I told him I wanted play the Cave, but the manager felt I didn't have the drawing power because he viewed me as a local act. I don't really know what happened, but as a result, a few days later, I received a call from Stan Grozina.

"I had a lot of really good breaks, but the one that got me into the business heavy was when I played the Cave. Everybody who was anybody played the Cave in Vancouver. It was *the place* to play. Once you played the Cave, you were just guaranteed all of the other A-rooms in Canada. You could ask for $10,000 a week in Edmonton, $10,000 a week in Calgary where only Lucifer's would pay that kind of money."

Securing a booking at the Cave had taken some dogged persistence. As Morris recalls, "I tried and I tried and I couldn't get in there, but I had some favors owed and finally I got in. I got the call from Stan Grozina. He said, 'Would you consider three days in front of Mitzi Gaynor?'

"I said, 'I'll be there in ten minutes,' and I was.

"I said, 'So, what are you going to pay me?'

"And he says, 'Five hundred bucks and the door.'

"About a week before I was scheduled to appear at the Cave, Stan phones me up again and says, 'Can you do the whole week?'

"I said, 'Yeah,' and I booted it over there, and he says, 'Mitzi can't open until the following Monday.'

"I said, 'Okay, what are you going to pay me?'

"And he said, 'Five hundred dollars and the door . . .'"

Morris agreed but he didn't merely roll over and capitulate. He didn't want to do all of the publicity himself. And he didn't want to play to empty seats. He wanted the same size ads in the dailies that he gave to his other feature acts.

"I told Stan that I wanted the same amount of promotion in the press that Mitzi Gaynor was getting," he relates. "I don't want some little one-line announcement saying that I'm playing the Cave. I told him that I would do it for $500, but I wanted my name all over the place."

Morris immediately geared up his own promotional campaign, putting up thousands of posters and passing out hundreds of complimentary tickets for the first three nights. "We wallpapered the town," he says. "I comped the first three nights. I sold my own tickets out of The Bicycle Shop, which was on the ground floor of my apartment building, and had my own people handle the door. I was getting 500 bucks and the door, and I wanted to pack the club, so I passed out complimentary tickets to

I had a lot of really good breaks, but the one that got me into the business heavy was when I played the Cave.

I passed out complimentary tickets to the Vancouver Fire Department, the Vancouver Police Department, and the Vancouver General Hospital staff.

the Vancouver Fire Department, the Vancouver Police Department, and the Vancouver General Hospital staff. The complimentary tickets were only good for the first three nights, but because I caused such a buzz, some of the comps couldn't even get in."

There were many obstacles to overcome. For one, mere days before Morris was scheduled to open at the Cave, his band staged a mutiny.

"I was using this young group of players," he recalls. "They wanted equal billing with me. They were backing me but they wanted to go out on their own. They were trying to use me to showcase themselves, and tried to sabotage me when I was going into the Cave. They stood their ground on the equal billing on the marquee. I said, 'No.' And I changed bands."

Morris was able to hire an even better lineup of older, more experienced sidemen — guys like Wayne Gust and Scott Anderson — who were already familiar with his repertoire. "We had to go into rehearsal," he admits, "and it was heavy duty, but we did it."

The weekend before Morris was to play at the Cave, he was able to take his new band into a small nightclub in North Vancouver, where he met Lyle and Grace Bobb, a young married couple who would become two of his biggest fans.

"We first saw Morris when he was at the Roadhouse in North Vancouver," Lyle recalls. "After the show, we went backstage and met with him and got to know him and visited for an hour. And then we went to see him at the Cave."

Monday night when Morris went on for his first show at the Cave, the club was packed, and there were people lined up outside the nightclub on the Hornby Street strip all the way past West Georgia.

Lyle and Grace benefited from being among the first to receive complimentary tickets to Morris Bates' opening night at the Cave, and they brought a slew of their friends along with them. Later, when Morris's fan club president Alma Cunningham realized what enthusiastic new fans they had become, they got a steady supply of tickets.

"We would get 50 tickets," Grace explains, "pass them out to our friends, and we would fill up that nightclub. All our daughters and their friends came, and our friends from my office, and Lyle's friends from Reliance, and we became really close to Morris."

"When we got to the Cave," Lyle remembers, "Morris asked to see us, and we went back and we met his mother, Phyllis. And she asked, 'Where are your relatives from?' I said, 'My mom is from Lytton and we got relatives up from past the lake.' It ended up that his mother and my mother were related.'"

"Morris had special feelings for Lyle," Grace recalls, "and he didn't know why. Lyle would go up to his dressing room and I would follow right behind. I was just crazy about his performances. He would come forward on the ramp of the stage and I would reach out and touch his hand. I've got about 30 of those scarves that he would give all the girls. Everybody would bring Teddy Bears. Morris got tons of Teddy Bears given to him, just like Elvis did. His fans treated him like he was Elvis. His performance was so good. He had the feelings. He had the moves. And he had the looks."

Morris Bates' appearance at the Cave resulted in many other friendships, including one very, special relationship with a young woman from his home stomping grounds. As Morris recalls, "Linda Fuller was from Williams Lake, and when I met up with her a few years after we had both left our hometown, she was working as a radiologist at Vancouver General Hospital. She was a beautiful young woman, and I thought she was special, but she wasn't interested. She didn't want to mess with anybody from Williams Lake."

Morris persisted and Linda was drawn to his shows at the Cave, where hundreds of women were screaming and rushing the stage in hopes of getting a brief kiss or a souvenir scarf. Their romance reenacted scenes from Elvis movies, where a clean-cut, young, sexual dynamo doesn't take no for an answer and ultimately wins the affections of a cool, aloof beauty.

Monday night when Morris went on for his first show at the Cave, the club was packed, and there were people lined up outside the nightclub on the Hornby Street strip all the way past West Georgia.

Their romance reenacted scenes from Elvis movies, where a clean-cut, young, sexual dynamo doesn't take no for an answer and ultimately wins the affections of a cool, aloof beauty.

Popular *Vancouver Sun* columnist Jack Wasserman provided a helping hand when he mentioned the lineups outside the Cave in his daily column. "Don't ask me why," Wasserman scribed, "but Morris is packing the Cave. That's not the finicky cat. He's billed as Canada's Tribute To Elvis — at which he's very effective — and the crowds are stumbling over each other to get in, which has Stan Grozina in a state of schlock, er, ah, I mean, shock . . ."

In those days, an endorsement from daily columnist Wasserman was like money in the bank, and no doubt ensured that the nightclub would be packed for the rest of the week as well. As Morris recalls, "At that time on Hornby Street, there were 14 clubs within a block and a half. On Thursday evening, I went down there in my Lincoln Mark III with the sunroof and everything, and at six o'clock in the evening they were lined up around the block. So I took the door for Thursday, Friday, and Saturday and I made $10,000 dollars in three nights. After that, I did two shows a night, and after the first show the people in there had to leave and make way for the second show crowd. People would buy tickets for both shows! So Stan was really making some serious money. After that I *owned* the Cave. It was the first time that I ever made $10,000 in one week. And Stan Grozina bought the show."

Over the years, Morris would return to the Cave many times before it closed. "I would come in there for one month at a time," he says. "Most of the other acts would come in for three days, or maybe a week or two weeks, but Stan booked me in there for a month at a time. I was a local boy and I was playing Vegas. I think I put 1,100 people in there for every show. The fire marshals didn't bother me. I probably played the Cave more than any other performer." Which, considering that some performers, like Mitzi Gaynor, for example, had been a perennial fixture there for more than a decade, was surely a noteworthy accomplishment.

"Then on Saturdays," Morris continues, "I would do matinees for the kids. Saturday afternoons all the moms

At Christmas time, when I would come up and play the Cave, I would take all those Teddy Bears to the Children's Hospital. I would go up there, just me and my guitar in my blue suit, and sing *Blue Christmas* to the kids.

would come down with their kids. There would be just tons of kids and they were so nice to me. I really had a built-in following. And my apartment was filled right to the ceiling with all the Teddy Bears they gave me. At Christmas time, when I would come up and play the Cave, I would take all those Teddy Bears to the Children's Hospital. I would go up there, just me and my guitar in my blue suit, and sing *Blue Christmas* to the kids."

This generosity of spirit merely added to Morris Bates' reputation. "I was in the press nearly every day!" he says. Following that first week at the Cave, Morris played to bigger and bigger audiences everywhere he performed in Canada. He was telling journalists that his show was "a piece of theater" now, and he was getting rave reviews wherever he performed.

"The Cave was really the turning point," he emphasizes. "It gave me the prestige. Once I played there, it just opened up. It was there for me."

Live at the Cave

Suspicious Minds

Morris among the stars.

*Top left: Charming his fans at a matinee
performance. Top right: Morris's number one
Vancouver fans, Grace and Lyle Bobb.
Bottom: Home for Christmas with his girlfriend,
Linda Fuller.*

Hound Dog

A World Tribute to Elvis

American Dreams

Breaking into the American market was a challenge for Canadians on the West Coast in those days but not an unattainable dream. In 1970, Susan Jacks became the first Canadian female vocalist to have a gold record in the States with her Poppy Family rendition of *Which Way You Goin' Billy?* Susan Jacks' husband, Terry Jacks, had the number one *Billboard* hit for 1975 with his hit record *Seasons In The Sun*. The Guess Who had hit it big in 1970 with *American Woman*, before band-member Randy Bachman formed BTO in Vancouver and hit the American charts with *Let It Ride, Takin' Care of Business*, and *You Ain't Seen Nothin' Yet*.

Little Daddy & the Bachelors' guitarist Tommy Chong had put aside his guitar and joined Cheech Marin as a comedy act that was about to make blockbuster Hollywood movies. Jazz guitarist Henry Young had played with Nina Mouskouri at the Cave and was invited to join her touring band. But the only Canadian entertainers to be booked as marquee attractions in Las Vegas were Ottawa-born Paul Anka and the little snowbird, Anne Murray. Morris's name would soon compete with their names up on billboards along the Strip.

In making the move from performing in Canada to bookings in Las Vegas, Morris faced a number of legal and strategic obstacles. He continued to manage his own career. He had hired one manager but that had not worked out. Now he had to sign with an agency that could book him into Vegas. There were several agencies that wanted to sign Morris, but he was wary of an ironclad contract with an agency that could stall his progress to Vegas or potentially even ruin his career.

Arm Wrestling Agents

Drummer Scott Anderson recollects that Morris would often relax after gigs by drinking a few beers and arm-wrestling with the guys from the other bands in whatever city he was playing in. "Before I met Morris," Scott recalls, "I was real young, out on the road with some real good jazz bands, and we all used to wonder why nobody was coming to see us. We found out that it was always because this Elvis guy named Morris had just come through town and broke all the bar records."

Anderson was only 17 years old when he met Morris. "I was born and raised in Surrey," he relates, "and I was in a club in Brandon, Manitoba with a band called Show Biz Kids. Wayne Gust came into the club with Morris. At first, Wayne and I were just horsing around. I got him in a headlock, and then he got me in a headlock — and then he introduced me to Morris. I remember Morris was always arm-wrestling guys. He would come in after his show and have a few beers and the guys would be arm-wrestling. Arm wrestling was popular in bars in those days. Nowadays the bouncers will come and shut everything down."

Friendship led to Anderson being hired to drum for Morris. "I filled in playing some dates with Morris around that time," he recalls, "and then I joined the band after that backup band Brass Tower quit; me and Kenny Nelsen, the bass player from Show Biz Kids, both started working with Morris at the same time. Morris and I got along real well right from the start. I grew up in Surrey and Morris was kind of a street-wise cat, himself, and we got along together real well."

We all used to wonder why nobody was coming to see us. We found out that it was always because this Elvis guy named Morris had just come through town and broke all the bar records.

Scott Anderson also offers some interesting insights regarding Morris Bates' relationships with agents and managers during those days. As he recalls, "I remember that Kenny and I were real young and we were sort of living in awe of the agents that would come into the bars we were playing. We respected them because they were the guys that kept us working and we were on our best behavior when they would show up. But Morris was exactly the opposite; Morris didn't treat 'em with kid gloves — he let 'em know exactly the way he wanted things. He believed that the way to treat agents was let 'em know where you were at — and if they didn't like it, screw 'em. It wouldn't work for just anybody but it worked like a charm for Morris. It was an amazing thing he had going, and, wherever he played, he always had people lined up around the block.

"Morris was living above The Bicycle Shop, right next to Lost Lagoon and Stanley Park," Scott recalls, "and I remember him grabbing this one manager he had in a headlock and rolling down the stairs with the guy. It looked like one of those old *Gunsmoke* movies. Robbie, I think the guy's name was . . . He was a guy that didn't last long as Morris's manager. I remember he drove a Corvette and he didn't last long.

I remember him grabbing this one manager he had in a headlock and rolling down the stairs with the guy. It looked like one of those old Gunsmoke movies.

One agent, intent on signing Morris before anybody else got to him, tracked the tribute artist down at the Mustache Club in Yorkton, Saskatchewan. Morris was in peak physical condition at the time, he was five feet and eleven and a half inches in height and weighed a trim 165 pounds. He could beat most men in an arm-wrestling match and figured he could surely beat this pesky agent, bragging that he could beat him left-handed — no problem . . .

"He didn't know I was left-handed," Dennis Compo recalls. "I beat him, and he signed a contract. It was a loose contract. Morris and I had a pretty good relationship. We worked with him for years and toured him all over the world. In one stretch, he was on the strip in Vegas for five straight years."

Dennis Compo was aware of Morris Bates' skepticism about

agents, but the two men soon discovered they were on the same page when it came to doing business. As Dennis recalls, "Morris was a very talented young man and a very talented businessman even in those days. His word was something we could stand by and we did the same thing with him. So we had a good relationship. He was tough, he wanted what he wanted, and we did our best to deliver what we could when we could. And he understood when we couldn't and why. It was a good, long-term relationship and we actually became pretty good friends over the years."

Morris was a very talented young man and a very talented businessman even in those days. His word was something we could stand by.

Compo's partner at the time was Richard Cheung. "Richard owned a couple of hotels and a cabaret in Prince George," Morris relates, "and he had begun working with Dennis Compo. Dennis booked me into Richard's cabaret, and Richard was paying me $3,500 a week. But then he discovered that I was making $3,000 a week from the photographs of myself and fans that came into the club. I sold them for $5 a photo, which was the same price that they paid to get into his nightclub. I was making $3,000 dollars selling photos and he and Dennis were not getting a percentage of that — so he told me he wanted to become my manager."

"I met Richard a few months before Morris met Richard," Dennis Compo recalls. "Morris was one of the first acts that I booked into Richard's cabaret in Prince George. And that was the beginning of the relationship. The way it developed was that Richard's interests up there in Prince George were sort of falling apart and I offered him a job to come into Vancouver and become an agent. That arrangement became a partnership that we called Compo-Cheung & Associates.

"Morris could have probably been a brilliant agent," Dennis Compo says, "because he knew good, bad, and indifferent and exactly what degrees of black and white it would be when you're playing it. He was really good at it. And he knew exactly how to arrange songs for the best results. A lot of musicians are very talented, but they are not intuitive when it comes to reading the crowd, whereas Morris had it down."

Booked

"I got myself booked into the Cave for the first time," Morris points out. "It was booked before Richard started working with me. He was just becoming my manager when I went into the Cave. And when Richard arrived at the club, my security guys told him that nobody could get into my dressing room before I went on and did my show. I had 28 French Canadian bodybuilders, muscle-builders from Langley, acting as my security. They all spoke French. The club was packed, and my security guys were all over the place. The dressing room at the Cave was upstairs at the back, and I had two guys on the door of the dressing room and one guy inside. They wouldn't let anybody into my dressing room. They wouldn't even let Stan Grozina, the owner of the club, in.

He knew exactly how to arrange songs for the best results. A lot of musicians are very talented, but they are not intuitive when it comes to reading the crowd, whereas Morris had it down.

"Stan came up to the dressing room to talk to me, but my security guy says, 'Nobody talks to *Maurice* in between shows. He's resting.' Stan says, 'Hey, I own the place.' And my security guy says, 'At this time, *Maurice*, he owns it.' And when Richard arrived, they wouldn't let him in, either.

"Richard was outside the dressing room telling them, 'I'm his manager, I'm his manager . . .' and they were saying, 'We don't care who you are, nobody gets in until after the show.'

"Richard kept on pestering them and finally one of the security guys knocked on the dressing room door and said, '*Maurice*, you've got some Chinaman out here who says he's your manager . . .'

"I said, 'His name's Richard, right?'

"And Richard said, 'Mo! Mo, I'm here!'

"When Richard got inside he said, 'Mo where did you get these guys?'

"The club was packed that night as it always was. Richard saw that I was the real deal and he became my manager."

During his Cave appearances, Morris continued to make his

Elvis tribute show even more spectacular. As he recalls, "We mounted one of those big strobe lights right in front of the stage, and in the song *Hound Dog*, where the drum break is like a machine gun, we would run the strobe light and I would shimmy. It was quite an effect. I would sing, 'You never got a rabbit and you ain't no friend of mine . . .' And the drummer would go rat-a-tat-a-tat-a-tat-a-tat . . . And I would shimmy . . . It was just great."

"Morris played the Cave more often than Mitzi Gaynor," Dennis Compo emphasizes. "It was a phenomenon; it really was. He used to take over the room. People used to walk out of there thinking they just saw Elvis. He was one of the best, if not the best Elvis act going — he had the act down to a science. He always had a good band and he really knew how to work an audience — and a band. He knew what he wanted and how to get it. He could tell them what to play and how to play it. He was a pretty amazing man. He was brilliant. He was a great entertainer. To this day I don't think I've seen a better Elvis act. I have seen better singers, but Morris knew what his capabilities were, and he made up for his limitations by the instrumentation in the band, and by being a brilliant entertainer."

> He was a pretty amazing man. He was brilliant. He was a great entertainer. To this day I don't think I've seen a better Elvis act.

The Elvis Look

Richard Cheung and Dennis Compo set up an agency office in North Vancouver on Pemberton Street. Richard had sold off most of his holdings in Prince George to concentrate on Morris's bid for fame and fortune. Richard proved to be a very wily manager, indeed. He helped develop Morris's "look" when he introduced him to Paul Minichiello, tailor to the stars, who had a shop on Lonsdale Avenue in North Vancouver.

"Paul Minichiello created custom-made suits for me for $800," Morris recalls. "He was the best in the business. He made suits for a lot of West Coast celebrities. Any celebrity in those days who was worth their salt, Paul Minichiello designed their suits. He made me a gold suit just like the one Elvis wore."

Minichiello also designed matching outfits for the band.

At the same time, Dennis was developing acts from Hawaii that could be tailored to play Vegas. As Dennis recalls, "I would fly to Hawaii and go to the armed forces base to meet some of the acts there. We would sign them and put them into a grooming situation in California and then tour them all over." These connections, combined with Richard's contacts with overseas tour promoters, would soon put Morris on the international stage.

In order to get Morris into the American market, Dennis and Richard signed a secondary agreement with a Seattle agency that had dealings in Las Vegas. The results were immediate. Morris and his band were booked to appear at the Playgirl Club in Los Angeles in the summer of 1977. The booking was not without its challenges as work visas for his Canadian band couldn't be secured and Morris had to put together a new band of American musicians. He chose Portland-based guitarist David Maitland, a musician Richard knew, to put the new band together. Once again, it was a smart move, as Maitland assembled a lineup of top-notch players.

As David Maitland recalls, "I got a call about an Elvis Impersonator who worked out of Vancouver, and they said, 'Do you want to do it?' And I said, 'Absolutely!' Of course, at that time I wasn't married and was prepared to do a lot of traveling. So I made some calls. It was the usual way that bands were put together in those days. You get a call and then you say, well, I got somebody and this guy and that guy . . . and you put the band together, blah, blah, blah. I made this call to a band that I had worked with before. I think they were called Blue Gin at that time. So I told them that I had a call about an Elvis Impersonator that had a lot of work out of Vancouver and do you want to do it? And they said, 'Absolutely.'"

To work out the kinks before the Playgirl engagement, the new band played a cross-Canada tour that ended with a two-week booking at the Cave in Vancouver. "I remember going up to Vancouver," Maitland explains, "and I believe Morris's girlfriend met

Any celebrity in those days who was worth their salt, Paul Minichiello designed their suits. He made me a gold suit just like the one Elvis wore.

us at the border. We jumped right into it when we got up there. We had the core of the band from down here, and I think we added some horns that were local horn players in Vancouver."

"We rehearsed and rehearsed and rehearsed," Morris reminisces. "I'm not kidding — 18 hours a day . . . We would sleep for six hours and start up again. We had a great band, but David was a rock and roll psychedelic guitar player and he didn't have a clue about Elvis Presley. I had to Elvisize him."

Right away, David learned that Morris had a complete vision of his Elvis Presley show. Morris knew exactly what he wanted from his musicians, and the guitarist rapidly came to believe that they could go all the way to Vegas and be successful there.

He wanted everything a certain way. On guitar he wanted to hear the Scotty Moore and James Burton licks.

"He had the drive to do it," David says. "By the time I met him he had already been at it for quite a while. Playing with Morris was the most professional job that I had played with. He rehearsed us all day for a couple of weeks straight. He wanted everything a certain way. On guitar he wanted to hear the Scotty Moore and James Burton licks. If anything else came out, he would turn around and look at you. We would rehearse that stuff for hours and hours and hours. I remember the first time we played the Cave it went over so well. It was really tight. And the effect on the audience was really noticeable."

"Within a week or so we played at this old hotel in New Westminster," David recalls. "Then we did three months going across Canada with those players. We started in Trail and we went all the way to Saskatoon, I think, a long way out there on the Canadian prairies. And then we came back and played the Cave."

The three-month Canadian tour — now billed as A World Tribute To Elvis — was the best Morris Bates' tour thus far. Every night now when Morris took the stage and paid tribute to the King his performance generated the same sort of Elvis-mania that the King himself generated. On a smaller scale, of course, but the excitement was always there. People really loved to come out to see Morris pay tribute to Elvis.

On stage, night after night with Morris, David Maitland believed that a marvelous transformation took place when they hit the stage. David was totally in awe of Morris's sincere portrayal of the King and his music.

"I remember one of the first times playing at the Cave and looking over at Morris," David recalls, "and, especially from the side, he looked exactly like Elvis. I'll never forget that. I went, 'Whoa!' From some of the shots I had seen of Elvis, Morris looked exactly like him. The show was so tight, and the people in the audience in the Cave were reacting so well. Boy, I used to love playing that place with Morris. The Cave had a great atmosphere. I remember we would pull up to the club for our first show and there would be a lineup around the block to get in. They would empty them all out after the first show and there would be another lineup around the block for the second show."

> I went, 'Whoa!' From some of the shots I had seen of Elvis, Morris looked exactly like him.

Fan Club

As David Maitland became more familiar with the star he was backing, he began to realize that Morris had his own fan base, fans who were Morris Bates fans even more than they were Elvis fans. Morris wasn't merely a Presley fan who dressed up like the King to pay tribute, he was a genuine star in his own right; and when he was not in costume, his custom-made Paul Minichiello suits provided him a wardrobe that was on par with visiting Hollywood celebrities.

"Everybody was impressed by the way Morris carried himself and the way he dressed," David points out. "He was always extremely well dressed."

Maitland also learned that Morris took care of his people and treated everybody fairly. "I remember he took the whole band to an Italian fellow who made boots. He had these boots made for us, these beautiful boots, because he wanted everybody just looking great."

"Reno was an Italian boot maker," Morris explains. "He made

boots for everybody — Little Richard, James Brown, Aerosmith. His shop was on Main Street at 12th Avenue or 14th Avenue and then he moved it down onto Broadway west of Main. Reno made me a pair of blue suede shoes. He made all my white stage boots. He took my footprint. And when we came back to the Cave after being in Asia or being in Vegas, he would have new boots for me, and he would bring them down there. One time, though, at the Cave, he brought me a pair of boots and I wore them on stage and they almost crippled me. After the show I asked him what was going on, and he admitted he had lost my footprint and he had made those boots from memory."

Another time, Reno came to Morris and asked him to judge a talent contest at the Italian Center on Grandview Highway. "I was headlining in the Cave that week. So he sent a limousine to pick me up. And when I got there the place was packed. What I didn't know was that he had put me on all the posters that were put up along Commercial Drive advertising me as his headliner. I thought I was just going there to be a judge at his talent contest. He was charging all these people $10 each to get into the show. The Italian Center is a big room — it holds more than a thousand people and they were packed in there that night.

"The Italian people had been very good to me, and I didn't want to let them down. But he had used my name to sell his show, and I had shown up in street clothes. So I sent someone in the limousine downtown to the Cave through rush hour traffic to get one of my costumes. The band had come up there with me because we had all been promised free food and drinks. They were in street clothes, too, but after a while they went on using the house band's equipment and played an opening set."

When the limo driver returned with the stage costume, Morris wasted no time and soon made his entrance. As he recalls, "I went on and did a couple of songs and I finished up with *It's Now Or Never*, you know, "Oh *solo mio*, it's now or never . . ." And the Italians loved me. Because I was olive skinned, Greeks thought I was Greek, Italians thought I was Italian, and some East Indians thought I was from India. I met Filipinos who thought I was from the Philippines — people thought I was a lot of things . . ."

Reno the boot maker and his talent show organizers made a lot of money that night and the funds raised went to a good cause.

Many of the people who worked for Morris over the years were first attracted to him through his shows. "He was electrifying like Elvis was," Gisele Kaufmann recalls, remembering the first time she saw Morris perform. "He was damn good!"

The first night that Gisele saw Morris, she was hooked; but unlike most of the women who came to see Morris night after night, week after week, Gisele wanted to become part of the show. Right from the get-go, she wanted to work with Morris's show. At the first show she attended at the Newton Inn in the Vancouver suburb of Surrey, she was distracted by her date, a guy that had just broken up with his longtime girlfriend. As Gisele recalls, "He asked me to go, and I was trying to watch the show because I thought it was fantastic, but all through the show this guy was crying on my shoulder. So I had to see Morris again and I went up and asked Maxine, the girl who was doing the lights at that time, where they were playing next, and she told me it was the Roadhouse, which was underneath the second narrows bridge in North Vancouver.

Because I was olive skinned, Greeks thought I was Greek, Italians thought I was Italian, and some East Indians thought I was from India.

"I went to the show at the Roadhouse with a couple of girlfriends, and I remember standing up on my chair with the other girls and screaming and saying to myself, 'I have to belong to this show.' Talk about the power of attraction! But I can remember that moment as clear as day. I didn't know how I was going to do it, but I knew I had to be part of his show."

"I kept going to the shows," she continues, "and I got to meet him one night. And then in New Westminster after a show at the Answer 2 nightclub somebody smashed all the windows in my car. Morris got them fixed for me and I paid him back by working at the coat-check in the club. From where I was standing at the coat-check booth, I couldn't see the show on stage, all I could see is Maxine running the lights. So while I was working at

Talk about the power of attraction! But I can remember that moment as clear as day. I didn't know how I was going to do it, but I knew I had to be part of his show.

the coat-check, I got to learn everything that she was doing, the timing, and everything."

Soon after that, Gisele accepted a job offer to work in northern British Columbia, where there was a booming local economy due to construction of an oil pipeline. She wasn't able to realize her dream of working with Morris, but she followed his career through monthly fan club newsletters she received in the mail from Morris Bates' fan club president Alma Cunningham. Morris's fans were about to follow him around the world.

Top: Morris and his managers, Dennis Compo (left) and Richard Cheung (right). Bottom: Sold-out at the Keystone Centre, Brandon, Manitoba

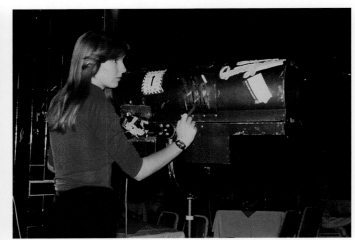

Top left: Band leader, guitarist, and MC David Maitland. Top right: Scotty negotiates a raise with Morris. Bottom left: The Show Biz Kids: (top to bottom) Kenny Nelsen, Michael Frye, Scott Anderson. Bottom right: Maxine Gradidge focuses the spot light on Morris.

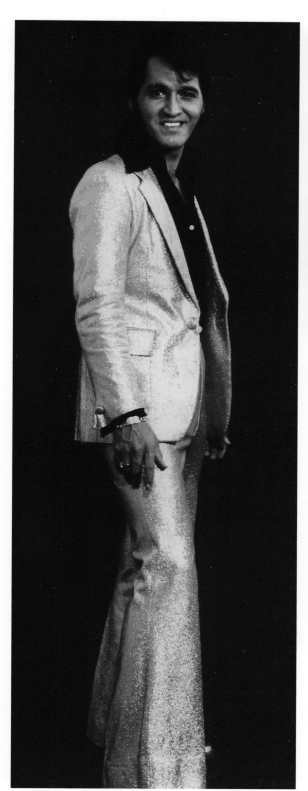

Morris's gold suit, designed by
Paul Minichiello

Polk Salad Annie

The Orient Tour

Playgirl Club

Now fully prepared to take on the world, Morris and his band traveled first to Los Angeles. "We debuted at the Playgirl Club, one of the best clubs in the Los Angeles area," Morris recalls. "We needed to play where that the agents could come and see us. A lady agent was handling us in LA and she had all the connections for Asia. We showcased for her and her clients. There were a lot of logistics that had to be put together.

"I had a really great time there. It was in Anaheim near Disneyland, and one night, after spending the day at Disneyland, when I came out to do the sixties set in my black leather I wore Mickey Mouse ears. When they hit me with the spotlight, I sang, 'If you're lookin' for trouble, look right in my face . . .'

"The place went nuts. It was packed and the audience was just outrageous. I was beginning to understand Annie Wilson's statement that 'if you go to the States, they are going to eat you up.' One night during my leather segment a girl walked right out of the audience to the lip of the stage, and, as I bent over to give her a kiss, she reached up and grabbed me in the crotch. I jumped back and nearly fell over the drum set. She turned around to face the follow the spot, put her hands up over her head in triumph, and the place went bonkers. Annie was right.

121

When the engagement at the Playgirl Club came to an end, the boys in the band had a few days off. As Morris recalls, "I went up to Hollywood on a Saturday and went into this bookstore and bought a copy of *Elvis: What Happened*, the book that Red West, Sonny West, and Dave Hebler put together. I went back to our motel and began reading that book the next day. Some of the guys from the band were sitting around on Monday afternoon and one of them said to me, 'When you get finished reading that book, can I read it?'

Just as a joke, I said, 'If this book is true, Elvis should be dead tomorrow . . .'

"Just as a joke, I said, 'If this book is true, Elvis should be dead tomorrow . . .' I just said it as a joke — I swear to God; and that was a Monday and Elvis died the next day. It was a weird day. It rained like crazy. It doesn't rain in southern California hardly at all, but that day it rained like crazy. It poured."

Asian Option

That day, Morris Bates' World Tribute to Elvis was in high demand. Richard Cheung and Dennis Compo had just signed an open-ended contract with the Asian promoters they met at the Playgirl Club. When Elvis Presley's death was announced, the Asian promoters called in their option. They wanted Morris Bates to fly to the Orient and begin the tour right away. "There was a lady agent handling us in LA. She had all the connections for Asia, and we showcased for her and her clients. There were a lot of logistics that had to be put together."

Behind the scenes, there was some dissension in the ranks. The band members David Maitland had recruited were initially told that they would be going to Vegas. Morris and Richard had scouted the Silver Slipper, the casino owned by Howard Hughes' Summa Corporation. There was some grumbling when a possible six-month tour to Southeast Asia was first brought up, and when the King's tragic death reversed the anticipated booking schedule, the dissension became outright mutiny.

As David recalls, "Richard Cheung and Dennis Compo came up with the Asian tour. I was all for it, but as it turned out, the rest of the band chickened out. Their girlfriends wouldn't let 'em go. The last gig that they played with us was down there at the Play-girl Club."

As bandleader, David had to make the call to Morris and tell him the bad news. "I remember the day that Elvis died," he explains. "I talked to Morris and told him that the whole band had quit. I told Morris that I would go back to Portland and put another band together, and that's exactly what I did."

"In the next few days everyone around me seemed to grow up," Morris says. "David put together the most professional rock & roll band in the world, and we got Scotty Anderson, who had drummed with me before back in Canada. Scotty was my Ronnie Tutt — he was the best rock & roll drummer I ever had in my show band. He watched me like a hawk. He never took his eyes off me. You see, I was always giving cues to the band, just like Elvis did in his shows."

After Presley passed away, Ronnie Tutt told a reporter, "I emulated and accented everything that Elvis did, just instinctively, every move, almost like a glorified stripper! And he loved that." Good show drummers must accent and punctuate an entertainer's moves; their role is quite different from the role of a good studio drummer.

Morris knew something about showmanship. He had played bass in a house band that backed strippers at the Penthouse nightclub in Vancouver. He had studied Elvis Presley's documentary film about how the King put together the TCB band and his Vegas show. And, like Elvis, he had studied martial arts. When Morris was on stage, every move counted.

"You had to watch the show," Scott Anderson explains. "You had to watch Morris. That was a big part of it. Morris was really into 'selling' the show and getting it over to his audiences. There was definitely some synch and some body language and the big fanfares. We used to do *Zarathustra 2001* and then the kickoff and the drum roll and the riff from *C.C. Rider* for the intro to the seventies section . . ."

> Scotty was my Ronnie Tutt — he was the best rock & roll drummer I ever had in my show band. I was always giving cues to the band, just like Elvis did in his shows.

Morris began his shows as Elvis had done with a rollicking version of *That's All Right (Mama)*, which was quite a bit faster paced than Presley's Sun Records hit single that he had recorded with Scotty Moore and Bill Black but without a drummer.

What was remarkable about Elvis is that he would throw bits and pieces of other songs that fit into the musical groove that his band had established — like a chorus from the Beatles' *Get Back* or his own *Little Sister*. That kept the rhythm section on their toes. Elvis had fun with it, and Morris was able to have fun with it, too, which is why so many people would come back night after night to see Morris do basically the same show over and over again. Even though most of the songs would be the same, both Elvis and Morris were loose enough that they never merely repeated all the same jokes and repartee as they worked their audiences.

"My band was so tight in those days," Morris explains, "that I could throw almost anything at them and they were right there with me. I would sing James Taylor's *Steamroller Blues* or the Clovers' *I Got My Eyes On You*. We lived it and breathed it. We were so tight that I could have sung *Love Me Tender* backwards if I had wanted to, and they would have been right there with me."

Not all Elvis impersonators were so tight – or so loose. "They didn't know what 12 bars were," Morris explains. "Wayne played with some of them and he told me that if the band changed anything, the guy they were backing wouldn't know when to come back in. They didn't know a bridge from a chorus. Some tribute artists, like Alan, for example, used to mimic the way Elvis spoke and tell all of the same jokes that Elvis told and that didn't always go over all that well with the audiences. Alan was a good singer. Don't get me wrong. He was just a little guy, but if you turned your head away when Alan was singing Elvis in the fifties, he had Elvis down better than I had ever heard anybody sing it. But Alan took himself too seriously. He thought he was Elvis. He could really sing, but he didn't have that appeal to women. He looked like someone you could cuddle — that you wanted to take home to your mommy or daddy. He looked cute. Where, when you saw

Not all Elvis impersonators were so tight – or so loose. "They didn't know what 12 bars were."

my show, if you were a woman, you didn't want to bring me home to your mommy, but mommy was probably at the show, too . . .

"I had a different approach. I saw that Elvis was having fun with it and that's what I did. Every show was the same show, but every show was really different, too. Some fans would come to all three shows that I did on the same night and then come back the next night and they never seemed to get tired of what I did because we always had fun with it, and didn't take anything too seriously.

"I appealed to a very wide demographic of people. I packed those showrooms for afternoon matinees. I had little kids coming to see me along with their mothers and grandmothers, and I also had teenage girls who were blushing after getting a scarf and a kiss. It always amazed me that little kids would come up and give me a kiss or a handshake and not be scared. They probably didn't know Elvis Presley from a purple Barney. Most of them were scared of Santa Claus. And then there were guys that liked me because they thought that I was a reincarnation of the Village People when I wore that leather outfit and that pink sports jacket.

> When you saw my show, if you were a woman, you didn't want to bring me home to your mommy, but mommy was probably at the show, too . . .

"Just about every show some guy would come up out of the audience to get a scarf and a kiss, mostly on a dare from his buddies. I'd bend over and put the scarf real tight around his neck, pull him to me and give him a big kiss right on his lips, and then spin him around and the spotlight would hit him. He would appear stunned and shocked and everybody would be hooting and hollering."

Morris realized that every audience was different, and by the time he got to Vegas, he had mastered the art of holding each audience in the palm of his hand and working them like a puppeteer works his puppets. His so-called fifties segment was not a journey back to the days of rockabilly when Bill Black's slap-bass compensated for there being no drummer and Elvis played rhythm guitar on every song. Morris's fifties segment was an authentic recreation of the way Elvis opened his Vegas shows.

"Basically," Scott Anderson says, "it was just a real fast Bo-Diddley kind of thing. And then 'ba duh dah . . . ba duh da.' And then we did *That's All Right (Mama)* in that kind of a treatment. We would use *C.C. Rider* or *That's All Right (Mama)*. Dave Maitland had a real professional radio voice and he would be announcing the beginning of the show. And Morris usually came out and did *That's All Right (Mama)*."

Scott had enjoyed playing shows with Morris in Canada and had been disappointed when he had been left off the roster when the decision to go with American players had been made. At that time he had no idea that a second chance would come his way as soon as it did, but the King's death changed a lot of things for a lot of people.

As Scott recalls, "The week that Elvis died, Richard Cheung called me up and said, 'You gotta get your passport.' Morris was going to Asia for a six-month tour and I was going with him! I was running to get my passport. I went down to Portland and lived and rehearsed in this cottage that was a hippie kind of place."

The young drummer was delighted to be working once again with bandleader David Maitland. "David was always writing and playing in lots of styles," Scott relates. "He could sound just like Carlos Santana or Jeff Beck. He was a pretty amazing guitar player all the way around."

With Scott and David both already familiar with the components of the tribute show, rehearsals with the new musicians were a snap, and by the time Morris arrived, they had the show rounded more or less into shape. "Morris came up to Portland," David continues, "and rehearsed for a few days and we went back to LA and played somewhere, it might have been the Santa Monica sports arena, and then flew out for our Asian tour. So there were two band lineups before we even went for our Asian tour."

Scott Anderson was pretty excited. He had taken a bus to Portland, but he had never flown anywhere and now he was going halfway 'round the world to exotic locations that were beyond his wildest imagination. He was pumped. "When we were done rehearsing," he recalls, "some of the guys drove down

The King's death changed a lot of things for a lot of people.

from Portland to Los Angeles, but Morris and I flew down. That was the first time that I was on an airplane. I was 19 at the time and I turned 20 when we were in Taipei."

Touring the Orient

Upon their arrival in Taiwan, Morris Bates' World Tribute to Elvis was featured on a live, one-hour TV Special filmed in Taipei. When his TV Special aired in prime time in Taiwan, Morris got higher ratings that the regularly scheduled *Donny & Marie Osmond Show.*

"The show we did was all in Chinese," David Maitland recalls, "all the introductions and everything, and you've got the girls dancing around us — I would love to see that again — it's got to be hilarious. We were there in Taipei for six weeks or so. "

When his TV Special aired in prime time in Taiwan, Morris got higher ratings that the regularly scheduled *Donny & Marie Osmond Show.*

"I was nearly 20 years old at the time," Scott Anderson recalls. "We got into some pretty wild stuff for a 20-year old. In Taiwan we all had to go and get haircuts so that we would be good role models for the staff in the hotel we were playing. They have a fairly conservative right-wing government there, and they were sort of always at war with the mainland Chinese communist regime. So we got the lecture about staying in line, and we all had to get haircuts.

"David had a pretty good Aerosmith kind of style and my hair was long. So Morris tells me, 'Scotty I'm going to take you for a real haircut.' This was a pretty normal thing in Taipei. You leave your shoes at the door and there are these beautiful 21-year-old Chinese gals waiting for you when you go in there. Some of 'em shine your shoes. And you sit down and they put a mask on your face and give you a pedicure and a manicure, and they trim your hair, and then it's time for the massaging in the back room. I think Morris put up a whole $10 for that 'haircut.' It was definitely the whole nine yards for a young Canadian boy, that's for sure. I think that Morris felt he was looking after me, sort of a big brother type of thing in those days."

Morris often took care of the boys in the band, but sometimes they found themselves taking care of their fearless leader. As Scott recalls, "I remember trying to wake Morris up for a show in Taiwan. We had this noon show at this fancy hotel in Taipei and we had been up for, like, 48 hours at this moon festival called Double 10 Day. And we were trying to wake Morris up and we had to throw him into a bathtub of cold water. We threw buckets of cold water over his head and he woke up and said, 'Swimming . . .' It was hilarious . . . we all got through that noon-hour show where they were all so formal and bowing and everything, but not too stellarly. I remember some funny things happening during our shows. They had their firecracker action going, and some flash pots that were supposed to go off during *Suspicious Minds* were going off during *Love Me Tender*."

> We threw buckets of cold water over his head and he woke up and said, 'Swimming . . .' It was hilarious . . .

While touring Southeast Asia had its glamorous moments, there were some hardships, too, and times when they all got more than a bit homesick. Other times they merely longed for a good old American cheeseburger and fries meal. "I remember," David says, "that they didn't have much American food, Western food, that we could eat in Taipei or that we could find. We were eating at a lot of sidewalk cafés, and we all had real good cases of creeping crud, the old Aztec two-step. I remember when we flew into Hong Kong with all the skyscrapers they have there and got into the cab it was total culture shock after where we had been. Then when were just getting to our hotel we saw the golden arches. We dropped off our bags and ran back to the golden arches, and, a couple of Big Macs later, we were just fine."

The contrasts between extreme poverty and opulent wealth would continue throughout their six-month odyssey. "We went to a lot of places," David notes, "Singapore, Kuala Lumpur in Malaysia, and Jakarta, Indonesia. We also went to some of the little islands off of the coast of Indonesia — Semarang, Surabaya. Some of them were pretty remote. We went to a lot of exotic locations. Some of them were real primitive, especially 30 years ago when they didn't see a whole lot of Caucasian people, evidently. But they knew about Elvis. You would walk down the street and hear Elvis music coming out of the shops. And you'd turn around and there would be a crowd following you down the street. There wasn't that much of a tourist presence at that time." Every time they took the stage, whether it was on a remote island, an exclusive urban nightclub, or a large outdoor venue where tens of thousands of fans were gathered, they discovered that Elvis Presley song lyrics were a sort of universal language. Everybody sang along in perfect English.

The boys in the band were well looked after for the most part. The tour promoters packed up their instruments and flew them to their next gig. The sound equipment and amplifiers were provided by local arrangements. As might be expected, some of the time the local equipment was not at all what they were used to dealing with. As David recalls, "They would provide PA systems and amps and that sort of stuff. And I remember at this military base playing in this one armory over there — cement wall, cement floor, everything cement, and the PA was a WWII vintage Bogen amplifier with a couple of horns for speakers. They just buzzed the whole time. You couldn't hear a thing. And a couple of real old Fender amps that just buzzed, too. I remember walking into what was supposed to be a dressing room and all over the walls and ceiling there were these four- to six-inch flying cockroaches. They were everywhere. Oh, my goodness, that was an experience . . . real glamorous, you know."

A good deal of camaraderie developed between all the players and technicians, and, then, just when you thought that you knew what was coming next, everything around them would become totally bizarre. As Scott Anderson points out, "There were some beautiful moments that's for sure, but, of course, you're just lookin' back through the haze of maudlin alcoholic reflections. We were just not used to that 30-degree heat. We were there during monsoon season and the floods would come up, and in the fish markets there would be crabs walkin' down the street. There was some amazing stuff going on. You could take a rickshaw, if

> I remember walking into what was supposed to be a dressing room and all over the walls and ceiling there were these four- to six-inch flying cockroaches.

you didn't want to wade in water up to your knees, and you'd be floatin' in the rickshaw . . . It was a watershed moment for a lot of young guys growin' up in the music business. It's one thing to be on the road at the local Holiday Inn in Canada with a show band. But it is another thing altogether to be traveling around the world with a show band with the language barriers and the exotic cultures that you encounter. In Indonesia, they had a military guard driving us in parades and people lined up along the streets and I don't think the people really knew if it was the real Elvis or that Elvis had actually passed away or what . . ."

On this one island in Indonesia, we played for the King and Queen.

"On this one island in Indonesia, we played for the King and Queen," Morris recalls. "I was awakened about 8:30 in the morning, and after I showered, they took me down to this restaurant to meet the Queen and her maids of honor. They sat around and looked at me and giggled and smiled. I had an interpreter, but they spoke a bit of English, and they asked me if I was married, and all kinds of funny questions. Later at the show, the King and Queen and their court sat behind the military general's family and staff. Guess you know who's in charge of the country . . . (pretty weird memories)"

Morris was also getting used to larger and larger audiences and situations that became less and less predictable. "There were four shows in Jakarta where 10,000 people showed up for four consecutive nights," Scott remembers. "It was humid and hot and the lights went on and we went up and did the show. Morris's shows were going over great. They were unique venues, almost like indoor arenas, but there were a lot of people that paid for tickets. And there were some outdoor venues almost like a Hollywood Bowl kind of thing. I can't really remember the specifics. At one time I was keeping a journal, but that was more personal notes kind of thing and then I lost it somewhere along the way."

"We definitely played some out of the way places," David admits, "along with Singapore and Bangkok. Boy, there are some stories that could be told about Thailand."

Morris never did become accustomed to the heat and humidity. "When I stepped out of the plane in Taipei," he recalls, "it was like walking into a blast furnace. We had never experienced anything like that. The heat and the humidity were brutal. I was sweating all the time, and I lost a lot of weight. By the time I got back to Canada, I had lost 40 pounds. All I did was sweat, day and night, for six months."

Despite his steadily declining bodyweight, Morris coped really well, but would sometimes be dumbstruck by the masses of people, their poverty, and the pestilence. Sometimes the sprawling ghettos were the only images he could remember when they had moved on to their next gig. When they arrived in Thailand, the bodies of victims of government suppression were strung up along the highway. As Morris recalls, "They drove us into Bangkok from the airport and we saw all of these bodies hanging from telephone poles, hanging by their heads. They were just kids. These students had been protesting and the army just went and scooped them and hung them up there."

> They drove us into Bangkok from the airport and we saw all of these bodies hanging from telephone poles, hanging by their heads.

Upon arrival at his hotel, Morris was told that there was a strict curfew in place and that because he looked more like a local than a white person, he was going to have to be very, very careful in Thailand. "As he recalls, "I was an Indian and on top of that I was really tanned so they couldn't tell the difference between me and the Thai people. This guy warned me that if the army or the police caught me out in the street after the curfew they would shoot me."

After these ominous beginnings, they discovered Thai people to be friendly and fun loving, though their culture was so exotic that it often took the young musicians totally by surprise. "I played a really big, beautiful dinner theater in Bangkok that Tom Jones had played when he was there," Morris relates. "Ray Charles was there at the same time that we were there, but he was playing a big, open venue, and we were playing in this supper club. We were there for two weeks. I remember they had these big, private balconies in there where people would sit and eat dinner and watch my show. It was the best nightclub in Bangkok."

> I played a really big, beautiful dinner theater in Bangkok that Tom Jones had played when he was there. Ray Charles was there at the same time that we were there.

Morris and the boys in the band did some exploring on their own whenever they had some time off, and they soon discovered a club called the Mississippi Queen, where all manner of exotic entertainment could be enjoyed if you were so inclined. "It was the only club in Bangkok where they played rhythm & blues," Morris remembers. "It was just tapes of rhythm & blues, but it was the only R&B that you could hear there. Scotty and some of the band went there quite a lot. It was a whole different world for us. If you watch the movie *The Deer Hunter* with Robert DeNiro, you will see the Mississippi Queen nightclub. Bangkok was R&R for Vietnam soldiers, and all of the girls called us *Joe*, which was short for GI Joe."

In those days in Bangkok, female companionship was readily available day and night, even in the swank uptown nightclubs. As Morris recalls, "Right in the club we were playing in, there was a corridor going to the men's room that had a wall with a 20-foot one-way window, and when you looked through that window, all you saw was these 100 girls sitting in there. Each girl had a number on her. So you could order number 88 and number 41 and before you got back from the washroom those girls would be at your table."

The first member of Morris's entourage to discover this window of opportunity, so to speak, was Scott Anderson. "Scotty went to the washroom," Morris recalls, "and when he came back he said, 'Morris, you are not going to believe this! There is a whole slew of women in the washroom, but they are behind one-way glass.' I said, 'I got to go see this!' And I went down there with him to the corridor outside the washroom, and sure enough, they were on the other side of the one-way glass of the window. It was a whole different world for us, and we never did get used to the way they did things there. We were only there for two weeks, and we were glad to get our passports back and get out of Bangkok because we couldn't quit thinking about those dead students hanging on the telephone poles on the highway to the airport."

"Morris, of course, stayed at the Sheraton," David recalls. "And when you are at the Sheraton and look out one of the windows all you see is just miles and miles of corrugated tin roofs. The band stayed in a place called the Rose Hotel. It was a small hotel a few blocks from the Sheraton where you couldn't drink the water. In one or two of those places that we visited, you couldn't use the water to wash with."

Japan and Hawaii

In Japan, they discovered another unique culture and conditions that were totally different than they had seen before this. "One thing I recall about Japan," Morris says, "was its' cleanliness, except for the hole in the floor of the washrooms – no throne, just handles."

David remembers that, "We were playing a very exclusive businessman's club in Tokyo in the movie theater nightclub district, and the band couldn't go out front. We had to stay on stage or in the back. We couldn't mingle. A beer was $300 or something like that. The businessmen would just put it on their expense accounts and write it off."

"One of the bigger venues," Morris recalls, "was in the Roppongi district of Tokyo. We showed up a couple of hours early to do a sound check in a tall, eight-story building. Each floor had a nightclub that seated more than 2,000. We went in the elevator and there was a roster of all of the performing acts in the theater complex. Rosemary Clooney was on one floor, disco on another, live theater on another, and so on. I just pointed to my picture on the elevator wall and the elevator driver took us to the appropriate floor. It was a beautiful theater with 500 hostesses and we were told very aggressively that we weren't allowed to mingle."

Meeting women that could speak English and were willing to chat with the boys in the band proved difficult in Japan. "I remember," Morris recalls, "walking down a street in Tokyo and seeing this blonde lady at one of the McDonald's sidewalk restaurants. I said to the guys, 'I saw her first!' as we hadn't met any American women for a long time. As we rushed over to say hello, she smiled her appreciation, but it turned out she was from Germany and spoke no English. So we were back to pointing and making gestures to communicate."

"All of us were single at the time," David points out, "and I remember the various places we went on the tour by the various luck that we had meeting women. A lot of places we did pretty well. But Japan was a little different. It would be funny. We would be playing the show and we'd be watching these girls down front trying to make eye contact. The girls would be singing along with every Elvis song, singing along with Morris. If we could get to talk to one or two of the girls, we discovered they couldn't speak a lick of English, but they knew every word to those Elvis songs."

After their two-week stint at the upscale club in Tokyo, the tour continued as relentlessly as before. "I remember taking the Bullet Train to Kyoto," David continues. "We played a regular nightclub in Kyoto. That was really interesting and seeing Mount Fuji and all that. Then they took us to other places like Hiroshima where we took a jet boat to some of the outer islands, and we played out there."

"In a theater in Nagasaki," Morris recalls, "we played a matinee and an evening show that was structured right off the old Ed Sullivan TV variety show. They had animal acts, acrobats, comedians, knife throwing artists, and, of course, my Elvis show. The audiences were always polite and receptive, with reserved enthusiasm, except in the nightclub settings where it was a lot more manic. We saw Mount Fuji and some really incredible ancient castles, and we were more touristy for a while, absorbing the rich blend of Japan's history and hi tech futuristic structures."

One day during their time spent in Japan, Morris noticed an advertisement for Morris Guitars, which were manufactured in Japan. Overcoming language barriers through a translator, he proposed a promotional sponsorship deal to the guitar company executives. "They were making cheaper copies of Martin Guitars," he explains, "and they were calling them *Morris Guitars*. So I got all these Morris guitars from them in return for promoting them."

> The girls would be singing along with every Elvis song, singing along with Morris. We discovered they couldn't speak a lick of English, but they knew every word to those Elvis songs.

Morris also noticed with some amusement and curiosity the Karaoke sing-a-long craze that was sweeping Japan and the high tech audio and video Karaoke equipment that was being used to facilitate novice singers getting up and singing with band tracks. He couldn't remember seeing anything like that in Canada.

The final stop on the tour was to be Hawaii. Once again David Maitland's recollections are vivid: "I remember we left Japan on Christmas Eve, and when we got to Honolulu it was Christmas Eve there, too, because we went over the international dateline."

"After being in Asia for so long, getting off the flight from Tokyo and landing in Honolulu had its own cultural shock," Morris notes. "People would talk to you and say, 'Can I help you?' And you were stuck for an answer. People said full sentences and wanted a response. Sometimes it took me a second or so to realize that I was in a conversation with a person who spoke English.

"Even stranger and more bizarre was that during my show I'd forgotten how to entertain the audience in between songs. I'd forgotten the patter of introducing the songs with little tidbits of Elvis trivia. After doing *Hound Dog*, which sold over a million copies, I would tell the audience the deejays played the B-side (*Don't Be Cruel*) and it sold three million copies. In essence kids went out and bought a record they already had. I had to remember to thank the audiences *in English* for the applause after the songs.

"Richard met us in Honolulu. My mom was with him. He was busy all over the place auditioning new backup singers for the show to return with us to Canada and then to go to Las Vegas as the Silver Slipper opening was being prepared. Having my mom with me was great. She looked like one of the locals, the Polynesians, at least, and everyone wanted to be her new best friend. On Elvis's birthday (January 8th), they made a big fuss about my show, and had me and my mom and our whole band visit the *USS Arizona* memorial, and even put our visit on the local TV news

They were making cheaper copies of Martin Guitars, and they were calling them Morris Guitars. So I got all these Morris guitars from them in return for promoting them.

On Elvis's birthday (January 8th), they made a big fuss about my show, and had me and my mom and our whole band visit the USS Arizona memorial, and even put our visit on the local TV news shows.

shows. It was a PR dream. The shows were packed and the act was hot, and we were back in the groove, although my mom did put a little damper on *some* things."

Morris played Le Boom Boom Club and was so well received that he and the band were held over for three weeks. "It was really a nice nightclub in back of the International Marketplace," David recalls. "You walked over this little bridge and you were in the club. There were no doors or anything. It was the Polynesian style, thatched roof overtop, held up by posts and no walls. It was really something. We played opposite a Polynesian show. One of the guys in the band became friends with one of the dancers in the show and a couple of years later moved to Honolulu and married her."

Morris got some very good reviews in Honolulu newspapers. One reporter raved that "within the soul of Morris beats the soul of Elvis. It's quite uncanny, the illusion. Morris is very good at capturing nuances of Elvis . . ."

David has many fond memories of the time they spent in Hawaii, not the least of which was that there were always plenty of women hanging around after their shows. "We had a very good time in Hawaii," he says. "It was like I later learned in Las Vegas. In Vegas they say, 'What happens in Vegas stays in Vegas.' And it was a lot like that in Hawaii, too. Girls would come down to the show with their friends. They would come in twos and threes. We ran into a whole lot of girls from Canada. It was the same thing as Vegas. They might have boyfriends back at home, but while they were in Hawaii they wanted to go out and party just the same."

Within the soul of Morris beats the soul of Elvis. It's quite uncanny, the illusion.

Upon returning to Vancouver from Hawaii, Morris played some western Canadian dates before flying to Nevada for his debut on April 18th 1978 at the Silver Slipper.

"The Cave was packed," Morris recalls. "I was a prodigal son, being Vancouver's first international star returning from an overseas tour — a major media story. They had me on *The Six O'Clock News* on TV. It was more than just a returning show; it was an event. The final touches for our Vegas debut would be rehearsed on the road before we went to Nevada."

Gisele Kaufmann had also come back to Vancouver after working up north. She was at loose ends, not really sure what she was going to do next, although she still day-dreamed about one day working with Morris. "I had been working up in Fort Nelson during the boom they had when the pipeline went in, and I had just got back to Vancouver. I wasn't quite sure exactly what I was going to do. I was sitting in my mom's kitchen wishing that Morris would phone and offer me a job. The phone rang and it was Morris, and he said, 'Can you come up to Terrace? Maxine is sick, she has hepatitis.' I said, 'Yes!' So I flew up to Prince Rupert and that was the start of it. Then we went and played the Cave and Lucifer's. I remember at the Cave Richard Cheung asking me if I wanted to go to Vegas with them. I was still really young in those days and it was just like something out of a movie. We all flew to Vegas together."

The Cave was packed. I was a prodigal son, being Vancouver's first international star returning from an overseas tour — a major media story.

Top: *At the Majestic Hotel, Taipei, Taiwan.*
Bottom: *Taping the Taiwan TV special.*

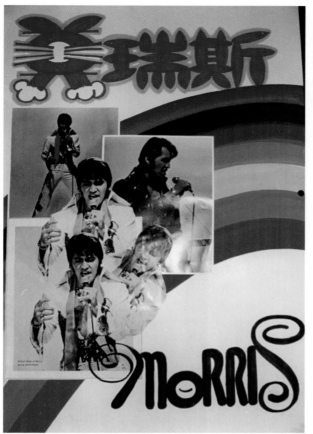

Top: Chinese poster with Morris's feline logo. *Bottom:* Japanese billboard announcing Morris

Top: Morris signs autographs at Vancouver International Airport upon arrival from Hawaii. Bottom: Richard Cheung, Morris's manager, guides his prize client past his adoring fans.

Back at the Cave, Morris trades kisses for Elvis scarves

That's All Right (Mama)

The Silver Slipper

Vegas Debut

Morris Bates' debut at the Gaiety Theater in the Silver Slipper Casino was reported in *The Williams Lake Tribune* by fan club president Alma Cunningham. "How proud you folks in Williams Lake must be," she wrote. "You already have your Williams Lake Stampede, and now you have one of your own on his way to becoming a great celebrity. That quiet, soft-spoken lad named Morris Bates, who graduated from Columneetza Senior Secondary School in 1969, is now appearing at the Silver Slipper in Las Vegas with his tribute to Elvis. Next door there is 'Big Chief' Wayne Newton and across the street none other than Tom Jones. Morris opened at the Slipper in April, and has a contract to appear there indefinitely. We are all hoping he will come back to the Cave in Vancouver for the month of December, and the Williams Lake Stampede in 1979 is a must. I have strict orders from him to make sure I keep you people informed."

"Alma was a wonderful, wonderful lady," Morris recalls. "When I first met her she was the mayor of Squamish. She came to see my show at the Cave and became a big fan, and she started the fan club. Every month she sent out a newsletter letting fans know where I was playing. She really helped me build my career. When she passed away a few years ago, my cousin Gloria Bates went up to Quesnel where Alma had been living and hauled away two truckloads of fan club memorabilia, all this stuff that she had accumulated and collected and kept there for me."

I worked hard in Las Vegas. It was just brutal. Three shows a night when I first started there.

Settling in for an extended engagement in April 1978 brought some stability to Morris Bates' life. He had just turned 28 years old. He had been on the road for eight years, performing 300 nights a year. Now he was able to unpack his suitcase. Still, the gig was hard on him. "I worked hard in Las Vegas," he recalls. "It was just brutal. Three shows a night when I first started there."

The years on the road and an even more strenuous Vegas schedule eventually exacted a toll on Morris's vocal chords, forcing him to resort to a common medical procedure used in Vegas — a cortisone shot in the neck before his nightly shows. "My vocal chords were damaged," Morris explains, "and the cortisone killed the pain so that I could go on and do my shows." The cortisone treatments eventually shortened his career. They were not a cure, they were an expedience, and, today, Morris speaks in a hoarse whisper. Former band members affectionately say that "Morris has that godfather voice now, like Marlon Brando."

"He was starting to have problems with that when I met him," David Maitland recalls. "But not as bad as it is for him these days. Richard Cheung told me that when Morris started out he really had the pipes, but he had just worked so much that he was beginning to have problems. I think he overdid it there for a while and he paid the price."

After being on the road with Morris in Canada and Asia for more than a year, Maitland was happy to be back in the USA and settled in for a good long stay on the Vegas Strip. He claims that his time spent with Morris was a complete education in the world of a professional musician. "Every night we did two or three shows and every time the curtain went up there was a brand new audience sitting there, and there would be some people that would come back and come back. There were some women that would be there 250 nights a year."

During their first season at the Slipper, they shared the stage with Kenny Kerr & his Boylesque Review. Kenny had begun doing a comedy routine and impersonations of Barbra Streisand before working up a full "Boylesque" show. Kerr continued on at the Slipper until it was closed in 1988, long after Morris Bates moved on, and was still playing Vegas in 2006, paired back to a solo act. The boys in this burlesque show took the boys in Morris Bates' band by surprise, as David Maitland recalls. "I remember the first time that we walked into the dressing room. We all shared the same dressing room — both shows. There was just a wall of mirrors between us. Those guys were something else! They had a great show."

One Vegas newspaper reporter marveled at the fact that for the first few months that Morris was playing the Silver Slipper his name wasn't on the marquee but his shows were always packed. "There is no fanfare built around his show," the journalist noted. "Morris doesn't even get space on the Silver Slipper's marquee. He gets a nondescript banner, hung out on the front of the building, but the place is packed all week, month after month."

Gisele Kaufmann remembers the initial excitement of their arrival on the strip, but there were some hoops that she had to jump through to keep her position running the light show and follow-spot. "We had no problem getting the H-1 visas that we needed," Gisele recalls. "We all had those, but they thought they were going to have a problem with me because I wasn't a member of their stage-hands' union in Nevada. But they convinced the union people that my lighting was so unique to the show that I was the only one who could do it. Their people came to watch a show at the Slipper and they said that there was no one that they had at that time that could do that — do what I was doing with the follow spot, each song had its own set of lighting cues."

She felt privileged to be there in the entertainment capital of the world during the final decade of the "old" Las Vegas when vaudeville and music hall traditions were still part of the best Vegas shows." It was such a fantastic show to be part of," she says, "because it had all that old Vegas show business feel about it. I'm

There is no fanfare built around his show, but the place is packed all week, month after month.

so glad to have seen that Vegas before everything changed because Vegas is completely different today."

Gisele had become a member of Morris Bates' show business family, getting to know the boys in the band and the extended family of relatives, fans, and friends who packed the showroom at the Slipper night after night. She shared an apartment with Morris and met both Linda Fuller, his Vancouver girlfriend, and some of the women he spent time with in Vegas, including Priscilla Presley-look-a-like, LA model Lisa Stacey. Gisele formed a lifelong bond with Linda and many of Morris's family and friends.

It was such a fantastic show to be part of, because it had all that old Vegas show business feel about it.

Richard handled the accommodations for band members and backup singers. The logistics of adding backup singers to the act had begun in Hawaii, where they had been auditioned, but their presence required some adjustments to be made. As Morris relates, "Having female backup singers in the show always proved challenging. Three girls accompanied us to Vegas. Although Richard had made it very clear that there was to be no fraternizing between band members and backup singers, it didn't take long for that rule to go by the way of the Dodo Bird. Everybody was shacking up with each other on the sly, or at least that's what they thought.

"To get the girls to agree on dress colors or shoes or anything at all was an 'it's just not me' syndrome. Finally, Richard would show up with show clothes and say, 'These are your outfits, bottom line!' When I had to reprimand someone for being late or not knowing their parts, I was not talking to a band member anymore but someone's newly acquired boyfriend or girlfriend. It was a true test of patience, but Richard was on top of his game. He rented six two-bedroom apartments and doubled up everyone who was already doubled up. So, we had two couples in one two-bedroom apartment, and the single guys got their own rooms in two-bedroom suites. Now everyone was happy.

"The opening was so exciting. None of us was prepared for the hoopla that Las Vegas gives to show openings on the Strip. The house was a-rockin'!"

Following a Vegas trend, Morris Bates contemplated a name change. "What was happening was that all of the major stars were using one name," he explains. "It didn't say 'Frank Sinatra'; it just said 'Sinatra'. And it didn't say Sammy Davis Jr.; it just said 'Sammy'. It was an era where if you were big enough, like Cher was, all you had to do was use one name.

"I was going to change my name. I really didn't like it. It's a very kind of 'formal' name. But I thought about it, and 'Elvis', that's what they name their dogs in the South. 'C'mon Elvis, c'mon Elvis.' That's what they call dogs down there. But his name was Elvis Presley. So I thought about it, and I thought, 'well, my name is 'Morris', what the hell am I going to do? It has an 'I-S' ring — like Elvis. And so it can be one name, I don't have to put Morris Bates I'll just put 'Morris'. Richard Cheung went out and made me a big neon sign."

The greater his success, the crazier the world around him became, and he was grateful to be surrounded by loyal friends and employees. "We went to Las Vegas for two weeks and we saw him every night at the Slipper," Grace Bobb recalls. "There were people that we knew there every night and we would all sit together." His mom was the matriarch of them all. "Morris's mom was like a second mother to the whole show," Scott explains. "One felt grounded after a chat with her. We all loved Phyllis." Phyllis Bates remembers that she would fly to Las Vegas every summer her son was entertaining there. She wasn't much of a gambler, but she would attend Morris's shows every night while she was in town. "Mom would play the nickel slots," Morris says. "She didn't spend much time in the casino except when I was in there doing my shows."

The extended engagement at the casino meant that the boys in the band were no longer living out of suitcases and waking up in hotel rooms. As Scott recalls, "I ended up living in a room that I rented from Toni Sandoval, the female bass player who played with Wayne Newton. She was in real estate, too, and she managed all of these properties. We had a real beautiful house in

The opening was so exciting. None of us was prepared for the hoopla that Las Vegas gives to show openings on the Strip. The house was a-rockin'!

Vegas that had been used by Howard Hughes' lawyers during the big court cases when they were trying to figure out his will. There were these big blown-up copies of his handwriting tacked up on the wall in the garage. Toni had played bass for Wayne Newton for a number of years and they were playing the Frontier Hotel, which is right next to the Silver Slipper, where we were playing."

We had a real beautiful house in Vegas that had been used by Howard Hughes' lawyers during the big court cases when they were trying to figure out his will.

On their breaks between shows, they were like kids in a candy store, cruising the nearby lounges and show-rooms where entertainment opportunities were unlim-ited. "The Slipper was right between the Stardust and the Frontier," Scott explains, "and we would walk out the back door and Wayne Newton would be doing these three-hour shows. Or you could see Mel Tillis or Glen Campbell or any number of people, and hang out with the musicians. It was neat getting to hang out with DJ Fontana; he was there playing with Ricky Saucedo, an Elvis impersonator who was playing at the Stardust."

Morris befriended Saucedo. "Rick was a real nice guy and he used to come over to my place and play his guitar and tell sto-ries," Morris remembers. "He was a good guitar player."

Las Vegas . . . I spent ten years there one night

"Since opening in Vegas in the spring of 1978," Morris relates, "until I got married in the little Wedding Chapel on the Strip on December 27, 1987, Vegas was my home. By showbiz standards, it was a relatively fast climb — it usually takes about 10 years to become an overnight sensation — but considering I came from a little Indian Reserve in Williams Lake called Sugar Cane, it was nothing less than phenomenal. In between his Vegas engage-ments, Morris played far and wide, from The Mad Trapper's Lounge in Inuvik, North West Territories to movie sets in South Africa. "They had to add extra pages to my passport," Morris jokes. "I have more memories than can adequately fill up one full lifetime and easily more than one book. I definitely did go touch the wall.

"If Las Vegas is considered to be America's playground, I was considered to be one of its schoolyard bullies, and, if Vegas is considered to be the center of decadence, sex, drugs and rock & roll, we definitely hit the mother lode. And, by the way, did I mention gambling? And it's open 26/7 – not a typo.

If Las Vegas is considered to be America's playground, I was considered to be one of its schoolyard bullies.

"I would usually come into the casino after the last show, sit at the end of the bar next to the security podium, and Sal the bartender would automatically bring me a Jack and a beer back. Richard had a souvenir stand in the corner where *Morris as Elvis* memorabilia was for sale, and people who had bought souvenirs would want them autographed. The atmosphere was quite relaxing and loose, and conversation ranged from interesting to funny to extremely bizarre. This one young lady always came to the show with a different older gentleman, and would always want her photos autographed. She was petite and very pretty, but didn't look anywhere near old enough to gamble. I told her she must really enjoy the show to have seen it so many times. She said she loved the show. She worked at one of the many 'ranches' on the outskirts of Clark County, and, whenever she got an 'out date', she insisted on seeing my show. With a smile and a twinkle in her eye, she added, 'If you ever want a date, *it's on the house.*' I smiled back, thanked her, and told her I'd keep that in mind.

Some girls wanted more than their pictures autographed. They wanted their souvenirs SIGNED. Sal the bartender would politely remind me to remind them that those signings were not allowed in the casino — maybe best done in the parking lot. Some women wanted autographs for their daughters or some men for their wives. Some just wanted an autograph. Some wanted to know my astrological sign, and if I knew Kenny Kerr, the star of the Boylesque Revue. Bob the security guard would sit on his perch in the security podium, keeping an eye on everything, just smiling and shaking his head.

"Once I left the casino I just melted into the bright swirl of

Once I left the casino I just melted into the bright swirl of Vegas lights. I liked to hang out at the show lounge at the Barbary Coast or the lounge at the Aladdin, where I knew most of the acts.

Vegas lights. I liked to hang out at the show lounge at the Barbary Coast or the lounge at the Aladdin, where I knew most of the acts. Sometimes folks would come up to me and say: 'Aren't you Johnny Harra?' or 'aren't you Rick Saucedo? And want an autograph. Some didn't know me. Some just wanted to mess with me. I'd just sign whoever's name they wanted. At least Wayne Newton had a mustache, sort of."

Richard and the Boys

"The core of my band prior to and in Vegas was Portland based guitarist and MC David Maitland, who may have thought *Morris* was the star of the *David Maitland Show*. Bass player Ken Nelsen was a tall, stoic redhead with a cutting sense of humor, who, at a distance, and with some imagination, could resemble Jerry Scheff, Elvis's bass player. Piano player and vocal arranger, Greg Perry, was probably one of the best rock & roll piano players in the business. The driving force of the rhythm section was Surrey, British Columbia born drummer Scott Anderson, who would rather pass out than drop time. He was 6'3", athletic, and a powerhouse when he played the opening drum intro to the show – you knew I was in the house. Elvis had also experienced the difference between a show drummer and a studio drummer when he had to replace legendary studio drummer Hal Blaine with Ronnie Tutt, who had worked with the Bonnie & Delaney band. New York born Zen Buddhist Tommy Cosmo was on saxes and flute. On trombone was a Brit named David Spence, who had written the song *Super Freak* for Rick James. First trumpet, Greg Marciel, became my conductor of our ever-increasing horn section, and would later become first chair with the Buddy Rich Orchestra. This was my core traveling road band.

The musicians all had their individual contracts and deals with Richard Cheung, the basic deal being the guarantee of 48 weeks of work a year including accommodation, transportation, wardrobe and a host of other perks that they may or may not have been able to squeeze out of Richard. Richard was known to 'make a buffalo squirm.' I had a rule that to play with me a musician had to be able to read charts. I was always getting horn players hustling me for a gig, especially in Vegas, and I would say, 'it's not that hard of a gig just as long as you can *read the spots off a leopard going ninety miles an hour in the dark*,' meaning you would have to memorize the charts, as my show required many quick stage blackouts where you literally had to play in the dark. When Elvis wanted to mess with the Joe Gershaw Orchestra at the Hilton, he'd simply change the order of the songs, and you could see the music charts a-flying as they struggled to keep up with the King and his rhythm section."

It's not that hard of a gig just as long as you can *read the spots off a leopard going ninety miles an hour in the dark.*

Competition for paying gigs in Vegas was fierce, and guitar slingers and out of work hot shots often came headhunting for David Maitland's job or one of the other cherry positions in Morris Bates' show band.

"My band was like the Rock & Roll School of Las Vegas," Morris explains, "and they were all graduates. The original guitar player for Kenny Roger's band, when he was doing the TV show *Rollin' on the River*, wanted to play guitar for me. At the time he was backing Roger Miller at the Silverbird. Miller was terrific, funny and a great fiddle player, too. His wife Marianne was singing backup. Between songs, Roger kept making wise cracks about this guy named Kenny who was playing up the Strip at the Riviera Hotel, meaning Kenny Rogers, who was Marianne's former husband. Buck Owens' wife Bonnie had been married to Merle Haggard, and so on. Some nights the whole town seemed incestuous. Roger Miller was using a native guy on drums who kind of reminded me of my old drummer buddy, Peter Hamlin. I was flattered that the guitar player wanted to play for me, but I didn't hire him because his credentials intimidated me. David was doing a perfect job for me, anyway. There was no reason to change."

The Merv Griffin Show

As August 1978 began, people everywhere were reminded that the first anniversary of Elvis Presley's death was fast approaching. Media producers had already begun gearing up for special presentations. A *Las Vegas Review Journal* story featured the three leading Elvis tribute artists who were playing the strip that month. The story was entitled "Kings of rock pack showrooms: Elvis impersonators keep memory alive." Morris was featured in this full-page story along with the older Johnny Harra, who was playing at the Silverbird, and the new kid on the block, Rick Saucedo, who was playing at the Stardust. "Locally," the *Review Journal* writer reported, "Morris seems to have the most fans. Kellie Flaherty, along with her sister Colleen and two other friends, Linda McIerney and Susan Benedict, have formed a Morris Bates fan club. The teenagers have each seen the show 38 times."

One night between his first and second show at the Slipper, Morris got a call from Merv Griffin. The veteran talk show host wanted Morris to perform on a show that they were taping at Caesars Palace the next day. It was to be part of a three-segment TV tribute to Elvis aired on the first anniversary of the King's death. It was a big deal to be asked to perform on *The Merv Griffin Show*.

"Merv Griffin's secretary told me to bring my musical conductor," Morris recalls, "and that I would be singing three songs with Ray Brown's Orchestra. She also told me that Merv would probably talk to me."

Between his second and third show, Morris heard a rumor that the casino where Johnny Harra was playing was paying the extra money so that he could bring his whole band on to the TV show. Morris went on and performed his 2:15 a.m. show, and he and the band went home to sleep. The boys in the band were burned and a little disappointed that they wouldn't be able to accompany Morris on the syndicated daytime

> Merv Griffin's secretary told me to bring my musical conductor, and that I would be singing three songs with Ray Brown's Orchestra.

TV show. However, in the morning Morris got another call, this time from Merv Griffin's production manager.

"He said that Johnny Harra was doing Elvis in the seventies in his white rhinestone suit," Morris remembers, "and asked if I would do Elvis in the sixties in my leather suit. I said I had no problem with that, as long as I got to bring my own rhythm section. The deal was done."

"The next morning," David Maitland recalls, "I was woken early by Morris's assistant, Ken, who said, 'Wake up, bring your stage clothes and our rhythm section. We are going to play the show.' We went to Caesars Palace, sat around for hours, did a dress rehearsal and run through; sat around some more, then, finally, the show started taping."

"We had a quick rehearsal with Ray Brown's Orchestra," Morris remembers, "and I asked Ray Brown if they knew the intro to *Trouble* in the key of C. Ray looked me up and down and reassured me they did."

Morris Bates' appearance on *The Merv Griffin Show* was another huge break for the Indian kid from the Sugar Cane Reservation, and, even though he had had very little sleep after doing his 2:15 a.m. set at the Slipper, he rose to the occasion.

Seventeen million people saw me singing on The Merv Griffin Show. It was the biggest break in my show business career.

"Seventeen million people saw me singing on *The Merv Griffin Show*," Morris says proudly. "It was the biggest break in my show business career. I was on the show with Roy Clark, Gavin MacLeod, the guy that played Captain Stubing on *The Loveboat*, Rick Saucedo, and Johnny Harra. I was wearing my black leather outfit. I opened with *Trouble* and closed with *Jailhouse Rock*, and I got a standing ovation. Merv came over and asked me, 'Aren't you hot in that leather?' Seventeen million people saw me on his TV show. All at once, I was a celebrity. After that, everything opened up for me."

Morris Bates' performance was the only one of the three Elvis segments to draw a standing ovation from the studio audience, but it had not been without its perilous moments for guitarist David Maitland. "Halfway through our first song I broke a string on my guitar. I couldn't stop the show to change strings, so I kept playing with five strings. I remember coming to a solo, looking into the camera, smiling, and somehow making it through the solo and the rest of the songs with five strings."

For Scott Anderson, whose father was a jazz drummer and had taken him to see Miles Davis and Cannonball Adderly when they came to Vancouver, the opportunity to play with Ray Brown was a career highlight he will never forget. "I got a chance to play for 60 seconds during the commercial break with the great Ray Brown, the standup bass player who had the orchestra on the TV show," he recalls, "and that was a real thrill for me, playing that walk-off with Ray Brown. We played *C-Train Blues*, and after that I got to talk with Ray a little bit in the dressing room. It was a big thrill for me because my dad was a professional jazz drummer who worked with pianist Bob Doyle on the CBC radio broadcasts a lot in those days and he was my biggest influence to play drums. Dad never got to play with Ray Brown but I did, and that was real special for me."

Some of Scott's most vivid memories come from that TV appearance. "Playin' the big shows with the lights and everything," he relates, "you don't really get to see anything beyond the stage. The scariest part for me was because of the TV cameras when we were playing *The Merv Griffin Show* at Caesars Palace. The house lights would go right up. So you would really see the crowd. The house lights would be up on the crowd, and I remember getting a bit of stage fright that I hadn't had for a long time."

A few days later, Morris was invited to tape a segment for *20/20* with Geraldo Rivera. Morris had become an overnight celebrity, but was becoming more cautious about agreeing to interviews. "I started to request a list of the questions prior to the interviews," he explains, "so I could get the tone and direction that it was going to go. The interview was set up in my dressing room. Geraldo did not ask me a single question on the list and started off by asking me, 'what did I think about Elvis's drug problem?' I was stunned. 'You should interview Elvis's doctor,' I responded. I was pissed off and it got worse as it went on. I had been set up."

The same sort of thing happened on a talk show with syndicated columnist Dick Maurice."I first met Dick Maurice when I was taping *The Merv Griffin Show*, I even had a picture taken with him. He was the Las Vegas columnist for Rona Barrett's LA gossip magazine. He would report on all the Vegas gossip, and he had a syndicated radio talk show that was broadcast from Caesars Palace at 1:30 a.m., nightly. The talk show was live with various Vegas entertainers appearing after their last shows. He also had a newly debuted TV talk show that was taped separately and shown at 3:00 p.m. in the afternoon, much like Oprah does today. I appeared on his syndicated radio talk show one night with Phyllis Diller. I talked with her for a while before the show and told her my mom's name was also Phyllis. She was sweet and told me she'd try to catch my show sometime. *The Dick Maurice Show* was also broadcast live inside Caesars casino from a kind of plexiglass bubble so the casino gamblers could watch and see the stars being interviewed. It was a phone-in talk show so that people could ask you questions about yourself or your show. The producer would screen callers, allowing for a 15-second delay. So you had time to prepare yourself for an answer.

'What's it like to make a living off of a dead man?' I went 'Whoa!' and started stuttering and stammering and looking at the producer.

"The question I was supposed to be asked was: 'What made you do a tribute show about Elvis.' When we were on the air live, the producer gave the caller his cue to ask his question, and he said, matter of factly, 'What's it like to make a living off of a dead man?' I went 'Whoa!' and started stuttering and stammering and looking at the producer. The producer was looking at Dick Maurice. I glanced into the casino, which seemed to be frozen mid-movement. Everyone was waiting for my response. I was trying to gain my composure. I finally calmed down and asked where the male caller was calling from, and I think he said he was from Texas. I went on to explain the void Elvis had left in the entertainment business and that I was simply filling it. And if I was not doing his music or his memory justice, people would simply stop coming to my show and there would be no market for this type of presentation. We talked for a while and finally he came around to say that, if he were ever in Vegas, he would be sure to stop by and check out my show.

"Dick Maurice also hosted a lot of celebrity parties at his home. I was invited to a couple of them. One of the parties was for Debbie Reynolds, an afternoon pool party for her birthday. Debbie held court beside the pool chatting with various well-wishers. Jack Jones was there, along with a lot of people I didn't recognize. It was mostly boy and girl dancers from her Vegas show and the Siegfried & Roy crew. I remember Debbie cutting into a couple of boy dancers that were teasing her. She tore a verbal strip off them that would make ten truck drivers blush.

"I was standing next to the poolside bar and I asked this lady who was standing beside me what her name was. With a very soft southern drawl she said, 'Bobby Gentry'. For those who don't remember, Bobby Gentry is the singer of the hit record *Ode To Billy Joe*. I spent most of the rest of the afternoon talking with her before taking off to do my first show.

"As time went by, I became a fixture on the Las Vegas scene. I performed month after month. People would say, 'We'll catch Morris next time we're in Vegas, he's always here . . .' I was even roasted by the Friar's Club of Las Vegas at the Holiday Inn Showroom. I had, basically, arrived. At the roast, however, nobody had anything really bad to say about me because nobody really knew me. I had kept to myself and stayed out of trouble with the tabloids and such. I was not gossip fodder. It was pretty surreal listening to Milton Berle telling jokes about me, and I remembered that Elvis had got his first exposure on West Coast television on Milton's show in the fifties. Shecky Green, Don Rickles, Rip Taylor, Carme, and a host of others took a run at me. Dave Barry said he got mixed up about who he was opening for – Wayne Newton or Morris. Most of the jokes were made about Elvis Impersonators waking up thinking they were Elvis. One of the comedians said that Morris woke up from

> It was pretty surreal listening to Milton Berle telling jokes about me, and I remembered that Elvis had got his first exposure on West Coast television on Milton's show in the fifties.

a nightmare and thought he was Johnny Harra. Or the reason that Rick Saucedo left town was that he couldn't afford to pay the Jordanaires' bunny ranch tab *or* DJ Fontana's gambling debts at the Stardust."

The rich and famous celebrities that congregated at gossip columnist Dick Maurice's soirees were not the only people that were drawn to the raw energy that Morris unleashed on stage night after night during his shows at the Slipper. He was also befriended by an ever-increasing number of people who worked in the industry and became Morris Bates fans. These new fans ranged from busboys and keno girls to lighting technicians, sound guys, musicians, and entertainers who were working in adjacent casinos. And then there were some people who simply loved living in the entertainment capital of the world and took a special interest in the kid from Canada.

As Morris recalls, "One of my biggest fans and supporters was the Hendricks family. Joe and Suzie Hendricks had retired to Vegas from Fort Lauderdale, Florida, and they had two sons, Joe Jr. and Harry Hendricks. They had Cadillac franchises in Fort Lauderdale and St. Louis, and Mrs. Hendricks' brother was in charge of the stagehands union in Chicago, which was run by the teamsters. Suzie Hendricks treated me like a son, and had her own table reserved in my showrooms whether she was there or not.

"After one of my early shows, Suzie Hendricks' son Harry asked me if I would accompany them to Eddy Arnold's 9:00 p.m. show at the Sahara. I tried to beg off as I wasn't really an Eddy Arnold fan, but she insisted, noting there was plenty of time before my 11:30 show. I was reluctant but gave in and wasn't prepared to see a truly unique performer. After seeing in-your-face productions, fast-paced reviews, and full-of-themselves star-studded entertainers, it was refreshing to see a real pro like Eddy Arnold walk on stage with a suitcase full of hits and deliciously funny stories. He was totally charismatic with the most crystal clear voice imaginable when he sang *Cattle Call*.

It was refreshing to see a real pro like Eddy Arnold walk on stage with a suitcase full of hits and deliciously funny stories. He was totally charismatic with the most crystal clear voice imaginable.

His effortless grace and ease with his audience was so comfortable. It was a feeling that it was just him and you in the show room. He taught me a lot that night about being able to hold an audience in the palm of your hand — truly a class act. After that night I always included an Eddy Arnold song in my show. *Welcome To My World*.

"Another night Joe and Suzie showed up with their two sons, and, after my show, they asked me and Richard to accompany them to the casino parking lot. There, they presented me with an almost brand new, light brown and gold metal flake, 1977 Brougham Cadillac. Harry threw me the keys and Joe Sr. said, 'just put insurance on her.' It was the beginning of a long and lasting friendship for both Richard and myself."

The first question he asked me was, 'Have you heard that Morris the Cat died in Hawaii?'

Part and parcel of Morris's newly acquired celebrity status was increased demand for him to appear on radio and TV talk shows, where he soon found himself being compared to his namesake, Morris, the finicky cat of cat-food fame. "I'd just arrived in Vancouver on a flight from Nevada," he recalls, "and was scheduled to appear on an early morning talk show. I was still half-asleep when he began introducing me on his radio show. The first question he asked me was, 'Have you heard that Morris the Cat died in Hawaii?' I guess he thought it would be a funny way to start the interview. I was kind of dumfounded not knowing what to say and I just looked at him and sighed and said, 'one down and one to go.'"

The New Showroom

Morris was already an accomplished self-promoter by the time he was playing shows at the Silver Slipper, but there were some things he was now being asked to do that he didn't always feel comfortable doing. "What Richard considered to be controlled publicity," Morris explains, "was for me to be seen everywhere and anywhere at local public functions representing the Slipper in a positive, family-type 'warm and fuzzy' atmosphere, which in his mind translated to 'the money you lost in the casino was being filtered back into the local community economy.' My scarves, for example, were made by a local Special Needs society. The Slipper also sponsored various local sports organizations."

Morris enjoyed turning out for local sandlot softball games, but he didn't feel comfortable when he was asked to sing the national anthem in a large stadium. "Vegas didn't have any professional sports franchises of its own in those days," he relates, "and a lot of pro basketball teams, such as the LA Clippers and Denver Nuggets, played exhibition games at the Thomas & Mack Center. There was a move afoot to promote professional baseball and get a triple-A PCL franchise, and a series of exhibition games were scheduled. One afternoon Richard showed up with the charts for the American national anthem. 'They want you to sing the national anthem at a baseball game, Mo,' he told me.

"'Oh, my . . . god,' I said, 'I don't even know it. You have to sing *a cappella* in those ballparks and you can't hear yourself singing . . . I'm a Canadian! Indians don't like baseball except in Cleveland, Richard! Don't you know I'm allergic to chalk?' When he offered no sympathy, I just threw up my hands in despair and said, 'Someone, anyone, please, help . . .' I moped and pouted all morning and then half-heartedly ran over the lyrics and melody to *The Star-Spangled Banner* with Greg, my piano player. We kept going until they couldn't stand it anymore and told me that I didn't have to sing it, they'd find someone else to do it. I was so relieved. Another time I was approached by a large church organization that wanted me to sing *Lord You Gave Me A Mountain* to their 1200 member congregation.

"I *did* perform at Nellis Air Force Base a couple of times and it was always fun. I'd sing *G.I. Blues* and march around the stage doing all kinds of antics. It was always loose and a guaranteed good time. They even offered to take me up in one of the Blue Angels' jets. They said I could go up and see the Pacific Ocean and be back in half an hour. I said I'd settle for a souvenir picture with the jet.

> I'm a Canadian! Indians don't like baseball except in Cleveland, Richard! Don't you know I'm allergic to chalk?

"One year there was a big police convention in Vegas. All the police chiefs of every major city in the USA were meeting at the Hilton Convention Center. It was packed. They'd asked us to perform a few songs and sent a couple of limos to pick up me and my band after our first show. I had also six or seven guys with me acting as bodyguards, and we were all ushered backstage. As I was nervously gauging the audience and deciding what songs to do, the curtain came up and I could see the audience of five or six thousand law enforcement officers and their wives sitting there at their tables looking prim and proper and stiff. The MC announced that Morris, the star of the Elvis Presley Story, was there to make a guest appearance. There was a ripple of applause and some hoots and hollers. I was just dressed in a suit with my hair combed into a fifties pompadour style. All the guys were hyped and cop jokes were a-flyin'. I had lots of nervous energy, then one of my buddies hollered out 'One hundred bucks if you open with *Jailhouse Rock...*' I said, 'right,' sarcastically, then thought about it for a nanosecond and told my guitar player David to announce me, vamp me on, and stop and hit the key of D. The band didn't even know what I was going to sing. They began vamping and I walked out into the lights, and, for a brief moment you could hear the air being sucked out of the ballroom. Then I grabbed the mike and leaned back and let go: 'The Warden threw a party in the country jail...'

"The lyrics hit them like an electric jolt, and, all of a sudden, the place was rocking. Couples were up and dancing and it was pure excitement. I moved on to a medley of *Teddy Bear* and *Don't Be Cruel*, and by the time I was singing *Love Me Tender* and closing with *Can't Help Falling In Love*, the dance floor was packed and everybody was dancing cheek to cheek. The mirror ball suspended from the ceiling was sparkling as it slowly rotated, and I got a déjà vu feeling that everybody was re-experiencing their first high school sock hop. Then the band was vamping me off to a standing ovation. I had a sneaky feeling that my second show at the casino was not going to be nearly as exciting, but then again who knew who would show up? I was learning that every day in Vegas was Christmas and every night was New Year's Eve . . ."

Meanwhile, night after night, Morris was packing the small showroom at the Slipper. His name was now featured on the marquee, and it didn't take management long to devise a way to further capitalize on their star performer's increasing popularity. As Morris recalls, "when we first started at the Silver Slipper, we were in the Gaiety Theater, which was on the main floor of the casino. I went on at 7:00, Kenny Kerr went on at 8:30 and 10:00, and I went on at 11:30 and 2:15 and so on. But we had to swap sets, and the stagehands had to strike the stage. So what happened was that they moved me upstairs. They built me a bigger showroom upstairs with separate dressing rooms and everything," Morris explains. "My dark night was Wednesday and that's when they had boxing up there. They really made it grand for me. They did a heck of a job building me a showroom so that we didn't have to set up and tear down to make way for Kenny Kerr and his revue after each show. It was dynamite!"

> I was learning that every day in Vegas was Christmas and every night was New Year's Eve . . .

"On Wednesday nights, they used to have boxing matches in the upstairs area, and that is where I met Redd Foxx. He sponsored bantamweight boxers who would fight up there, little Mexican boxers, and, man, they could really fight. On fight night there would be 600 or 700 people up there, laying bets on the fights. One night one of the sponsors had this fighter by the name of Tyrone — he was touted as the next Muhammad Ali. Tyrone was from Nevada, he was about six foot three and he weighed about 225 pounds, and the other fighter was this guy from east LA who was about six foot one, 210 pounds. The shorter guy gets in the ring with the next Ali and knocks him down three times, beats the crap out of him. Then the judges put up their cards and the big guy from Nevada was the winner.

"The whole place erupted. Guys were jumping into the ring. Guys were beating up the judges. It was like a fight scene out of a John Wayne movie. It was unbelievable. Then they got everybody separated and calmed down and the two fighters and their entourages went back into their dressing rooms. Wayne Gust and I were sitting there watching all of this, then all of a sudden they came back out and the place erupted again just like in Mel Brooks' movie *Blazing Saddles*. They were all fighting and screaming and beating on each other because it was such a bad decision."

Casino manager Bill Friedman explained that the fights were just another attraction. People gambled after the fights before they left the casino, just like they gambled after they attended Morris's shows. As Morris recalls, "Bill Friedman told me, 'Morris, every time a person walks in this place he walks out ten dollars short. There will be ten dollars less in his pocket when he walks out . . .'"

I'll Sing His Songs

When a Vegas songwriter asked Morris if he would record a demo tape of a song the writer wanted to pitch to Kenny Rogers, he couldn't refuse. "I could sound like a whole bunch of guys," Morris explains, "and these songwriters wanted their song demo to sound like the star they were going to pitch the demo tape to, so they hired me. Sometimes we would go into a professional studio, but mostly they were just done at their home studios."

Recording songs that were going to be pitched to big name recording artists got Morris thinking about what he was going to do after his Elvis act. "I wanted to transform myself, to spring-board myself out of being merely an Elvis tribute artist to something that was different," he relates. "They worked me really hard in Vegas. They worked me too hard, and I wanted to branch out. I wanted to transform my act. That's why I put my name up there so big on that neon sign. I wanted them to remember '*Morris*'. After a while the promoters never put anything about Elvis on the marquee, they just put 'Morris'.

"I wanted to branch out, but they couldn't find anything for me to branch out into . . . because people came to hear me do Elvis. When I moved over to the Landmark, I would be the only

All of a sudden they came back out and the place erupted again just like in Mel Brooks' movie *Blazing Saddles*.

guy in Vegas whose show was grossing up to $40,000 and $50,000 a week. I would be making more money than Tina Turner, Freddy Fender, and Roger Miller, but they also made a lot of money from record sales. I was making all of my money from performances. So I decided to record an album before I opened at the Landmark. It was just going to be an album that we sold at shows."

Morris recorded his debut album in Vancouver when he returned there to play the Cave. Mostly, he recorded covers of Elvis songs, but added two originals that he penned with Wayne Gust. "Wayne and I had begun to write songs together before I went to Vegas," Morris recalls. "Wayne would come up with a concept and run it by me and I would add to it. It was a weird process. Wayne and I never actually sat down together and wrote songs. Wayne would write stuff. I would write stuff. And then we would fit it together. And when it got down to the recording sessions, I would come up with an arrangement.

That's why I put my name up there so big on that neon sign. I wanted them to remember 'Morris'.

"We wanted to come up with a song that would do what Ronnie McDowell's song *The King Is Gone* did for his career, so we put together *I'll Sing His Songs*."

I'll Sing His Songs turned out to be an Elvis tribute ballad with big production and plenty of pomp and circumstance, but, sadly, it wasn't released as a single and promoted to radio as McDowell's offering had been. Their second effort was *Getting Back To Memphis*, an up-tempo country rocker that evoked the days when Elvis and his Memphis Mafia sidekicks traveled back and forth from Tennessee to California on a regular basis.

"When he was young, Elvis didn't like to fly," Morris relates, "so he bought himself a Greyhound bus and he would drive it and everything. They would drive from Memphis out to California to make movies. He would take his whole gang with him. And when the movies were done, they would drive all the way back to Memphis. He never flew much at all until he began touring in 1969. And in 1975 he bought a Convair 880, which he chris-

We wanted to come up with a song that would do what Ronnie McDowell's song The King Is Gone did for his career, so we put together I'll Sing His Songs.

tened *The Lisa Marie*, and a small JetStar, which he called *Hound Dog II*."

The sessions were done at a small recording studio near the Compo-Cheung offices on Pemberton Street in North Vancouver and the album was titled *I'll Remember You*. "I was playing two shows a night at the Cave," Morris recalls, "and in the afternoons we would go over to North Van and cut a couple of tracks. The band was working even harder than I was, laying down tracks."

Dennis Compo remembers that his first office when he moved from Edmonton to Vancouver had been above Bill Snow's recording studio on Pemberton. "Then Richard and I got the bigger offices further up the street," he recalls. The tracks were logged at Snow's facility, and Wayne Gust was onboard for the duration. "Wayne wasn't the ideal guitar player for my shows in Vegas," Morris admits. "He was real good at fifties and sixties stuff, but he wasn't a perfect fit for the whole show, and I always had a hot-shot lead guitar player in my band. Wayne would just show up some nights and plug in his amp and guitar, and he was there for all of the recording sessions.

"Wayne went in with the band in the afternoons and sang the vocals like he was me. Then they would do the background vocals. That way I didn't have to wear out my voice too much. And when they were almost done, I would come in and sing the lead vocal. After that they would add the horns and we would mix the tracks. We ran out of time and money before we got the horns recorded for *If I Could Dream*, but the rest of the album is a lot more finished sounding."

The album features Elvis standards — *Treat Me Nice, Don't Be Cruel, Money Honey*, and *I Want You, I Need You, I Love You*. The band is incredibly tight and vocal harmonies recall the days when the Jordanaires wound their vocal styling around the King's husky baritone on the early RCA records. Greg Perry's piano, Maitland's guitar, and the tight, economic horn arrangements all contribute to a very smooth big band sound. Also included are

> In the afternoons we would go over to North Van and cut a couple of tracks. The band was working even harder than I was, laying down tracks.

the ballad *I'll Remember You* from one of the Hawaiian Specials and Joe Mock's version of the Clovers' *I Got My Eyes On You*, which Joe taught Morris way back when they were playing in the Bachelor's Three in Williams Lake in 1970.

Morris Bates' only regret is that he didn't go in with the band and record his own live-off-the-floor vocals right off the bat. "What I should have done," he explains, "is have an audience in front of me when I recorded. Once I was in front of an audience, that's when I transformed myself. I couldn't transform myself in a studio because there was just me and a microphone in the sound booth and I couldn't get that 'attack' that I had when I was in front of an audience.

"That's what Elvis did when he first made his come-back on the NBC Special in '68. He sang live to a studio audience. He had that thing that you have when you are singing to people as opposed to just sitting in a sound booth singing to tracks. Some guys can really do that. But I never did enough of it that I became good at it. I should have done my recording in front of an audience.

"When Elvis recorded his Christmas album in June and July so that they would have the record ready for the Christmas market in December, they transformed the studio. They had a Christmas tree and lights, and when he walked into the studio, it looked like Christmas. It felt like Christmas Eve. That's what they did to make it feel like it was Christmastime in the middle of summer."

There were other small details that escaped his notice until too late, like Greg Perry's piano introduction to *Don't Be Cruel*. "It should have been David Maitland playing that intro on guitar," Morris points out, "but they did that track on their own and when I came in to listen to it, they had already moved on. It's good but it's not the way I wanted it to be." Still, his fans bought plenty of tapes once Richard Cheung had them dubbed up and sent to Vegas to their merchandise sales agent.

I couldn't transform myself in a studio because there was just me and a microphone in the sound booth and I couldn't get that 'attack' that I had when I was in front of an audience.

New Line-up

When relationships between backup singers and band members soured, their discord began to affect shows and rehearsals. Richard had to act ruthlessly before things got really out of hand. "It was difficult working up new material for the show," Morris recalls, "because we had to pay a minimum of four hours overtime to our two union stagehands to turn on the power and lights in the showroom. I used an electric drummer and an acoustic guitar to run over the arrangements in my apartment. Greg, my piano player, was supposed to be working on arrangements for the horns and backup singers. At this one particular rehearsal in the showroom at the Slipper, we were going to clear up some arrangements and lighting cues, and go over *Way Down*, Elvis's last charted hit while he was still alive.

It was difficult working up new material for the show, because we had to pay a minimum of four hours overtime to our two union stagehands to turn on the power and lights in the showroom.

"As we were getting ready to run over the tune, I could feel some sort of tension as they were not talking to each other. As I was running over the lighting cues with Gisele, Richard came by, which he seldom did, and said, 'Let's get going, time is money, it's costing a fortune for the stagehands to sit around.'

"Scotty counted the song in and I hit my vocal and went to the chorus where the backup singers answer my "way down" with one of their own whenever I sing those lyrics, but there was nothing but a muted whimper from the backup singers. I put up my hand and stopped the song and said, 'Let's take it again from the top.' There wasn't much improvement. I was starting to lose it. I said, 'What's going on here?' One of the girls started to cry. Greg got up and left the piano bench. I told them all to 'take five.' After the guys trouped out, one of the girls told me that Greg and the other girl singer weren't getting along anymore and the other couple was quarrelling, too. When Richard came back in to find out what was happening, you could cut the tension with a knife. By the time the dust settled, the girls had been given two weeks notice and Greg was toast. His contract was not being renewed. Richard flew to LA and came back with three black girls, a gospel trio who were just fantastic, and a piano player named John, who used to work with Buddy Miles."

Bookings

For any entertainer from Canada becoming a marquee star on the Vegas strip in the seventies was a major accomplishment. Anne Murray and Paul Anka had secured their Vegas engagements because they had number one hits on the radio. Morris had got there because he was a gifted entertainer with a terrific management team.

Dennis Compo had revolutionized booking tours in western Canada by using what he has always called his "secret weapon." As Dennis recalls, "When I got into the agent business and went on my own, I got excited about computers. Those were the days when everything was done in MS-DOS, and I had my whole agency programmed. My assistant and I would plug all the bands into the databank, and none of the other agents could figure out how we managed to put tours together so fast. We had it all computerized. We were probably the only agency in the world that was totally computerized that early on — I just took a shine to computers. Nowadays in the 21st century, pretty well everything I do is online, online marketing and everything. And back in the day it kept Morris busy as well as a whole lot of other bands we were working with."

We were probably the only agency in the world that was totally computerized that early on — I just took a shine to computers.

Morris Bates had undoubtedly benefited from this technological advantage. A mere glance at his booking schedule during the seventies quickly points out that after signing with Dennis his tour schedule improved by quantum leaps. "We had great results putting tours together," Dennis confides. "I was part of an association called the Great Canadian Touring Organization. A whole series of agencies from Vancouver to Halifax got together and we would meet all the time. I would put the data from all of the tours into our database. Then I would phone everybody and say, 'I know you have an open date here and here and here, and I have an act that would fit perfectly.' With that computer it was like having a staff of 30 people, but there was just two of us at that time."

Dennis Compo and Richard Cheung were on a roll that gamblers the world over usually only dream about. "At one time, we had seven or eight Vegas acts," Dennis explains. "We groomed the acts, trained them, and booked them into Vegas. They were mostly California acts. And after they played Vegas, we toured them all through Canada. Some of them still live up here; they liked it here and became landed immigrants. They were all nightclub acts — my agency had exclusive contracts with hotel chains that had nightclubs and showrooms right across Canada."

Dennis Compo and Richard Cheung were on a roll that gamblers the world over usually only dream about.

Of course, within the most successful organizations, there will always be power struggles, strategic decisions, and frequent redeployment of resource management personnel — which is precisely what happened during the time Morris was performing at the Silver Slipper. Many years later, Dennis Compo is gracious enough to merely dismiss this reassignment of roster personnel to a casual mutual decision made by himself and his partner. "We split up the company after a few years," he reminisces, "and Richard managed the acts that we had in Las Vegas." Richard Cheung now completely controlled Morris Bates' international booking and management.

Not long after this, Cheung seized an opportunity to release Morris from his contractual obligations to the Seattle agency he had signed with years ago to get a Vegas booking. A release secured when an agency representative was in dire need of a few thousand dollars. That release was handwritten on the back of a keno ticket, and the Seattle agency representative was paid in money obtained from the casino cage. When the rep returned to Seattle and faced his superiors, he denied everything and the agency sued, but Cheung couldn't find the keno ticket. Meanwhile, the casino held onto the weekly money that was owed to Morris, and Cheung and Bates searched week after week, month after month for the keno ticket. It was ironic. They owned homes in Vegas and LA. They were driving Cadillacs. But they didn't have any cash and they couldn't meet their weekly payroll to band members. Loans had to be taken out.

At last, the keno ticket with the scribbled contractual release signature was found. It held up in court, the casino cage released the pay money that been held back for so long, almost a year, and Richard Cheung continued on as Morris Bates' manager. The arrangement lasted for several more years.

The next melodrama that would be played out began with an offer from South African promoters. As Morris recalls, "Movie producer John de Kock and some South African concert promoters came to Vegas and signed me to do a movie and concert tour."

When the idea was first pitched to Morris and Richard, it seemed like a good opportunity. Like everybody else in North America in those days, they had heard about apartheid in South Africa, but they had no idea what the conditions truly were. If the African promoters didn't see a problem, then it was probably all right. They had most likely seen Morris on *The Merv Griffin Show* and decided to sign him up for their R2 Million TV movie and live concert promotional package.

"Morris was the number one Elvis impersonator ever to hit Vegas," Dennis Compo asserts. "The main competition that Morris had at that time was Alan, but Alan was very slight in stature . . . He sounded like Elvis but he was just a little guy . . ."

"I was one of the hottest acts in Vegas at that time," Morris relates, "and I guess they just assumed that I was a white man. Richard was Chinese and I was a Shuswap Indian, but we didn't think it through all that much. It happens all the time. While we were putting this book manuscript together, Celine Dion finished her five-year engagement in Vegas — and where was she off to next? South Africa! However, when I went there in 1979, things were a whole lot different — Nelson Mandela was still in jail and I didn't know much about him."

They were driving Cadillacs. But they didn't have any cash and they couldn't meet their weekly payroll to band members.

I was one of the hottest acts in Vegas at that time, and I guess they just assumed that I was a white man.

The promoters were impressed with his show at the Slipper, but Morris was totally unprepared for what they told him just before the contracts were signed. "I had these three wonderful black women singing backup with me at that time," he explains, "and they were incredible. When these girls sang, I thought I was Elvis — they were that good. I would sing *In The Ghetto* and their voices were just so beautiful! They were some of the best backup singers I ever had. But when the promoters came to see us in Vegas they said, 'Okay, we have got all of the contracts here for you to sign. We like your show and we want to do the movie, but you will have to get rid of the colored backup singers.'"

The promoters surprised Morris even more by actually using the inappropriate "n" word that has become even more inappropriate since that day in 1979, but they got their message across — the African American backup singers would not be able to make the trip to South Africa.

"Those three girls were like sisters to me," Morris confesses. "They were so nice to me, and they worked so hard on all their parts, we didn't even have to rehearse them. Richard hired them. They were big girls, gospel singers, and when I did *C.C. Rider* they would just punch up my lines — they were fun to perform with and they were great singers!"

At the time, the decision was made to let the gospel singers go because the movie deal was deemed to be too good to turn down. Upon hearing that they would not be going on the South African tour, one of the backup singers quit. "So," Morris explains, "we had to hire three white girls to fulfill our contract. But we only really needed two girls for the tour, so Gisele Kaufmann put on one of the singer's costumes for the promotional photos that we had taken to send to South Africa."

That summer Morris went home to entertain family and friends and everybody else who showed up at the Williams Lake Stampede on the first of July, Canada Day 1979 holiday weekend. Lyle Bobb remembers that "when Morris went back to Williams Lake for some reason he was a bit nervous and he asked us to come up there with him. In those days, it was a huge party because the police blocked off pretty well every entrance and exit to Williams Lake. We had a motel room just outside of town and after the shows it would take us quite a while to get back to our motel. The Williams Lake Stampede with the rodeo and everything was a big deal in those days."

Thursday night, Morris dedicated the first of his two sold-out grandstand shows to his mother. With plenty of free time during the daytime hours, Morris visited some of his old haunts. Scott Anderson and some of the other boys in the band were invited to come along. As Scott recalls, "I remember going downtown in the middle of the afternoons with Morris for a beer in one of the local taverns, and he would be visiting with his old buddies. Of course, he was a huge celebrity there in Williams Lake. Morris liked to play pool. There was some pretty hot pool-players there in his hometown that weekend, and I guess they figured they were going to show him a thing or two. I remember a kind of cool came over Morris and a champion spirit. He ran the table. He looked like one of the British guys on *Billiard Champions* on TV. I had played pool against Morris in the past, and I would beat him sometimes, maybe one time out of ten, but I had never seen him shoot that good and make the kind of shots that he did that afternoon. He didn't have 'choke' in his vocabulary. He never had 'I'm sorry' in his vocabulary, either. He never would apologize. And that afternoon he just didn't take any prisoners — he ran the table!"

Morris dedicated the first of his two sold-out grandstand shows to his mother.

Morris played a second grandstand show Saturday night, again dedicating his performance to his mother, Phyllis. He told the hometown crowd that his band members hailed from Canada, the USA, and England, and, that following the Saturday night show, he was flying to London and on to Johannesburg, South Africa. A show had been booked at a London club, but then it was discovered that to coordinate the flights from the States to England, then from England to Africa, there would not be enough time to do the London show.

His triumphant return confirmed in everybody's mind that he was a big star in Vegas, but he had not forgotten where he came from.

Morris would be back performing shows at the Cave in Vancouver in the fall, he told his fans. Hundreds of young women rushed the stage during *Suspicious Minds*, his finale, and Morris rewarded them with his usual gifts of scarves and kisses. He was a hometown hero, and Phyllis Bates was very proud of her son. His triumphant return confirmed in everybody's mind that he was a big star in Vegas, but he had not forgotten where he came from, or the friends and neighbors who had helped him on his way.

Morris lights up the Strip

Morris in neon

Three grueling shows a night

*At the Merv Griffin Show, Morris's first national
exposure (seventeen million viewers)*

Morris is welcomed home
by Chief George Abby.

Love Me

The South African Tour

Movie Star

On July 8, 1979, Morris and his band, bodyguards, and manager arrived at Jan Smuts International Airport in Johannesburg and faced a throng of South African curiosity seekers, Elvis fans, and reporters. During his lifetime, Elvis had never traveled to Africa. Morris Bates' arrival on the continent was much heralded, and he encountered autograph seekers wherever he went. "It is a 13-hour flight from Heathrow to Johannesburg," Morris recalls. "It was a long flight, and when we arrived at the airport in Africa, they had a room that I could go in and wash up and shave because there were all these reporters and TV camera crews waiting there to interview me."

Daily newspapers reported that the Canadian singer was in their midst to perform concerts and film a movie with producer and director John De Kock as part of the R2 Million Live Show Motion Picture Package. De Kock had already been touting Morris as "the new Elvis" and told newspaper reporters that he was going to "bridge the gap between South Africa and the rest of the world" by making no less than three made-for-television films during Morris's scheduled six-month tour.

Morris's leading lady, Lisa Stacey, arrived on a separate flight but often shared the spotlight at press conferences

> De Kock had already been touting Morris as 'the new Elvis' and told newspaper reporters that he was going to 'bridge the gap between South Africa and the rest of the world.'

179

with him. "Lisa is an LA model," Morris told the press, "and she looks just like Priscilla Presley . . ."

"She's too small to be a professional ramp model," a reporter for the *Durban Daily News* told his readers, "yet beautiful enough to grace the covers of glossy magazines around the world. She's left her home country only once before on a short holiday and she feels most comfortable in jeans and tennis shoes." All of the South African writers raved about her resemblance to "Mrs. Presley." The man who was pretending to be the King looked even more like the King with Lisa Stacey at his side while directors called out, "Lights, camera, action . . ."

"The most I remember," Morris recalls, "is the director hollering, 'Don't look into the camera! You're not on stage in this scene . . .'"

Lisa Stacey had been hired to play Priscilla alongside Morris Bates' Elvis in at least one of John de Kock's three productions, a feature film to be entitled *If I Were King*. "They are stars without an image," de Kock suggested, "and are sufficiently flexible to be carefully molded as they have not yet been exposed to film media." In molding the image of Elvis, De Kock apparently did not recognize the African American roots of rockabilly and rhythm & blues, let alone Elvis's and Morris's native heritage. No mention was made of Presley's role in fusing black music with white music in the Deep South, let alone his Cherokee bloodline to his great, great grandmother, Morning White Dove. Nor was there any mention that Morris Bates was a Shuswap Indian from the Sugar Cane Reserve. No doubt, Morris and Richard Cheung were in no hurry to reveal his aboriginal heritage, especially after they became familiar with the racial prejudice and strict cast system that was in place in South Africa in 1979.

Morris got his first introduction to the apartheid political policies and racial inequality that prevailed in South Africa the day after he arrived and went down for breakfast in the hotel restaurant with his girlfriend, Linda Fuller. "They took me to one of these luxury hotels," he recalls. "Sun Hotels and Lucky

> Nor was there any mention that Morris Bates was a Shuswap Indian from the Sugar Cane Reserve.

Strike cigarettes were sponsors of the movie and tour deal that we had with the promoters. The first time that I noticed how it was there was when Linda and I were in the elevator in the hotel and the elevator operator wouldn't look me in the eye. He kept looking at his feet. We went into the hotel restaurant and Linda ordered an omelet and I ordered steak and eggs. And I remember when the waiter brought our food he said, 'Steak for the master and omelet for the missus.' That really threw me. I thought, 'Whoa!' Before that I hadn't seen or heard anything like that. But that was the way it was everywhere we went."

Morris was assigned an East Indian driver who filled him in on some of the realities that people faced in Johannesburg. "He was a great guy," Morris recalls, "and he would go out between my first and second shows and bring me back take-out food. But it was always curry dishes, and I asked him, 'Isn't there anything else?' He explained to me that he couldn't go into the white restaurants. He could only go into East Indian restaurants. To this day I still have a craving for East Indian cuisine. South Africa is a spectacular, beautiful country, but in those days there were a lot of ugly things that people were doing to each other."

Shooting the film was not without trepidation for Morris – not the acting but the helicopter flight to the set location. "I would get up at seven o'clock in the morning," he explains, "and they had a helicopter that would pick me up on the top of the hotel. I was scared of heights. And every morning we would fly to the location where they were filming that day. I never got used to it. It was pretty scary for me.

"One morning we had to do this scene where I would land at a racecar speedway where there was actually real races going on. I was to make a live appearance, which was to be filmed as if to appear that the thousand and thousands of race fans were there to see me. It was a low budget way for me to make an appearance and capture the hysteria using thousands of unpaid extras on film. The day was bright and sunny and the helicopter they were using had a complete see-through plexiglass floor so that you could

> South Africa is a spectacular, beautiful country, but in those days there were a lot of ugly things that people were doing to each other.

look through your feet and see the tops of the skyscrapers of Johannesburg. The choppers they had been using before this had coverings so you couldn't really see the ground. The helicopter pilot could tell right away that I was real nervous when I climbed onboard. To reassure me that everything was going to be all right he said, 'Don't worry, son. Elvis died in his bathroom, not in a helicopter.' After the appearance at the speedway, I demanded that I be driven back to my hotel in a car. No way was I getting back into that glass-bottomed helicopter."

To reassure me that everything was going to be all right he said, 'Don't worry, son. Elvis died in his bathroom, not in a helicopter.'

Photos of Lisa Stacey and Morris Bates were frequently featured in daily newspaper stories with tantalizing headlines that read: "Look-a-like Lisa fears for the future" and "She's frightened playing Mrs. Presley may make her a star . . ."

Lisa spoke of her empathy for Priscilla to reporters. "Priscilla was married to Elvis's career," she told one reporter. "There were only so many clothes she could buy, only so many things she could spend their money on. She wouldn't see Elvis for weeks at a time. She spent her days on a pedestal. He would call her down when he needed her, then back she would go, until she was needed again. That can't last forever."

The specter of Morris's heritage did not go undetected for very long. "Things went along smoothly until the promoters learned that I was an Indian," Morris remembers. "They didn't know that I was an Indian, and when they learned about that, they were still going to ram it through. They didn't like that my manager was Chinese and I was an Indian, but they had made an investment and they were still going through with it."

David Maitland speculates that the tour promoters were connected with the financiers of the movie somehow, but he was never told what the arrangement was. "I do remember doing a lot of shooting for the movie," he says. "Morris did much more than we did. I remember spending a couple of days in this real nice theater doing the crowd scenes and the onstage scenes. I remember going to dinner with the promoters of the tour. But I don't think I was that involved with the movie itself. We did a month's worth of shooting and then, I think, the financing ran out is what happened . . ."

The movie simply faded away. Morris has talked to people who have seen "that John De Kock film" in Europe. They raved about it, but he has never seen it. Today, little is remembered of that film. "I saw some of the dailies," Morris explains, "and then we went on with the tour and they never showed me anything else."

Morris has talked to people who have seen 'that John De Kock film' in Europe. They raved about it, but he has never seen it.

Apartheid Times

While shooting the movie, Morris was booked into topnotch venues where some of the best acts in the world had played. As he recalls, "I followed Tom Jones in South Africa and Van Halen was following me. We played in all the same venues and theaters." Despite his initial enthusiasm for playing these venues, Morris soon became disillusioned by apartheid attitudes.

The first time that Morris stepped over the invisible line that existed between people of color and the ruling white elite was when he kissed a young black woman who rushed to the front of the stage out of an all-white audience during one of his shows. "I thought they were going to throw me in jail," he recalls, "but we talked our way out of that. I hadn't meant any harm. But the people there were very, very uptight."

"Everywhere you went," David Maitland explains, "everything was either black *or* white — all the way down through stores, transportation, drinking fountains to beaches, everything." David remembers "playing in Johannesburg, the first place we played, and they told us, 'No fraternizing!' The hotel we were staying in, all the people staying in the rooms were white and all the maids were black. And I remember that we had this tall, goofy looking keyboard player and he liked black ladies and started getting involved with them and it became a worry there for a while."

They all treaded as lightly as they could, but as Morris recalls, "about three months after we got there I did something that they

Everywhere you went everything was either black or white — all the way down through stores, transportation, drinking fountains to beaches, everything.

really didn't like. We were on a really hectic schedule. We were very busy. Shooting this movie for John de Kock and doing concerts and flying all over the place. And one Sunday we had a day off and I went to this big, beautiful opera house in Johannesburg to attend this all-black concert. I wanted to see Wilson Pickett who was headlining the show. There were a lot of people in there. They had balconies and boxes and the place was packed with black people."

Memphis Soul singer Wilson Pickett was fully aware that Morris was in Johannesburg making a film about Elvis. Morris was in the headlines nearly every day in the daily newspapers and they were talking about him on television. Morris was a celebrity and Pickett felt kinship with him. In the spontaneity of the moment, he just got up and went up on stage. In retrospect, if he hadn't wanted to irk his financiers and promoters, he wouldn't have gone to the all black concert at all.

As Morris explains, "I didn't understand the rules of their apartheid politics. I was just there because I loved music and I loved Elvis Presley. I went to the opera house with Lisa Stacey and an entourage of white people, and we were sitting down front and we were the only non-blacks there. There was about eight of us, and we were sitting in the tenth or twelfth row right in the center in front of the stage. They put a follow spot on me, and Wilson Pickett said, 'Morris, I hear you're here doing a movie. Would you come up on stage and sing a song?'

"I wasn't expecting it, but what are you going to do? Say no? So my security people walked me down the aisle and I got up on stage with Wilson Pickett. I said, 'Wilson, I only know one song of yours and that is *In The Midnight Hour*, but I do it in the key of D.' And he said, 'Morris, it is *my* song. I do it in the key of D.'

"We stood shoulder to shoulder on stage and we sang *In The Midnight Hour* together. We swapped the lyrics back and forth. To me it was a huge highlight. I mean to be standing there singing that song with Wilson Pickett in that opera house in front of all of those people — that was something! But politically speaking, with the backers and promoters and filmmakers it pro-pelled my career downward. That is when I became aware that Nelson Mandela was still in prison and how bad things really were in their country. That is when it was explained to me what it meant to them for me to go on stage with Wilson Pickett in that all-black venue — what it meant to the apartheid regime that was in power.

"Before that moment, I had been kept away from it, I guess. They took me by helicopter from the roof of my hotel to where they were shooting. And they took me by plane and limousine to these exclusive resort hotels where we did our shows. And they kept me away from it."

South Africa's apartheid regime had transformed certain regions of the country into independent states, where topless dancing, gambling, and other "immoral" activities could be car-ried on with impunity. The infamous Sun City resort was built in Bophuthatswana for this purpose. The promoters Morris was working with in South Africa regularly booked Vegas acts like him and other stars, such as Elton John and Queen, into these sanctioned venues.

I can't begin to explain how horrible it was down there at that time.

Determined to see what was going on in the country outside of the white hotels and casinos, Morris made a trip into Soweto, where riots had erupted when the white government tried to enforce Africaans as the official lan-guage taught in ghetto schools. Millions of disenfranchised black people had been confined in the South Western Townships, where there was only one hospital and rebellion against ongoing repression had reached a boiling point. More than 500 people were shot dead during the first riot in 1976, and three years later in the summer of 1979 conditions had not improved.

"I can't begin to explain," Morris says, "how horrible it was down there at that time. The white people drank all of these really good South African wines and they had fancy liquor stores. The black people had a little shack out back where they could only buy this rot gut wine that was really bad but it got you drunk. If you weren't used to it, it would make you sick. The laws were horrible. If a black woman got into bed with a white man, she went to jail. If a black man got into bed with a white woman, he went to jail. It was worse than that, but you get my drift."

Even though Morris, his band and entourage were challenged everywhere they turned by culture shock that they never really got used to, Morris managed to keep his sense of humor, especially when he was performing. Just like Elvis had done in his shows, Morris always kept his musicians on their toes by segueing into songs that were not exactly on the set list. One night, at the Victoria Theater in Johannesburg, he decided to have a little fun with Gisele Kaufmann, too.

Just like Elvis had done in his shows, Morris always kept his musicians on their toes by segueing into songs that were not exactly on the set list.

"It was a big theater," Gisele recalls, "and I was way up in this lighting booth. They had these arc lights, which were new to me. The theater was so big that Morris seemed like an ant on stage to me. And this one particular night he was going to play with me. He was doing that all of the time to all of the guys in the band. I think it was in the song *Polk Salad Annie* where it goes black and then I do this 'flash, flash' with the spotlight. I saw this reflection off the rhinestones on his belt and I knew he had jumped to his left. So I moved the spot to my right and did the 'flash, flash' — and he was staring up at me with a look that said, 'How the hell did you know I was here?' I was so proud of myself that I saw that, because it was pitch dark down there. And I saw this one glint off one of his sequins or something that showed me that he moved. I just loved the look on his face. He was stunned."

After more than a month in Johannesburg, the tour moved on to other cities. "I didn't care much for Johannesburg," David Maitland admits, "but some of the other places we went were much better. They would take us to these real nice hotels . . .

We took this long bus trip from Johannesburg down to Cape Town, which is one of the most beautiful cities I have ever seen in my life. It's where the Atlantic and Indian Ocean meet. It is incredible. The trip down there was something else. The bus ran out of gas in some desert area, and I remember sitting by the side of the road watching these ostriches. Getting gas, especially at three o'clock in the morning, the bus driver would have to stop and knock on somebody's door and get 'em to come out and give us some gas. Then we drove back up the East Coast of Africa and played in Durban.

"Every morning we were reminded that the conditions privileged white people enjoyed were not the same for black people. Our hotel was not far from the railroad yards. I remember, every morning the trains would come in, and there would be a sea of black people walking by our hotel on their way to work. Every evening at a certain time, they all walked back down our street and got on the trains and left again."

Band on the Run

When it finally got back to the financiers of the film that Morris was a Shuswap Indian, they were far more angered than they had been by the Canadian star kissing black girls and getting on stage with Wilson Pickett. It's ironic that Elvis had played frontier half-breed Pacer Burton in *Flaming Star* in 1960 and Navajo rodeo rider Joe Lightcloud in *Stay Away Joe* in 1968, but to the repressive South African regime in 1979, Elvis was a white guy and Morris Bates was a man of color. Three months before this, Morris had arrived at the Johannesburg airport a conquering hero, hailed as the next Elvis. "By the time we got back to Jo-Burg," David emphasizes, "there was a change in attitude."

Elvis had played frontier half-breed Pacer Burton in Flaming Star in 1960 and Navajo rodeo rider Joe Lightcloud in Stay Away Joe in 1968.

"All at once," Morris says, "it got real funny. I don't know if it was the funders that pulled out or what it was. They had taken our passports away from us. It started getting real sticky, and Richard and I could feel it. The production slowed right down. We had been invited to see some of the dailies — some of the film they had shot each day — but that wasn't happening any more. They were working me real hard. I was doing two shows a night and I had to get up real early and go off to these locations that they had picked out and begin filming. So when it started happening we didn't know exactly what caused it. We didn't know if it was because I sang with Wilson Pickett. It started getting weird and it all started falling in on itself. Richard and I didn't have any real control. They had discovered that I was an Indian and that their promoters had really messed up.

"The financiers became disenchanted with the producer's concept of 'Using Elvis to Bridge the Gap', which was merely apartheid propaganda designed to persuade the outside world that South Africa was a great country to live in and invest in despite the racial unrest. The biggest mistake of all in their minds was that they were using a North American Shuswap native Indian to play the role of Elvis. In retrospect, I might have bridged the gap, but then Nelson Mandela was still in jail. The longer I stayed there the crazier it got.

When Diana Ross came to Johannesburg to attend the premiere performance of *Oz*, her all-black version of *The Wizard of Oz*, she was refused admission to her own premiere.

"When Diana Ross came to Johannesburg to attend the premiere performance of *Oz*, her all-black version of *The Wizard of Oz*, she was refused admission to her own premiere. Diana and I had very nearly shared a duet moment of our own when Richard and I were in Vegas scouting the Silver Slipper in the summer of '77. It was the first show we saw at Caesars Palace and she had this song she performed, *Reach Out And Touch Somebody's Hand*, where she walked through the audience and wanted everyone to hold hands and sing. She came up by our booth in the showroom and I started to freak out imagining that she was going to single me out and have me sing with her. But when she got closer, she could see I didn't want any part of it and walked on by, and I was left wondering why someone with a long scar across their shoulder and back would want to wear a backless gown.

"Ironically, when Diana flew to South Africa to promote *Oz*, the film was being premiered at an all white movie theater, and when she was told to leave and put up an argument with the theater manager, it was reported in the press that the manager had knocked her down and pulled her by her hair. I guess he simply didn't believe that she was the star of the show. Reading about what had happened to Diana Ross was not reassuring. Our situa-

tion with our producers and our financiers wasn't getting any better. We were prepared for anything. We
were prepared to get out of there real quick. But I
wanted to make sure that my band got out of there
okay, too."

We were prepared for anything.
We were prepared to get out of
there real quick.

David Maitland and the boys in the band were even more in
the dark than Morris and his manager. "I remember they got real
picky about the hotel bill," David recalls. "I remember sitting in
the lobby at one point and they had confiscated some of our gear.
They were holding on to it. I remember freaking out about that.
But Morris took care of us. He always did."

"My primary concern was for my band and crew," Morris says.
"We were all real worried, but Richard took care of everything
and we all got out of Johannesburg on the same flight."

The return flight, through an airport in Nairobi with a
stopover in New York City, did not go as smoothly as their
flights to London and on to Johannesburg. Morris recalls that
when they disembarked at Vancouver International Airport,
they discovered that their luggage was not on the same plane
that they were on. "When we came back from Africa my clothes
ended up in New York. So did all of the band guys' clothes. I
had one suit with me. They just had the clothes on their backs.
And we were scheduled to do a show at the Cave the next night.
So I gave everybody money. I gave the girls money and said,
'Go buy something nice.' David Maitland, who was my MC,
went out and rented a white tuxedo with tails, and he wore it on
stage. I had my white jumpsuit, but I didn't have any white
boots."

Backstage

During the month-long engagement at the Cave, Gisele Kauf-
mann told Morris that she was leaving the show to marry Peter
Yates, a soundman she had fallen in love with while on tour in
South Africa. "I left the show," she recalls, "and went back to
South Africa, because I missed Peter so much." Morris asked her

to hang in there for a few more weeks because they were scheduled to play the grand opening of the new showroom that had been built for him at the Silver Slipper. As Gisele recalls, "Morris asked me to do the opening of the new showroom upstairs at the Slipper. So I did the first week in the new showroom at the Slipper and trained Delphine, Ken Nelsen's wife, to do the light show."

Gisele's romance was not the only one going on behind the scenes in South Africa. As Gisele Kaufmann recalls, "When it was found out that Lisa Stacey was down there, I think Linda Fuller would have been on a plane, like, that second, but she couldn't. She did a really fantastic job of staying and working it through. Initially she was so upset. It was hurtful to see her so upset, when the rest of us knew. To be someone's good friend and to know that, and you can't say anything, and then when you see how it comes out and how hurtful it is . . . you don't know whether you should have said something — that was difficult for me to deal with." Linda had been Morris's girlfriend for years, standing by her man as he made his way to Vegas, but loyal to her job as a radiologist in Vancouver. Hollywood actors like Rock Hudson, Dean Martin and Frank Sinatra had often been caught with girls in their closets, under their beds, and behind the shower curtains in their movies. Elvis often had two love interests in his flicks. Morris seemed to be following in the King's celluloid footsteps as well.

Like the King, Morris had never been without female admirers who wanted more than merely a kiss and a scarf. Even before Morris started dressing up like Elvis, his sexuality energized his shows, a power he reserved, most of the time, for the stage, not his backstage groupies. Now that he was in the movies, just like Elvis had been, his personal life appeared to have become a series of scenes from Hollywood romantic comedies. Not everyone in real life laughed at his predicaments.

Hollywood actors like Rock Hudson, Dean Martin and Frank Sinatra had often been caught with girls in their closets, under their beds, and behind the shower curtains in their movies.

The Native Question

Despite the malicious Afrikaaner response to his race, Morris hasn't regarded his native heritage as a disadvantage. In 1979, he told Sylvia Woods, a young aboriginal reporter, "I don't think my native heritage has hindered, but it may have helped in a lot of ways because it gave me an attitude. When you're living on one of those reserves, there's nothing to go back to. So I worked hard to get out of there, to be successful, and I keep working at it because I don't have a place to go but to go back there, and I don't want to go back there. I want to be big in the entertainment business. I want to make it, that is what I'm striving for."

At the time, pride in their heritage was emerging within the BC native community. During the sixties, Salish chief Dan George had became a role model for many native boys, especially if, like Morris Bates, they were from the Cariboo. Chief Dan George played the regular character Ol' Antoine on the weekly CBC TV series *Cariboo Country*. Chief Dan George was named chief of the Burrard Indian band in 1951. He starred as the father of the title character in theater productions of George Ryga's *The Ecstasy of Rita Joe* in 1967. Morris became an admirer of Chief Dan George when he saw the feature film *Little Big Man* starring Dustin Hoffman and Chief Dan George, who was nominated for an Academy Award for his supporting role.

> I don't think my native heritage has hindered, but it may have helped in a lot of ways because it gave me an attitude.

On the occasion of the celebration of Canada's 100th birthday, Chief Dan George recited his defiant "Lamentation for Confederation" to a crowd of 35,000 assembled at Empire Stadium in Vancouver. His famous speech began as a searing indictment of white men, their ways, and their treatment of aboriginal people, but ended with an inspirational prayer.

The prayer section began: "Oh God in heaven! Give me back the courage of the olden chiefs. Let me wrestle with my surroundings. Let me again, as in the days of old, dominate my environment. Let me humbly accept this new culture and through it rise up and go on."

And continued on in a similar inspirational vein: "Oh God! Like the thunderbird of old I shall rise again out of the sea; I shall grab the instruments of the white man's success — his education, his skills — and with these new tools I shall build my race into the proudest segment of your society."

The next verse envisioned a day when "our young braves and our chiefs" would be "sitting in the houses of law and of parliament."

Morris first heard this remarkable speech when Chief Dan George recorded an album with country rock band Fireweed, called *In Circle*, which began with "Lament for Confederation."

Sometime during the mid-seventies the acclaimed activist and actor became a Morris Bates fan. "I was playing a cabaret in Chilliwack," Morris recalls, "and Chief Dan George came in with a small entourage of people. He came right up on stage and asked me if I would sing him that Kris Kristofferson song, *For The Good Times*. I knew the song, but I hadn't done it with my band. On the break, I took my guitar into the kitchen and rehearsed it with my drummer and bass player. When we came out for out last set, I sang *For The Good Times* and dedicated it to Chief Dan George. He stood up and began clapping and everybody stood up and they gave me a standing ovation." Morris kept on singing *For The Good Times* throughout his career, and he always dedicated the song to Chief Dan George.

Chief Dan George continued to be an avid Morris Bates' fan until his death in 1981. "He would come to my shows at the Cave every December and August," Morris recalls, "and sometimes he would lie down and rest in my dressing room upstairs in the nightclub. He was nearly 80 years old by that time, but he always came out to my shows, and after I had done my Elvis songs, the audience would always still be screaming and yelling for me to come back out and do more. One time I had taken off my sweaty

Chief Dan George came right up on stage and asked me if I would sing him that Kris Kristofferson song, For The Good Times.

costume and hung it up and got into my bathrobe and they were still stomping and hollering. I was standing there and they wouldn't stop so I just went out on stage in my bathrobe and dedicated *For The Good Times* to Chief Dan George, and that became an encore tradition at the Cave."

So I just went out on stage in my bathrobe and dedicated *For The Good Times* to Chief Dan George, and that became an encore tradition at the Cave.

The Grind

Upon his return to the Silver Slipper Casino after the time spent in South Africa and playing the Cave in Vancouver, Morris received better promotion, and his hectic work schedule was made somewhat more manageable by a new arrangement with the casino. Morris would do two shows on weeknights and three on weekends.

Morris packed the bigger showroom, as he had the 350-seat Gaiety Theater, but by the time Morris and his band mates settled in for this second engagement in Vegas, the novelty had worn off and the grind had begun. When they were not performing, they often found themselves in a recording studio cutting demos. Everywhere they went there were temptations, young women eager to perform sexual favors in return for complimentary tickets or access to backstage areas, and perhaps even to help them make it through the night.

In the company of groupies who swirled around them, there were plenty of notorious characters and downright dangerous dudes. While they were in Africa, the severed head of one of the groupies they had met turned up in Red Bluff and the rest of her body was found in a vacant lot in Lake Meade. "It was brutal in Vegas," Morris says. "There was always a lot of shit going down. I had quite a few people looking out for me. They were looking out for me because I was taking care of them. After my second show, I would go out front to our memorabilia sales area and sign autographs. But after my first show, I had a valet who looked like Elvis who would walk out one of the doors and all of the groupies

While they were in Africa, the severed head of one of the groupies they had met turned up in Red Bluff and the rest of her body was found in a vacant lot in Lake Meade.

would run after him. And I would make my getaway out another door and into my Lincoln that my driver had waiting for me. It wasn't a normal life." There were more and more hustlers showing up and pitching all sorts of good, bad, and ugly opportunities to Richard and Morris.

One night Morris had to discipline a bass player who had violated band-policy and been caught "fraternizing" with one of the female backup singers. Instead of accepting a fine, he picked up his bass guitar and walked out the backstage door into the parking lot mere minutes before their next show was to begin. Right away, Morris told Bill Friedman that he couldn't go on because he didn't have a bass player. "I told him that I didn't have the bottom end of my rhythm section," Morris relates, "and he said, 'Well, you're goin' on. We've got people here and they have bought tickets . . .'

"So I decided to do a show that was a little lighter than my regular show. Bill said, 'Just do the show.' And I went out and started the show acoustically, singing *That's All Right (Mama)*. It was like what they later called on MTV, unplugged. The band was right there with me, but we played it all acoustically. We gave it a light touch. I played guitar, and I sang songs like *Are You Lonesome Tonight*, all the songs that I could do without the pounding bass, and after the show Bill Friedman said to me, 'Morris that was a great show! Now we are going to find that bass player and kick his ass back to Canada.'" Richard replaced the fired bass player with Kenny Nelsen, who had been with Morris in Canada. Right away, Kenny fit in seamlessly, and the shows got better.

Redd Foxx

He was just nuts, but that foul-mouth routine was all in his act. We would sit in the keno lounge and he was just a real gentleman.

During the years that Morris spent performing at the Silver Slipper, he befriended Redd Foxx, the star of the TV sitcom *Sanford and Son*. Foxx was one-quarter Seminole, one of the first black standup comedians to entertain white audiences on the Vegas strip, and he took a shine to the young Indian guy who was paying tribute to Elvis at the Slipper.

On stage and on TV, Redd Foxx was known for his off-color jokes and raunchy personality. His Vegas routine was rated triple X on the Landmark casino marquee, but some people paid no heed and were offended by his four-letter-word standup comedy routine – which would be a factor that led to Morris Bates to replace the comedian at the Landmark.

"He was just nuts," Morris relates, "but that foul-mouth routine was all in his act. We would sit in the keno lounge and he was just a real gentleman. He would ask me, 'How are you doing in your show?' He was so nice to me. And all the time I spent with him, I never heard him swear. Not one word."

People always wondered how Redd Foxx had taken it when he learned that Morris was going to replace him in the Landmark showroom. "He was okay with it," Morris says. "He had been there quite a while, and the numbers were not good. He wasn't putting people in the chairs anymore. One of the many shows that I saw, he had the Step Brothers opening for him. The Step Brothers were an old, vaudeville tap-dancing act like Gregory Hines would later rejuvenate. There were about 30 people in his showroom. He was very gracious to me, and I would not have pushed him out. He was on his way out when I came in. I really respected him."

The Eagle Cape

Renowned LA stage costume designer James Wiggins remembers that when he first met Morris, the Canadian tribute artist was not overly impressed. "I went to Las Vegas to promote another entertainer," Wiggins recalls, "and I saw Morris at the Silver Slipper. I went backstage and asked him to let me try to make him a suit for his show, but he wasn't too interested. I told him I would make it with no obligation." It was an offer that Morris couldn't refuse.

The first costume Wiggins designed for Morris was Presley's signature eagle outfit. "That eagle suit was my final touch for the

That eagle suit was my final touch for the show. I'd done all the songs from every era. I just needed to find the right costume for the seventies segment.

show," Morris told *The Los Angeles Herald Examiner*. "I'd done all the songs from every era. I just needed to find the right costume for the seventies segment. That eagle costume was seen by a billion people on Elvis Presley's *Aloha from Hawaii via Satellite* TV Special. I wanted it duplicated."

He was furious. You could hear him screaming in Los Angeles from the balcony of my Las Vegas apartment.

Wiggins duplicated the original costume down to the fine detail in the multi-colored rhinestone embroidery. Morris was hooked after that. "James Wiggins made two more identical costumes," Morris relates. "They had absorbent cotton liners that fit inside the jumpsuits. If the rhinestone studs absorbed my sweat, they would rust. When I took the suit off, my dresser would pull the absorbent liner out — it was stuck in there with Velcro flaps — and he would hang it up to dry and to wash. Every time I came off stage I was sweating and those liners were soaking wet.

"The first eagle suit didn't have a cape. I said I wanted one with a cape, and he said it would cost $2400. I said, 'Make it.' He came back about six weeks later with the new suit with a cape, but the eagle on the back of the cape looked more like a parrot than an eagle. I told him I wanted a full eagle, just like Elvis had on the back of his cape. Wiggins told me that the Velcro strips were not strong enough to support a full eagle cape, and that the suit would have to be redesigned to hold the weight of the cape with eyehooks and fasteners instead of Velcro. He also mentioned that someone would have to put the cape on me and then remove it during the show. I told him I'd work out the logistics. I wanted it for the opening of my new show at the Landmark. He said it would cost $3500. I said, 'Talk to Richard.'

"When Jim Wiggins showed up with the newest suit, he brought with him a writer and photographer from *The Los Angeles Herald Examiner*. They were working up a story about him designing costumes for Las Vegas entertainers. They also did a story on my show at the Slipper and put a full color photo of me in one of my black leather outfits, which I wore during my sixties segment of my Elvis show, on the cover. They put the picture of me and Wiggins and the eagle suit on about the fourth page in black and white. The way they presented these images it looked like he had designed both the eagle suit and the black leather jacket and pants, which I had bought off the rack. He was furious. You could hear him screaming in Los Angeles from the balcony of my Las Vegas apartment. When I spoke with him on the phone, he blamed me for ruining his costume business. He was totally hysterical. I tried to explain that I had nothing to do with the picking of the photos or context of the story, but he sure was hot. That was the last Elvis costume he made for me. Today, that eagle cape is displayed in the Williams Lake Museum."

Breaking Up

When Linda Fuller arrived in Las Vegas on December 31, 1979, she told Morris that she wanted to reassess their relationship. "Linda was with me when I arrived in Las Vegas to open at the Silver Slipper Casino in the spring of 1978," Morris recalls. "We had been together a long time and known each other since high school. I wasn't a recording artist, I was an entertainer, so Vegas was about as good as it was going to get. Linda loved to travel. I took her to South East Asia. I took her to South Africa. She saw a lot of places. Linda was working at Vancouver General Hospital as a radiologist, working double and extra shifts, to bank the hours in order to come to Vegas or catch up to me on the road.

The long distance romance was falling apart. I don't think either one of us was to blame — it was just falling.

Linda was very ambitious and planned to go back to school to advance her career. I was also ambitious, and really cared for her and didn't want to destroy her life and career. We were on very different paths. My life was so chaotic and unstable, and, as the saying goes — you're only as good as your last show. I wasn't ready to make a commitment, and I'm sure she was also seeing the writing on the wall.

"The long distance romance was falling apart. I don't think either one of us was to blame — it was just falling. I flew to Vancouver to be with her and my family at Christmas. The day before Christmas, out of the blue she decided that she was going

I arrived at LAX, and Jesse Floyd met me with a limo. He had some of the Coasters and their backup band with him, and the party was on.

to drive to Salmon Arm to spend the holiday with her family — so much for Christmas together. The original plan had been for us to fly back to Las Vegas because I was to reopen my show on New Year's Eve. The day after Christmas I got up and went for a jog around Lost Lagoon in Stanley Park. When I got back, I phoned a travel agency to see if they had a flight that afternoon to LA. They did. I phoned Jesse Floyd, the leader of the Coasters, and he said he'd pick me up at LAX that evening.

"I called a cab and was running late when I got to the Vancouver airport. I tried to hurry through customs, but they recognized me and wanted my H-1 visa. They didn't believe that I was just going to LA as a tourist because I was on the cover of *Las Vegas Star* magazine, which was in every magazine holder on every plane seat in those days, and they held me up because I didn't have the work visa with me. Then the customs officer said, sarcastically, 'There is no way you are going to LA today.' I remembered that immigration couldn't refuse me entrance to the United States if I had my Indian status card. I quickly showed him my status card and he said, 'You better get moving. I don't think you are going to make it.'

I was panicking when I reached the accordion section of the boarding ramp and saw the plane backing out onto the runway. I was running and hollering to the attendant to stop the plane. He was saying matter-of-factly that I had missed the flight. I was saying, 'Pick up the phone and tell him that I have to be on that plane.' I could see the pilot and he could see us toe to toe, screaming at each other, and it was just about coming to blows. Then all of a sudden the plane stopped backing out and began pulling back in. The attendant said he had worked there a long time and never seen that happen before. We apologized to each other, and I boarded the plane, thanked the pilots, and wished them a Merry Christmas. I was off to LA — one of the few perks of being an Indian. 'Double Scotch, please!'

"I arrived at LAX, and Jesse Floyd met me with a limo. He had some of the Coasters and their backup band with him, and the party was on. After all, it was Christmas. I spent a couple of days in LA, saw some friends, and flew to Vegas for my New Year's Eve shows.

"Vegas was packed, and both shows were sold out, some people buying tickets for both shows, but I didn't know if Linda was there. I came out after and saw her in the casino. It was nuts in there, but, after all, it was New Year's. We thought we'd find some place to talk that was quiet, so we walked next door to the Stardust Hotel and went into the Sportsman's Lounge. We talked for a long time. We knew it was over, but we still laughed and cried about all the crazy memories. Linda had got a room at The Castaways Motel, and we walked up the Strip past all the glittering lights that make Vegas look like daytime at nighttime. People were drinking on the streets, which is legal, partying, and wishing complete strangers a Happy New Year. It was a long walk and we'd had a long run together. It broke our hearts, but we both knew it was the best decision. She flew back home to Vancouver the next day."

"They were going in different directions," BJ says, summing up a situation that many family members had hoped would turn out quite differently. "Linda is happily married with a beautiful daughter, and is still part of our family today. Just doesn't talk to Morris."

Cutting Loose

Other personnel changes were afoot. Scott Anderson recalls that at times "there were a lot of older musicians that played in the band, especially horn players when we were in Vegas. They could all play, but some of them I think we got through the methadone program out of Los Angeles. They weren't really part of our little inner circle of guys who had been in the band with Morris for years and years." "I had to let some people go," Morris explains, "because they weren't getting the job done — gigging in Vegas can be a hell of a distraction."

Morris would ask the guy, 'How many notes are you playin'? Am I paying you by the note?'

Scott also remembers that "Richard Cheung handled all of the business stuff, and he ran it a little bit like the army. There were a lot of guys in the band and three or four girl singers. Richard had rules — you had to be there 30 minutes before the gig with your suit on, and you got fined a dollar a minute for every minute that you were late. There was a $30 fine for yawning on stage — that kind of stuff. I remember the pay scale got kind of funny sometimes. Morris looked after me real well, but sometimes a horn player who was just playing fanfare riffs from our charts would get heckled. Morris would ask the guy, 'How many notes are you playin'? Am I paying you by the note?'"

"If it wasn't written on the chart," Morris explains, "they wouldn't play it. So I had to get my point across to them without bringing a lot of negativity into our shows and rehearsals."

"Morris always had a lot of fun with things," Scott says, "even though we were all professionals and what we were doing was a job. He always had fun with it."

Despite the close friendship between Morris and Scott, the young drummer left the band during this long engagement at the Silver Slipper. No one wants to remember any of the details. Anderson would rejoin Morris further on down the road, but at the time it was merely the way the dice rolled. The parting of ways was emotionally draining for both men. "When I cut Scotty loose," Morris admits, "it was the hardest thing that I had ever done — I picked him up when he was 17 or 18 years old. He was just a kid."

The beginning of the end of Scott's tenure in the band started on a high note when Scott got lucky. As he recalls, "The day I turned 21, I hit seven out of seven on a keno ticket and won $3,500 and that was a lot of money back in those days. I owed Morris $1,200 on a loan he had advanced to me so that I could buy this big set of Pearl drums with the double bass drums that I used on the shows. I was able to pay off that loan. It was a beautiful thing because it was on my birthday and if I had won it 12 hours earlier I wouldn't have been able to collect. Anything you win that is over a $1,000 you have to pay out-of-state taxes and you have to show ID and I would not have been able to collect. I was 12 hours legal."

"Scotty wasn't allowed to gamble for the first two years we were in Vegas," Morris remembers, "because he wasn't 21 years old. And when he turned 21, he only had, like, 50 cents in his pocket. So he went to his mom, Marion, and he borrowed 25 cents and put 70 cents on a keno ticket. He won $3,500. Scotty owed me for the drums and right away he paid me. I was flabbergasted. I thought I would be getting $20 a week for the rest of my life."

Scotty owed me for the drums and right away he paid me. I was flabbergasted. I thought I would be getting $20 a week for the rest of my life."

Phyllis Bates remembers being there at the Silver Slipper the night that Scott Anderson got lucky. "If he had won that money a few hours earlier," she says, "he would have had to get one of the other guys in the band to go and collect it for him. Everybody was so happy for him." Unfortunately, winning big changed Anderson almost overnight, as Morris recalls. "When Scotty won, he started believing that he could gamble and win whenever he wanted to, but it doesn't work like that in Vegas. He was real young and winning kind of screwed him up for a while. He was a very lucky young man … it happened once. But it doesn't mean that it is going to touch you twice. He didn't understand that. His work ethic started to slip after that."

As Scott humorously puts it — he got traded to Johnny Harra's band. The two bands swapped drummers. "Johnny Harra was working at the Silverbird Hotel," Morris explains, "but he had to go out on the road. I stayed in Vegas for a very long stretch, but most of the other guys had to go out on the road. There was this very good R&B drummer by the name of Nardo Lee working there in Vegas for Johnny Harra, and Nardo told me that he wanted to stay there in Vegas and work with me. Nardo looked just like Ronnie Tutt, and he had paid a lot of money for the TCB band arrangements, plus he wanted to bring his piano conductor Jake Jacobson with him. We literally got a couple of heavyweights. I wasn't happy about trading Scotty to Johnny Harra's

I wasn't happy about trading Scotty to Johnny Harra's band, but it was a good deal because I got Nardo and his TCB band arrangements.

band, but it was a good deal because I got Nardo *and* his TCB band arrangements. We didn't have to rehearse everybody when they joined the band; we could hand them the arrangements. It expedited things."

Soon after Scott Anderson joined Johnny Harra's band, he was cut loose and sent back to the minor leagues in Canada. Due to his experience playing shows with Morris, he was sought after by promoters who had Elvis imitators out on the road, but he soon learned that there were good, bad and ugly productions. "In the mid-eighties," he recalls, "I drummed for a show that was called 'Elvis, Elvis, Elvis.' They had three guys doing Elvis with one pared-down band backing up all three of them. There were horns and girl singers for the second and third segments, but after being on the road with those guys for a while I had a whole new respect for Morris."

The hectic pace and demanding schedule in Vegas had its toll on band members. David Maitland recalls that "I made up a list and there were more than a hundred players who went through the band while we were in Vegas." He also remembers that the rapid turnover often meant that, as bandleader, he had to work overtime to keep things together. "At that time, including the backup singers," Morris reiterates, "we had a 17-piece orchestra."

"The thing was," David explains, "that you would have three singers that would be around for a while. They'd leave. You'd work up three more singers. We went through a few drummers, a lot of keyboard players. Playing in Vegas that many years you get a lot of transient musicians. They are there for a while and then they are gone. Being the bandleader I got to rehearse nearly everyone of those people. It was a lot of work. Year after year, two to three shows a night, for six nights a week. And then having to spend my mornings and afternoons going over *Hound Dog* with a keyboard player or some singers for the umpteenth time, I earned my money, put it that way." Morris recalls that to save his voice he videotaped segments of their rehearsals so that David could play these segments for incoming band members.

> I made up a list and there were more than a hundred players who went through the band while we were in Vegas.

Morris Bates' bands continued to have topnotch personnel throughout the decade he spent in Vegas because Morris was able to offer them the stability that other acts could not provide. "The reason I was so popular with the good musicians in Vegas was that they got to stay in Vegas," Morris says. "People raised their children around me. I had musicians who had played with Elvis, the Righteous Brothers, Buddy Miles, Rick James . . . They didn't want to go out on the road for six months — they wanted to stay home and raise their families."

> People raised their children around me. They didn't want to go out on the road for six months — they wanted to stay home and raise their families.

Living with Lisa

With Linda Fuller no longer coming to Nevada to visit Morris, Lisa Stacey's visits became more frequent. They would eventually share a house together. As Morris reveals, "After the long distance relationship between me and Linda came to an amicable end, I was by myself but not alone . . ." Not that he had all that much spare time on his hands to spend with a girlfriend. His work schedule had not been this hectic since the days when he worked all day at a sawmill and nearly all night as a bass player in the house band at the Ho Ho Thunderbird Room.

"During the duration of my stay at the Slipper," he explains, "we were the only act on the Strip that had a 2:15 a.m. show. By two o'clock in the morning the other entertainers had finished their shows or were just finishing, and some nights they would slip into the back of my showroom to relax and kick back. My late-late show was far looser than the earlier shows. It was easygoing, relaxed, funny, and usually the most entertaining of the three shows we performed. In the casino behind the 40-foot bar was a full-length window so you could sit at the bar and actually see into the showroom. The bar would be packed three or four deep with people trying to get a cocktail, and when we started the show they would close the curtain and everybody would grab their drinks and head into the showroom. There were many times my 2:15 a.m. show would do better than my 11:30 show.

The whole approach was super casual. I would wear one of my Minichiello suits, and usually only took requests from the audience, making goofy answers to goofy questions. Stuff like: 'What's your favorite Elvis song? The last one you clapped for.'

In Vegas, everyone stole jokes from each other. If it was a good joke, everybody up and down the Strip would be telling it by the midnight show.

"In Vegas, everyone stole jokes from each other. If it was a good joke, everybody up and down the Strip would be telling it by the midnight show. I stole a joke that was a bit risqué from Englebert Humperdinck and told it one night when M-M-M-Mel Tillis was in the audience, and he up and walked out. I don't know if it was the joke or the nature call or maybe he thought I stole it from him. The musicians from the Frontier Hotel Orchestra that were playing next door would come over in their tuxedos after their show backing Wayne Newton. They would say, 'Are you doing a tribute to Wayne Newton or Elvis?' or 'Is Wayne doing a tribute to Morris? Because if he is he could save us a lot of rehearsal time by buying us your charts . . .'

"I usually didn't introduce other entertainers or celebrities in the audience during the 2:15 show because I felt if they were attending my late-late show and didn't know who they were, it wasn't up to me to point it out unless I was prompted to do so. One night I was told that Priscilla Presley and some of her people had come into the showroom after the show had started and that they had left before the lights came back on at the end, but I never knew if it was the truth or just a rumor.

"The late, late, late night action got started around 5:00 a.m. in the morning at a real popular disco called the Brewery, where I often ended my evening with breakfast at about 7:00 a.m. I'd get home at 8:00, check my messages, answer calls, and head off to bed until about 5:00 p.m., when I would get up and start my routine all over again."

Return to the Cave

Morris Bates' semi-annual return engagements at the Cave nightclub in Vancouver were occasions for numerous newspaper reviews and interviews. In March 1979, for example, music critic Kevin MeKeown wrote, "it was just like the so-called good old days last night at the Cave, the full house, the screaming crowds, the seen and be seen jostle of first-nighters. It's what the Cave was built for and a mood that can be reproduced in no other club in town. The event was the gala first-night for Morris Bates who just wrapped up a record-breaking eleven-month gig at the Silver Slipper Casino in Las Vegas."

"I was too much of a punk when I arrived in Las Vegas," Morris told McKeown, "and I couldn't figure out what the people there wanted from me. It was maturity that they were looking for and I think working there matured me a lot."

Morris Bates' shows at the Cave were an occasion for his extended family to continue getting to know each other. Many of his Vancouver fans had shown up at the Silver Slipper and all of them turned out during his December engagement in the Cave. Their presence provided Morris with a special feeling every night when he went on stage.

"Phyllis became friends with Scotty's parents," Grace Bobb reminisces, "everybody who went to his shows became friends. Morris outsold all of the other performers that came to the Cave — Mitzi Gaynor, Bette Midler, Ginger Rogers, Roy Orbison, all of them. I remember that we were living in North Vancouver in those days and one night we had two busloads of people come in from Seabird Island and we packed the Cave that night, the whole main floor of the Cave."

"It started out small," Lyle explains, "and it snowballed and it ended up being two buses full of people."

> It was just like the so-called good old days last night at the Cave, the full house, the screaming crowds, the seen and be seen jostle of first-nighters.

Posters for the South African tour

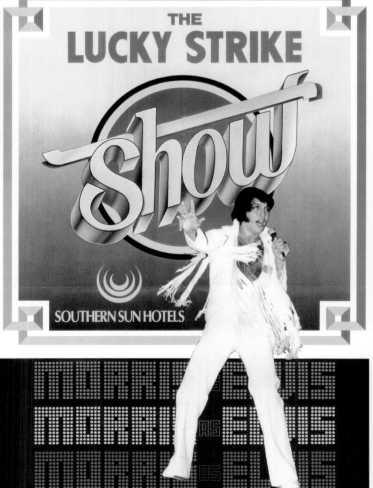

Morris Bates, alias Elvis Presley, arrived at D F Malan Airport yesterday for a series of shows in Cape Town, during which he and Lisa Stacey will shoot a film of the "King's" life. Presley's name is not mentioned in the script, according to the producer and director, John de Kock. Lisa plays the part of Elvis's wife, Priscilla. The Canadian-born entertainer's show ran in Las Vegas for 14 months.

Top: South African tour band. Middle: Morris's leading lady, Lisa Stacey. Bottom: Celebrity reception.

Players in the band: David Maitland (top left), Kenny Nelsen and Delphine Nelsen (middle right), Gisele Kaufman (bottom)

Backup: Greg Marciele, David Spence, Tommy Cosmo (brass); Paula, Suzie, Roxanne (right), and Sylvia and Debbie (vocals)

Strong women in Morris's life: Linda Fuller, Alma Cunningham, and his mother, Phyllis

Top: *Album cover for* In Circle *by Chief Dan George and Fireweed. Bottom: Morris sings a command encore performance of* For The Good Times *for Chief Dan George*

All Shook Up

The Landmark

Ultimate Showroom

As time went by, Morris was less and less satisfied with performing in the upstairs showroom at the Slipper. He had his sights set on the big showroom in the Landmark Hotel, which seated 780. There were some political games to be played out before he could make the move, but as he had done in Vancouver when he had successfully negotiated his way through show business politics and secured a booking at the Cave nightclub, Morris was equal to the task. First, he had to convince Richard Cheung that it was the right move for his career.

"Richard was one amazing dude," Morris explains. "It seemed like he never slept. Once I was secure in the Slipper, he became tight with Bill Friedman and the Summa Corporation. We were off and running. I was on an excellent weekly salary. I also had a daily per diem and a $5,000 line of credit at the casino cage. Together we owned the show.

"My only responsibility was to be in perfect form to perform. Richard assigned a valet/driver/bodyguard to me, usually 24/7. He didn't want me getting into any conflicts, no drinking and driving, no mention in the tabloids or gossip magazines, no problems with women. He just wanted good, controlled publicity. He was coordinating tour junkets from San Francisco, Taipei, and Hong Kong. At this

213

time, he was working for Summa, Caesars, and the Hilton. He was booking the Hilton Lounge using Dennis Compo's acts -- Freshwood, the Rocky Vasalino Show, and a girl band called the Party Dolls, just to name a few. He also had control of Caesars Lounge booking the acts that played on the barge in the casino.

For about a year, I lived between the house on Decatur and a penthouse suite at Caesars.

"We shared a two-bedroom apartment for a while before moving into a home on Decatur Street. For about a year, I lived between the house on Decatur and a penthouse suite at Caesars. Richard always had comp rooms at Caesars because of the number of high rollers he brought in. He'd say, 'Here's the room key, I'm going to Frisco for a week.' I could sign for food, bottles of wine, Courvoisier, you name it. One of the suites even had a baby grand piano. He had set up an office just a block off the Strip on Sahara. You could look up 'workaholic' in the dictionary and see Richard's smiling face.

"Although I'd become a local institution in Vegas, my career seemed to be standing still. The rumor eventually got around that I was feeling unhappy and stifled at the Slipper. When Richard got wind of the rumor, he showed up after my last show on a Tuesday night and said, 'Let's get out of Vegas — we'll fly to LA and get a change of scenery.' It was a good call. I didn't have to be back in Nevada until my first show on Thursday night. Over the next two days Richard and I had some long talks. He explained all of his business connections and how everything would change if I were to play in a major showroom. With me at the Slipper, there was no conflict of interest for him with the major hotels he was dealing with. The Slipper was considered to be for locals, as it didn't have hotel rooms to accommodate gaming junkets. My show was not viewed as a threat as it would if I were to move to the Landmark.

Playing the Landmark might be my only chance to present my show exactly as I envisioned it with the three segments set up completely differently.

"I told Richard I was determined to go, no matter what. I told him that I wanted that big, beautiful showroom that seated 780 people. It was perfect for me. Playing the Landmark might be my only chance to present my show exactly as I envisioned it with the three segments set up completely differently, with the standup bass in the fifties trio through the sixties with the scrim curtain to the full blown production in the seventies, all in one 90-minute show. I told him I was going with or without him.

"At the time, the union help at the Slipper was about to go on strike. I had made a deal with Bill Friedman that, if I stayed on through the strike, Bill would release me from my contract at the Slipper 30 days after the strike was over. I'd also made a deal with Gary Baldwin to open at the Landmark 30 days after the strike was over. Gary wasn't sure if I could get out of my contract with the Slipper so he had requested a $50,000 deposit and a thousand dollar a day penalty if I didn't open on time. I had all the money in a cardboard box under my bed; I didn't even have a bank account. I just went home, got the money, brought it to Gary, and he took it to the cage and gave me a receipt. We were in business.

"After Richard and I returned to Vegas, the strike began. I ran into Bill in front of the entrance to the upstairs showroom, the one that he had built for me. He made some small talk about my numbers being good and that the strike would soon be ending. Then there was a long pause, and he looked at me like a father looks at a son. He said, 'Morris we have spent over a million dollars promoting your name and your show . . .' I stood there looking at the floor, knowing I'd burnt this bridge forever. Bill shook my hand, said goodbye, and we never spoke again.

"Richard said he wasn't going to be able to be my manager because of all the conflicts. It looked like I was going to be on my own. He'd hired a local agent to be my manager, but what I didn't know was that behind the scenes Richard was quietly putting the production for the Landmark showroom together with Kenny Nelsen, my bass player. Richard got the set designer from the MGM Grand to design the new stage. As the days went by after the strike and I was counting down from 30, I was getting more and more nervous. Finally, it hit the press two days before I was to open in the new venue. After my last Slipper show on Tuesday

> Behind the scenes Richard was quietly putting the production for the Landmark showroom together with Kenny Nelsen, my bass player.

night, I walked down to the casino cage and in my mail box there was a single white envelope. In it was a letter releasing me from further commitments to the Silver Slipper and the Summa Corporation, signed by casino CEO Bill Friedman. That was it.

"Someone said, 'Richard's looking for you, Morris . . .' I put the letter in my pocket and began to walk out of the casino, but before I even started to look for Richard he caught up with me. He was standing there in the parking lot, and I told him I had got the letter. He said, 'I know, I know. Come on, Mo, I want to show you something.' We jumped into his Cadillac and he drove to the Landmark. When we got there they had just finished changing the marquee and it now said: '*Morris* presents a tribute to Elvis (with special guest, Robert Allen),' but right at the top in small letters it also said 'Richard Cheung presents'. I gave him a big hug and just about started to cry. Richard said, 'Come on Mo, I got something else to show you . . .' We climbed back into his car and he turned up the Strip — they were putting up billboards of me all over town. He had paid for 20 billboards that lit me up all over Las Vegas. It was one hell of a night.

I would open in the Empire Theater at the Landmark Hotel & Casino Thursday night at 9:00 p.m. with all the pomp and ceremony that Vegas had to offer, searchlights in the sky and all. It was my dream and I lived it every night. I had touched the wall."

Opening Night

"Opening night at the Landmark was just a blur," Morris recalls. "We only had Wednesday day and night and Thursday to have practice run-throughs and sound and lighting checks. It was 'don't stand there, don't touch that, you are wasting too much dry ice . . .' Delphine was explaining to the lighting men to make the neon *Morris* sign flash as I sang the phrase 'neon flashing' during *Viva Las Vegas*, and to black out the stage and just hit the flute player during the solo in *Dixie*, and 'yes, the flute player is the same guy as the sax player.' Meanwhile, I was conquering my great nightmare, going up and down the white stairs as they individually lit up. I think Kenny Nelsen had designed some sort of pressure plate to light up each stair as I stepped on it. I survived the stairs and got great reviews."

The move from the Silver Slipper to the Empire Room in the Landmark Hotel casino meant that Morris was now entertaining more than 1500 fans a night in two shows. "It was like night and day," David Maitland recalls. "The Landmark was much larger. Nice casino — and the Landmark was a *landmark* in those days — being right across the street from the Hilton and everything. The stage was huge. Kenny Nelsen, the bass player at that time, helped build the set, and, after Morris left, Kenny stayed and became a set-builder or a stage manager there in Vegas. He created all the scenery for shows."

Kenny Nelsen had been with Morris on and off since he and Scott Anderson joined the band in the mid-seventies. He met his wife, Delphine, at a Morris Bates show in a nightclub in Yorkton, Saskatchewan. They became key members of Morris's extended show business family. Kenny played bass in the band, while Delphine ran the light show. At the Landmark, she wasn't allowed to run the lights because she wasn't a union member and eventually became Richard's left hand girl.

Morris and Richard faced many challenges at the Landmark; in fact, all of their people had to make adjustments. As David Maitland recalls, "It was totally unionized. You couldn't move your amp on and off stage. If you did some guy would come and yell, 'Hey, that's my job!' If you asked him to do something that wasn't his job, he would just sit there and look at you. So it took a little while to get used to it. But it was really a great education. You had to be on top of it. There was a reason everything was so tight and organized."

As he had throughout his career, Morris continued to improve his show. "I concentrate on details in my show," he told *The Las Vegas Mirror*. "I want every detail in my show about Elvis to be accurate and honest. I don't want anybody in the audience to feel

And the Landmark was a landmark in those days — being right across the street from the Hilton and everything. The stage was huge.

cheated. I went to the extra trouble and expense to custom order an exact copy of Elvis's ebony Gibson Dove guitar. It was one of his trademarks, like that eagle suit."

Having the original band arrangements from the TCB band made things a whole lot easier for David Maitland. He had a healthy respect for Morris, his knowledge of Elvis's music, and vision of what he wanted from musicians in his show. "He controlled stuff, man," David says. "It was his way or the highway."

"David Maitland was without a doubt one of the best guitarists I worked with," Morris confides, "a disciplined professional with a great attitude. I had very talented musicians, but they often felt stifled due to the constraints of my totally structured show. It's difficult to not become stale and jaded doing basically the same show twice a night. You have to keep in the back of your mind that you need to present the show as if it's the first time you ever did it. To keep the freshness and excitement each and every time, you have got to remember that there will always be people in the audience who have come from all over the world and will be seeing your show for the very first time. Even if they have seen the show before, they want to see if you can do it again and maintain the energy and vibrancy."

> I went to the extra trouble and expense to custom order an exact copy of Elvis's ebony Gibson Dove guitar. It was one of his trademarks, like that eagle suit.

From a Jack to a King

"The transition from the Silver Slipper to the Landmark went relatively smoothly," Morris relates. "I had rehearsed it over and over in my mind for 10 years. The Elvis Presley Musical Story was about to unfold. You don't go to Vegas to make records; you go there to set them — attendance records. You don't go to Vegas to mine the coal; you go to polish the diamond. The musical part would stay relatively the same, but production got a lot bigger, elaborate by 1980 standards, and I don't think it's been duplicated or equaled by a single Elvis act since then. I was 30 years old, a perfect age to play a 21-year-old Elvis performing *Heartbreak*

Hotel all the way through to a 33-year-old Elvis in the '68 Come-back Special, and on to the seventies segment in the eagle suit. The logistics of the quick costume changes, to the striking of each stage-setting to match the era, had to be carefully thought out in order to make the produc-tion look as if you were watching a movie – true theater. When David made his opening announcement, 'Ladies and gentlemen, the Empire Showroom proudly presents Morris' Tribute to Elvis in the fifties, when Elvis was the swivel-hipped King of rock & roll,' the curtain went up and the audience didn't really know what to expect.

You don't go to Vegas to make records; you go there to set them — attendance records.

"As the curtain rose on this huge stage, they saw a three-piece rockabilly band – standup bass, three-piece drum set, and a guitar player pounding out the rhythm to *That's All Right (Mama)*. And, as I made my entrance, I could feel the audience squirm in their seats, thinking, 'Is this what I paid $10 for? And stood in line for? And tipped a maitre de for?' Then as four of my horn players qui-etly slipped on stage to sing the Jordanaires' parts to the fifties songs, it at least filled out the stage. As I exited the stage at the end of *Jailhouse Rock*, the curtain came down and David began his second announcement, saying that Elvis had retired from live performances in 1961 to perform in over 33 movies, and then decided to do the '68 TV Special. These were some of the songs from that *NBC-TV Special*. While David was making his announcement, a standup piano and a B-3 organ were pushed on stage, and Jake, our keyboard player, and a second guitar player hurried into position. As the curtain rose, the audience saw the horn section and the backup singers through a scrim see-through curtain giving the stage the appearance of a chapel setting.

"When I came back in that black leather outfit and opened with *Trouble*, accompanied by the sound of a full orchestra, you could feel the audience starting to churn. By the time I finished the second set with *If I Can Dream* and *Lawdy Miss Clawdy*, the audience was starting to get on their feet.

"While David was making the announcement for the third segment, the strains of the overture from the movie *2001 A Space*

Odyssey was beginning. David would announce: 'This is the show that changed Elvis from the most controversial performer to the most popular . . .' Backstage was running like a well-oiled machine, and, while I was downstairs changing, the stage was being struck again. The drum kit atop of the white staircase and the interactive staircase itself was being uncovered. Would I trip and fall down those stairs . . . I could envision the headlines – 'Morris's 9 Lives Run Out, Elvis Breaks Neck, Morris Dies at Landmark, Fans Run Screaming From Showroom . . .' What made it even more unnerving was that as I came down the stairs in the dark, I couldn't see the next step until the one I had just stepped onto lit up.

"The audience was happy, screaming and hollering, knowing they were getting the full impact and production of the show they had come to see, and I was nervously taking each step one at a time. Elvis didn't have this much production, but then again he didn't have to – he was Elvis. Now a gigantic picture of me was being lowered from the ceiling. During *My Way*, my big neon *Morris* sign lit up and the audience gave our show its full approval. As we became more comfortable with each other, I exchanged small talk with the audience. David Maitland would later say that 'the most fun part of the show was in between songs.' By the time that I introduced the band, sang *Viva Las Vegas*, and was bathed in a cloud of fog during *Dixie*, I had the audience on their feet. When I finished with the scarf giveaway during *Can't Help Falling In Love*, the audience was giving me a standing ovation and the curtain was coming down.

"I went backstage. I was spent. I touched the wall, grabbed some oxygen, made my mark on the wall to indicate another standing ovation, and went downstairs to rest, to get ready to do it all over again at midnight. I never gave encores in Vegas. Elvis hadn't done them, either, and when the curtain came down, the King had definitely left the building."

Living the High Life

"Prior to Las Vegas, my band played the opening set. In essence, they were my opening act. As the show progressed, we used various opening acts — comedians, ventriloquists, dancers, and magicians. I remember Richard telling me that Lyle Wagoner from *The Carol Burnett Show* was going to open for me at the Cave. None of us really knew what he did other than being a famous TV personality. He brought a potted plant onstage with him. Then he'd take the leaves off and blow through them making bird noises and whistling tunes. To this day I don't know what it was all about, but I was backstage and didn't get the whole gist of his act.

"It wasn't hard to find opening acts, but it was difficult to find acts that fit with the show. Standup comedian and magician Robert Allen, who opened for me at the Landmark, was a good fit.

"An opening act is designed to warm up the audience. It also gives you an opportunity to read the audience before you hit the stage. I remember one show in particular at the Landmark. When Robert came off, I was standing in the wings as my overture was beginning. He told me that the audience on stage left didn't respond to any of his jokes. They just sat and stared and didn't even clap.

"Usually, I'd hit the stage and do two songs before I'd welcome the audience to the show. Most times I'd ask, 'Is anyone here from Vegas?' I'd get a few hoots and hollers and people would say, 'New York! Chicago! LA! Texas! Canada!' And so on. So I went over to the left of the stage and asked, 'Where are you folks from?' The showroom got real quiet for a few seconds, and then someone hollered, 'Sprechen Sie Deutsch!' And then they all clapped and a couple of them shouted 'Vooden Heart! Vooden Heart!' They were all on a junket from Germany and didn't speak much English, which explained why they didn't understand Robert's jokes. They were a great crew and loved the show.

It wasn't hard to find opening acts, but it was difficult to find acts that fit with the show.

"Robert could not only make people laugh, he also provided great family entertainment. The kids loved his magic routines. I had become one of Las Vegas' premiere babysitters because Vegas was becoming a vacation destination for Middle America only to be rivaled by Disneyland."

"I was performing at the Landmark," Morris recalls, "when I got another invite from Dick Maurice to attend an opening night party for Suzanne Somers after her show at Caesars. The invitation said, 'Bring a Friend.' So I asked my opening act, Robert Allen, if he wanted to go to the party, and he said 'sure'. After my last show, we went up to Dick Maurice's place, which was packed. It seemed like the whole Strip was there. Paul Anka was in the kitchen wearing a red satin touring jacket that just said "Anka" on the back. Suzanne was floating around, talking with everyone, and her husband Alan Hamel was following in her wake. Lola Falana was bopping here, there, and everywhere. At one point, someone cracked a joke to Paul Anka about coming home off a tour and the toilet seat being up. (Paul has a wife and seven daughters)

"Liberace showed up with his companion and they went directly into the washroom, and there were funny whiffs in the air. Siegfried & Roy, Jack Jones, Debbie Reynolds, Tom Jones, Marlene Ricci, Bob Anderson, Bill Medley . . . everybody who was anybody was there. Suzanne Somers was one of the few acts, other than Ann Margaret, who could hold down a gig at Caesars who didn't have a hit record and wasn't previously known as a live performance entertainer, although she soon changed that image. I lost track of Robert Allen sometime during the evening and drove home alone in the gray light of early dawn.

"Later that same year Dick Maurice stirred up the entertainment scene with some gossip that would cost him his career. Dick was taping a TV show with a well-known physic he was promoting. The psychic lady had made some over the top predictions that were getting some entertainment bites, and after taping *The Dick Maurice Show* she went home and saw on TV that President

> I had become one of Las Vegas' premiere babysitters because Vegas was becoming a vacation destination for Middle America only to be rivaled by Disneyland.

Reagan had been shot. She got hold of Dick Maurice and they went back into the studio and re-taped the TV show, inserting her predictions that there would be an attempt on the President's life. They swore the technicians to secrecy and released the show for broadcast; however, when it was aired, television viewers noticed that the set was different, the plants had been moved, and she was wearing different jewelry. That show was found out to be a hoax and got some ugly national press for trying to capitalize on a tragedy that had happened to a well-liked president. Dick Maurice lost his show, his home, his dignity, and neither he nor his psychic pal was heard of again. Sensationalism sells.

Siegfried & Roy, Jack Jones, Debbie Reynolds, Tom Jones, Marlene Ricci, Bob Anderson, Bill Medley . . . everybody who was anybody was there.

"Every once in a while Dick Cavett would critique the Las Vegas scene on his TV show, talking about who was hot and who was not, up and coming acts, and shows that were hits and misses. In one of his critiques, Dick mentioned that I was the longest running one-man show to play Vegas other than Wayne Newton. He was right. After the summer of '78 no one had come to town with an Elvis tribute that rivaled the production of my show at the Landmark. In fact, during my seven years of performing my tribute show in Vegas, five years on the Strip and two years at the Union Plaza, the only other show of any notoriety to have an Elvis performer was the Legends Show at the Imperial Palace, and the Legends' Show Elvis segment was just one of many celebrity impersonations performed by a cast of unacknowledged performers who were frequently replaced by the producers.

BBC Special

The move from the Slipper to the Landmark also brought a whole new set of tactical challenges created by the unions — stagehands (run by the Teamsters), the Culinary Union, and the Musicians' Union. "The casino gaming personnel were not unionized," Morris notes, "except for maybe the big union in the sky called THE DESERT. The whole town is basically in bed with each other. If one union goes on strike, the others show solidarity. During the union strike of 1979, the Slipper was not affected because our showroom was not fully unionized. At the Slipper our only lighting technician was Delphine Nelsen. At the Landmark it took three unionized lighting personnel to try to do Delphy's job. As the comedian Robin Williams once said, 'Cocaine is God's way of saying you're making too much money.'

Most entertainers like Frank Sinatra and Sammy Davis Jr. traveled only with a musical conductor and didn't bitch if someone was paid 'not to play'.

"The union spot operator at the Landmark was always a hoot. I would introduce the guitar player and he'd light up the drummer. When I made jokes or teased them, they'd get their revenge by turning off my stage monitors. Joe, our stage manager, was cool, a big father-figure of a man with a heavy presence and usually solved the situations 'toot suite'. Because the Landmark showroom didn't have a house orchestra, I was allowed to use my own band. If you were playing at any of the other major showrooms in Vegas, you had to use the local musician's union house orchestra. If you used your own bass player, the house bass player would still be paid full union scale not to play. Most entertainers like Frank Sinatra and Sammy Davis Jr. traveled only with a musical conductor and didn't bitch if someone was paid 'not to play'.

"Not Cher, however. At the beginning of her show, she would introduce and thank her 'girlfriends' for stopping by to help her with the show. Then she would introduce Diana Ross and Bette Midler lookalikes, and the audience would go wild, not knowing they were female impersonators. When the audience finally figured it out, they felt duped but were forgiving. At the end of the show, Cher would introduce her personal band and then make the Caesars orchestra stand up and take a bow while introducing them as the 15 laziest men in Las Vegas. After the first few nights of pulling that stunt with the orchestra, the union stepped in and told her to 86 that part of her show, which she did. In the Nevada tabloids she took some heat and lost some respect, but not as much as I, or Las Vegas, was going to get or lose later in the summer of 1980 while I was at the Landmark.

"Things were going really well for Richard and me that year, even though the rest of the economy had begun to experience an economic recession, and they only seemed to be getting better when a BBC-TV film crew arrived in Vegas and the producer decided to feature my show in the documentary movie they were shooting."

BBC-TV producer Sandra Gregory decided to feature Morris's show at the Landmark as the best example of how good Elvis impersonators had become since the King's death. At first, the opportunity seemed golden, but as Morris and Richard learned more details, they discovered that there were some serious obstacles to be overcome.

"The producers wanted to shoot my show and tape an interview with me for their production, *Elvis Lives*," Morris relates, "but the BBC didn't have a budget to pay the extra fees due to union musicians if they were used in the footage chosen for their final cut of the film. So they met with Richard to work out a solution. They would be allowed to shoot the show if we were given possession of the raw tape footage so that we could make a TV commercial. There were to be no close up shots of the individual members of my show other than my personal core band. Then Richard came back to us and told us that the film crew was going to shoot two shows and interview me in my dressing room after the shows. When three of our union horn players inquired about being paid extra for the night the BBC-TV cameras would be in the house shooting the shows, Richard explained that they were shooting the show for a TV commercial and I would be the focus of the camera. It would be just another normal performance.

"So the show was shot, we were given a copy of the raw footage, and I was told that that they would send me a copy of the broadcast product at a later date. We said farewell to the BBC people and returned to our daily routines. Richard was in the process of buying a home for me in the northwestern part of Vegas on Crazy Horse Way. It was two homes on two acres. The

BBC-TV producer Sandra Gregory decided to feature Morris's show at the Landmark as the best example of how good Elvis impersonators had become since the King's death.

house I got was beautiful, a 2400-square foot two-bedroom ranch style home with a sprawling living area that could easily accommodate 20 people watching sports on the five-foot TV screen I'd gotten for my birthday. Lisa Stacey, the lady I'd been in the movie with in South Africa, was living in LA but she had been moving in with me one sock at a time since we had returned from Africa. We were seldom seen in public together except now and then at show openings. Lisa spent her time in both Vegas and LA and sometimes went home to Kentucky. She preferred hanging out with her girlfriends and watching soaps on TV to living the Vegas nightlife scene. She let me sleep all day in my air-conditioned cavern and seldom woke me before five in the afternoon.

This one morning in the summer of 1980, Shirley phoned Lisa and told her to run out and buy *The Las Vegas Review Journal*. I was on the front page.

"Sometimes we would hang out with Jim and Shirley Gardner, a beautiful older couple I had met when I first debuted at the Slipper. The Gardners were an extraordinary couple, totally in love with each other and married since they were 14 years old. They were from Arkansas where you can do that. They were just newlyweds when they moved to Nevada. Jim had worked on the construction of the Hoover Dam and they had raised a beautiful family. When I met them, Jim was building some of the major hotels in Vegas and Shirley was a caregiver. Jim had a fire engine red Corvette and Shirley had a lime green Cadillac Coupe de Ville that you could spot in parking lots from two blocks away.

"Lisa and I spent a lot of great days out on Lake Mead water skiing with Jim and Shirley, and when my mom came down from Canada, they entertained her. Along with Joy Shadaheh, they frequently attended the Joe Dolan Show at the Silverbird. They were older than me but at heart they were a lot younger. At any given time it seemed they could fill half my showroom with just their family and friends.

"This one morning in the summer of 1980, Shirley phoned Lisa and told her to run out and buy *The Las Vegas Review Journal*. Lisa ran out and got five copies and laid them out on the kitchen table. Then she knocked on my bedroom door and said maybe I should get up and look at the newspaper. I was on the front page . . .

"The night before this I had been cutting through the casino on my way backstage before my first show and ran into a scrum of reporters at the stage door entrance. At first I didn't realize they were there for me. I was in a hurry. If I didn't keep on truckin' I was going to be late, but they were shouting questions about musicians not being paid for a TV special, which brought me to an abrupt halt. I told them I didn't know anything about that, as Richard, my manager, handled all of the business aspects of the show; they should talk to Richard. I remember one young cub reporter hollering at me, 'Aren't you in the musicians' union?' I told him I was in the union because I played guitar in my show, and to appease the union I had joined, although, as a featured vocalist it was not necessary to be in the union. At that time I didn't know that Richard had me join the union in order to make me leader of the orchestra so that he wouldn't have to pay leadership wages to one of the sidemen. My first thoughts while I was waking up and splashing water on my face was that some of my musicians had gone to the union and complained that they had not been paid extra wages for the time the BBC TV film crew had taped two of our shows, and, accidentally, opened up a can of worms.

"Similar union circumstances had occurred at the taping of *The Merv Griffin Show*. The producers of Merv's show would only pay for the guest artist and a musical conductor, not his whole band. When the Silverbird offered to pay Merv Griffin Productions the cost of using Johnny Harra's whole band and back up singers, the producers accepted their offer. And when I made a separate deal to do my leather segment instead of the segment wearing my eagle outfit, they agreed to pay for my rhythm section to play with the Ray Brown Orchestra. After the show, my musicians and I received our checks from Merv Griffin Productions, and, not knowing that the rule of thumb was to return them to Merv, my band guys went to the casino cage and cashed theirs. Later, at the

Similar union circumstances had occurred at the taping of *The Merv Griffin Show.*

Slipper, one of the guys from Merv's show phoned and asked me if my musicians had handed back their checks, and I told him that we didn't know we were supposed to do that. I asked him if he wanted my check back and he said, 'It's okay, keep it, Morris.' I had done a good job for them and it wasn't a big deal that my band had cashed their checks instead of handing them back to Merv's people.

"Of course, the Landmark TV taping was a completely different set of circumstances. We didn't know if and when the footage was to be used, or if it would be used at all. Three band members complained to the union saying they wanted to be paid regardless of what the BBC-TV producers were doing with the footage. In retrospect, most of the footage was never used at all and the footage that *was used* in the BBC documentary was never broadcast in North America. Not in the US and not in Canada, a decision that the producers eventually made in order to avoid conflicts with the Elvis Presley estate and possible copyright infringement. But the local press had made a big issue out of the local union musicians' complaint, spinning what was basically a non-issue into a bad press, front page issue, which was not the sort of press that Richard wanted. I was about to face the music.

"When I came into the kitchen, Lisa pointed to the newspapers on the table and my heart sank. I was stunned. It was one hell of a rude awakening, that was for sure. Headlines alleging wrongdoing with the union payroll stared back at me from the five copies of the *Review Journal* that she had laid out for me to see. The old cliché 'there is no such thing as bad publicity' didn't give me any relief at that moment. In retrospect, some of the locals *may* have lost some respect for me or for my show — my mom does remember hearing some catty statements in the casino now and then — but otherwise it was business as usual. I survived the scandal because tourists rarely have time to read the local Vegas newspapers or watch local TV news shows, and the story wasn't picked up by the networks and broadcast nationally."

Morris did a lot better than merely survive the momentary

scandal, and, despite the bad press he had become one of the higher paid single acts in Vegas. "My run at the Landmark was probably the best year of my life," he says. "Everything I wanted and worked for had just fallen into place. The shows were selling out and the audiences were fantastic. I could do no wrong. I mentioned in the taping of the BBC-TV Special that we were there in Vegas for 27 performing months. I had been keeping score. After every performance I had put a mark on the wall beside the stage if I had got a standing ovation. I think I had 29 straight standing ovations before I missed one and had to start all over again.

> I think I had 29 straight standing ovations before I missed one and had to start all over again.

"While I was having the time of my life on and off stage, Richard was also a very busy man. Being the producer of my show, he also controlled the Landmark lounge entertainment. The lounge was one of the nicest show lounges in Vegas and it could seat up to 300 people on a good night. The Landmark was a gorgeous hotel. The tower looked like a space needle and the disco and restaurant on the 26th and 27th floors were packed every night of the week. We turned the Landmark into one of the hottest Vegas venues that summer and I was just 30 years old. No one had ever done that or has done it since."

The final cut of the BBC-TV documentary *Elvis Lives* featured some outstanding performances by Morris and some interesting interview clips, as well. "I think in my own little way," Morris said in one clip, "I experienced some of the craziness that Elvis experienced for 25 years of his professional entertainment career. I mean, it gets to me sometimes and I'm nowhere at the level that he was. And it does get to you sometimes, people walking up to you in the bathroom asking you for an autograph. I mean, some of this stuff does get on your nerves and tends to wear, but then you hit the stage. I love the songs and I love the show."

During the course of the interview, Morris also let the BBC-TV audience know that he never ever confused the role he was playing on stage being Elvis with his real life. "I try to leave as much of the character in this dressing room, along with the suits," he said. "I mean, I leave here and I am Morris Bates. I see

I leave here and I am Morris Bates. I see too many people working too hard to try to be Elvis off the stage.

too many people working too hard to try to be Elvis off the stage. I can't do it because I work so hard onstage. If I was trying to be Elvis in the daytime, I wouldn't have anything to give to the people when I got here . . ."

Unfortunately, because of possible legal hassles, *Elvis Lives* was not broadcast in North America, but he now had a strong contingent of fans in the UK, where his name is still revered by Elvis fans.

On a Roll

"As summer was winding down," Morris continues, "I broke all the house records for attendance on the Labor Day weekend. You couldn't get near the show. The ticket brokers were selling out and requesting more tickets and all the comps had to be canceled except those personally authorized by Richard. I had to get Richard to pull juice with the hotel just to get rooms on the 25th floor for my friends when they came in from LA. Richard was definitely making hay when the sun wasn't shining.

"As we coasted through the fall months with solid numbers, Richard was in negotiations with the Landmark management to extend the contract into the New Year. With a recession happening all around us, and the trouble we had with the unions behind us, Richard had some tough decisions to make. He reassured me that everything would be fine as he was also in negotiations with a brand new 500-seat showroom opening in Bob Stupak's Vegas World, and, he added, there were no unions.

"The next knock that I was to hear on my bedroom door before five in the afternoon was when I heard Lisa saying, 'Morris, the MGM is burning! I jumped up, had a look at that big TV screen in my living room, and saw people leaping from the top floors of the MGM. I ran to the back door of my house and looked toward the sky and I could see black smoke billowing over the skyline of the Strip. It was surreal running back into the house to see the chaos on TV, and then running back outside to look at the skyline. I told Lisa I was going uptown and she said,

'Don't go, they are advising everyone to stay away, the whole strip is being closed down . . .'"

The MGM Hotel fire on November 21, 1980 was the worst disaster in Nevada history with 87 dead, mostly due to smoke inhalation, and more than 650 injured. It was the second worst hotel fire in US history. "It was the proverbial straw that broke Las Vegas' back," Morris says. "It changed a lot of things, and, with Vegas' image covered in soot while fire depart-ment investigators examined the disaster scene, Richard told me it was time to make our move. He said, 'I've booked the show into Dallas for three weeks, and made a deal with Bobby Stupak to open with Trini Lopez at Vegas World on New Year's Eve. After the month of January, we'll stay on and run it for him indefinitely.

The MGM Hotel fire on November 21, 1980 was the worst disaster in Nevada history.

"I don't remember much about Texas except that we played at a beautiful club called Yorick's for an oil company, and that all the waitresses were ex-Playboy bunnies. Dallas was definitely a much-needed breath of fresh winter air. I do remember follow-ing Ricky Nelson, whom I'd met previously in Vegas, into the club, and being in Dallas on December 8th when John Lennon was shot.

"After Texas it was back to Vegas for Christmas and preparing for Vegas World. My mom and brothers were all down for the holiday and it was great having the whole family and all my friends around me during the festive season. Christmas week you can shoot a cannonball through Vegas and not ever hit a taxicab. It is dead. The acts booked during the week before the holiday usually just die. No one goes out. The hotels save their heavy hit-ters for New Year's Eve. The hotels begin to fill up on Boxing Day and by the 31st there isn't a hotel room or a show reservation to be had.

"I was cutting through Caesars to meet a friend of mine and a pit boss caught hold of me and said, 'I've got some comps for Sinatra . . .' He insisted that I go. I had seen Sinatra's show many times and wasn't really in the mood, but he insisted again, so I said, 'Okay,' and as soon as I stepped into the showroom I realized he was just papering it because there were only 67 people in the audience. I counted them. I couldn't believe it. Regardless of the size of the audience, Frank put on a fantastic show and he wasn't even his usual cocky self. Of course, a few days later Caesars was sold out for New Year's, but the Strip was definitely headed for a recession, and the unions that had been wagging the dog were in for a rude awakening — Vegas was changing.

Christmas week you can shoot a cannonball through Vegas and not ever hit a taxicab. It is dead.

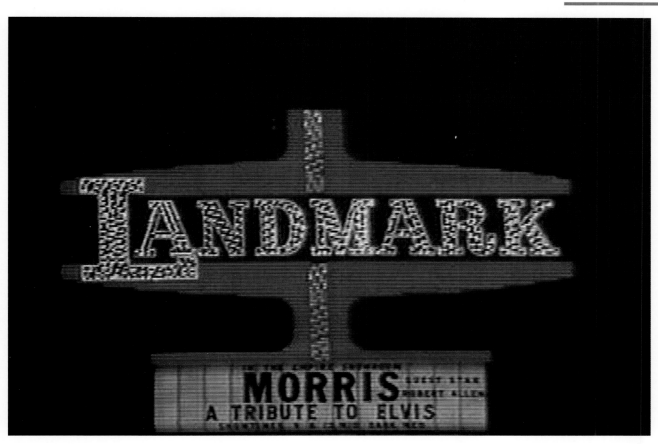

Morris lights up the Strip again

Death-defying stairs

In the spotlight at the Landmark

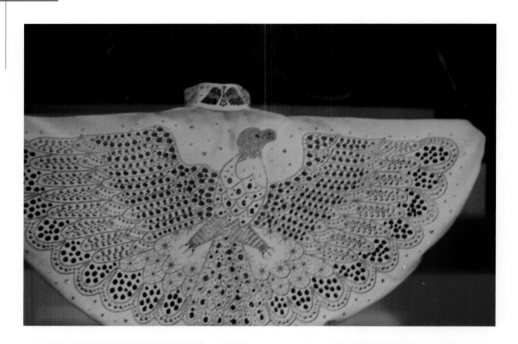

The celebrated Eagle cape

Morris's guests: Eagle cape costume designer James Wiggins (top right), comedian and magician Robert Allen (bottom), and Lyle Wagoner of the Carol Burnett Show *(middle left).*

An American Trilogy

Vegas World

On Top

Morris Bates was sitting on top of the world, driving a different model or color of Cadillac depending on his daily mood. He had access to half a dozen Caddies, which Richard used for his high rollers, and owned houses with Richard in Vegas and LA. He had a record-setting streak as the longest running Elvis impersonator to be booked on the Strip. But the strain and stress of performing two shows a night for 12 months a year except for Wednesdays — when his showrooms were dark — had begun to damage his body and soul. Nightly injections of cortisone, shot into his neck to relieve the pain from his damaged vocal chords, were the most brutal of all of the compromises he had made in order to stay on top of the game, but a four-wall lease in a casino to run specific games of chance was his downfall.

Many people have marveled at how long Morris was able to extend his Vegas engagement, moving from the Silver Slipper to the Landmark and then on to Vegas World the next year. He was a continuous presence on the strip from 1978 to 1982. No doubt, Richard Cheung's wily ability to negotiate deals had a great deal to do with this remarkable achievement, but Richard could not have made any of those deals if Morris had not packed Vegas showrooms night after night, month after month, for all those years.

Many people have marveled at how long Morris was able to extend his Vegas engagement, moving from the Silver Slipper to the Landmark and then on to Vegas World the next year.

Morris's stand at the Landmark lasted only one year because of lease and union complications, and a slumping economy. The lease that Richard and Morris had signed with the Landmark was called a four-wall agreement. As Morris explains, the intricacies of four-walling were not exclusive to the casino showrooms in Vegas. "'I'll take the door, you take the bar' is a common form of four-walling. In Canada and the US, most clubs that hire bands just pay the entertainment out of the profits from the bar, plain and simple No cover charge. No hassle. If your bar can't afford entertainment, then you don't have any. The more popular the act, the bigger the venue; then things start to get complicated. If a venue doesn't feel it can turn a profit on just the bar sales to pay the band, they add a cover charge. The club usually kicks in the amount they would pay a band if they didn't have a cover charge, in case the gig goes completely sideways. Then at least the band has gas money to the next gig. Remember, you're doing it for the music, not the girls.

"LA is tough — a lot of clubs will not book an act unless they pay the club a deposit. If they lost money on you and you don't make more than they would normally make if they didn't have entertainment then they keep your deposit, and no one knows what is normal. So you pay the club to play, and if you end up playing to tables and chairs, they keep your money. A lot of clubs want a current fan club list to insure someone is going to come and see you and not drive out their steady customers with your 'waiting to be discovered' new sound. Remember the girls. Amplify that concept 1000 times and you have got a Las Vegas four-wall.

"Vegas truly is a complicated city with words like 'high roller', 'juice', 'connected' and a slew of others, but I'll cut to the chase — it has to be the right act for the room. Vegas has become so big now it has the luxury to specialize. When I was in Vegas, the only specialty venues were Sam's Town and Circus Circus — cowboys and clowns. Today it has the world from New York to Paris, but the bottom line has not changed – you still have to put people in those chairs. And it's not just people; it's people that gamble. Certain entertainers attract a certain clientele, and that's the reason some acts make it in Vegas and some don't.

"A simple explanation for a four-wall is that the act accepts the cost of running the production for the showroom receipts, and the casino makes its money from the gaming. Then it starts to get complicated, with percentages of the gross to cover comp show tickets, hotel rooms, comp drinks, advertising, ticket brokers, maitre de's and a host of side-table deals, plus the three powerful unions that keep a relentless thumb on Las Vegas. And you roll the dice. Remember, it's about the money.

"Whatever money your show makes belongs to you. It goes to the cage, and, after taxes, it is yours, however, union arrangements can be a major issue. In a fully unionized venue like the Landmark, you have to pay the culinary union, the stagehands union, and, of course, you have to pay the musician's union."

By the time Morris was performing at the Landmark, his weekly costs had reached $17,000 a week. The boy from Williams Lake did well there, and there were no problems taking care of the payroll, but union problems arose and the engagement did not run longer than the original one-year deal.

Morris and Richard moved on quickly, negotiating a four-wall agreement with Bob Stupak to secure the first extended engagement offered to any entertainer at the newly constructed Galaxy Showroom in Bob Stupak's Vegas World Casino. Located at 2000 Las Vegas Boulevard, just north of Sahara Avenue, halfway between the original Strip and Glitter Gulch, Vegas World later become the site of the much-ballyhooed Stratosphere.

> By the time Morris was performing at the Landmark, his weekly costs had reached $17,000 a week.

The Sky's the Limit

Bob Stupak was a kindred spirit to Morris. Born in Pittsburgh during a bygone era when crooks and cops coexisted as colorful Damon Runyan characters, Bob tried his hand at many vocations. He discovered a passion for motorcycles, cut some singles that didn't become hit records, and then found his niche with two-for-one coupons. He hawked them in Vegas in the mid-sixties, tried them out briefly in Australia and was deported, and moved back to Nevada where he purchased a dilapidated Ford and Mercury dealership on a 1½-acre property, which was on Las Vegas Boulevard but not inside the Strip itself. The acreage was in a seedy, crime-ridden area strewn with rundown motels that had become a haven for street prostitutes and junkies.

In 1974, Stupak opened up a restaurant and slot machine joint, which he named Bob Stupak's World Famous Historic Gambling Museum. Despite the many unorthodox gimmicks Stupak employed, not all that many paying customers were lured inside his tiny operation. The massage parlors in the area were all said to be raking in more dough than Bob was.

The massage parlors in the area were all said to be raking in more dough than Bob was.

When the museum burned to the ground, Stupak used the insurance money and a bank loan to begin construction on his 'Bob Stupak's Vegas World' casino and hotel. Bob realized he would need to offer special incentives if he was going to be successful luring gamblers away from the brightly lit marquees of the super hotels. So he offered VIP packages where — for less than $400 — patrons received a room for two nights, an unlimited drinks pass, good in any casino bar, and several hundred dollars worth of chips that were only negotiable in his Vegas World casino.

Vegas World décor was a low budget version of *Star Trek* with faked moon landing movie sets that featured a genuine moon rock displayed in a glass case. Huge outer-space murals adorned outside walls and inside ceilings were studded with tiny lights meant to be stars twinkling in a night sky — casino wallpaper and carpets blended seamlessly with the polyester and plaid outfits many of the paying customers wore in those days. An aggressive direct mailing campaign of two-for-one coupons and vacation value package offers was so successful that Stupak's Vegas World hotel and casino turned a healthy profit in its first year. Stupak put the profits to work, building more hotel rooms and adding the 480-seat Galaxy Showroom, where Morris Bates would perform after leaving the Landmark.

The Vegas World motto, "The Sky's The Limit," was displayed in big letters outside the casino above the obligatory rocket ships that sat on top of the entranceway awning. Stupak was always promoting slogans — "Don't come to the big place with the small bankroll, come to the small place with the big bankroll." He kept upping limits at his gaming tables and offering bigger and bigger slot machine prizes. Double exposure blackjack and crap-less craps would be succeeded by endless quirky gaming variations. Many people thought Stupak was nuts, including, he has said, mob guys who tried to bring him into their fold. He reached a hundred million a year in profits by the mid-eighties and then he topped that mark.

Author of a book on gambling with the inspiring title *Yes, You Can Win!* Bob Stupak often referred to himself as the Captain Kirk of the only casino in the world that was designed like a starship. He had a 100 percent scale model of Skylab, the first US orbital space station, built, and hung it up in his space lobby, where it would be the first thing patrons saw when they entered his casino.

"In the game of life," Stupak advises in the introduction to his book *Yes, You Can Win!*, "the house edge is called Time. In whatever we do Nature charges us for doing it in the currency of time. So we must take advantage of every moment. Every moment in life is so very precious. You only get a fling at life for a while then the house collects. We must get all our thrills and all our experiences while we have the opportunity. We have to go for it now! And only by taking advantage of time in this way can we get the best of it — win or lose."

Morris Bates' backwoods philosophy was less boisterous but essentially the same. Morris had taken a chance on life and he had never looked back. He had come a long way from humble beginnings. Morris had dared to believe that he could walk in the King's footsteps. He had made some giant strides of his own.

Stupak put the profits to work, building more hotel rooms and adding the 480-seat Galaxy Showroom, where Morris Bates would perform after leaving the Landmark.

Now he was headlining in the Galaxy Showroom. As Morris recalls, "I opened at Bobby Stupak's Vegas World on New Year's Eve with Trini Lopez. His hits were *Lemon Tree* and *If I Had A Hammer*. He had a great voice and a red Gibson sunburst guitar. He was a nice guy and he had a hit with a cover of Neil Diamond's *Love On The Rocks* while we were there at Vegas World. I like that song. I've sung it a few times."

Bob Stupak and Morris got along famously. Life at Vegas World was looser than it had been at the Empire Room in the Landmark, and Morris was impressed as he watched the dollars roll in and the hotel tower being built floor after floor from the profits. "When we had a good weekend, like on a Labor Day weekend," he explains, "another two floors of the hotel got windows. Bobby was a gambler. It was in his blood. I used to sit up in his office there with him and I would see two cockroaches on the floor and I would say, 'Okay, I got my money on the right one. A hundred dollars says my cockroach gets over to there . . . before your cockroach.' And he would bet with me. He would bet with me on anything. One day I told Bobby I wanted new lights for the showroom, and he says, 'Morris I'll put new lights in the showroom if you can beat me at Pac-Man.' I said, 'Bobby, I'm not very good at Pac-Man, but my piano player JT is pretty good at it.' He says, 'Okay, then JT will represent you . . .'

"They got to playing Pac-Man in the back room and they got really close to the end and Bob was losing and he threw up his hands and said, 'I'm done.' And JT quit. But Bob was back in there like a dirty shirt and finished him off. He faked JT out, and I paid for the lights."

Whenever Morris tells any of his Bob Stupak stories his eyes are merry and his voice soars melodically as he recounts each successive absurdity. "I would be sitting up there with Bobby watching the monitors and shooting the breeze," Morris relates, "and he would all of a sudden say, 'Okay, there's a hard hitter down there,' and he would get up and go down there. He would sit down at the table, take over from his dealer, and play the next

> I would see two cockroaches on the floor and I would say, 'Okay, I got my money on the right one. A hundred dollars says my cockroach gets over to there . . . before your cockroach.'

hand against the gambler that was getting lucky. If you were winning $5,000, $6,000, $7,000 thousand dollars, he would play you himself. He didn't screw around. He was the owner. If you wanted to win at Vegas World, you would end up playing against Bob Stupak. It was his money that you had been winning. He would just tap his dealer on the shoulder and take over.

I was already performing at the Galaxy Showroom at Vegas World when it happened — when Richard and I lost three and a half million dollars on Pai Gow poker.

"He spent most of his time in a corner booth in the restaurant drinking coffee and chain smoking, sometimes two cigarettes going at the same time. He told me he was going to build Vegas World into the tallest structure in Vegas and call it the Stratosphere and put a rollercoaster on it. I thought he was nuts, but he did it.

"In Vegas not all betting is done under the bright lights of the Strip. There is a lot of out-of-the-way, behind closed door gaming — dog-fighting, cock-fighting . . . This one guy ran a private poker game and to keep everyone entertained they put a rooster in an eight-by-eight cage and you would pick where the rooster would shit. There were squares and numbers on the floor of the cage. The rooster would go in there and you would put your money on square number 49 or square number 14 and while you played poker you would wait to see where the rooster made his next dump."

Amused by Stupak's unbounded energy for the Barnum and Bailey approach to doing business, Morris was totally unprepared for what came next. As he recalls, "I was already performing at the Galaxy Showroom at Vegas World when it happened — when Richard and I lost three and a half million dollars on Pai Gow poker in the Landmark Hotel casino during Chinese New Year's week."

The Game of Las Vegas

When asked to explain how this could possibly happen when Morris himself seldom gambled, he sums it all up by simply saying, "I learned the game of Las Vegas. Richard had moved on from just bring in gambling junkets from Frisco and Hong Kong

"We haven't been paid for two weeks, Morris," David said. "What's going on?"

to specializing in heavy hitting Asian high rollers from all over the Pacific Rim. The high rollers like to play Pai Gow and Baccarat, which were not available at the Landmark Casino. Richard used his Cadillacs to move the high rollers from the Hilton to Caesars and sometimes to the Landmark because they didn't like to use taxis. The Landmark began to realize the money these people had and agreed to back Richard in getting a gaming license. They agreed to let him four-wall his Pai Gow poker game for a percentage of the take. He explained it to me that just getting the gaming license and controlling the games was a win-win situation. He put up our houses and cars and all the cash he could lay his hands on in order to be liquid for about three and a half million dollars, which in retrospect was not much money at all. After I left the Landmark show room, I hardly went back there at all. I remember dropping by to see Richard one night and watching him in his embroidered silk Chinese suit overseeing the Pai Gow games, and thinking we'd come a long way since we first met with me selling and signing pictures of myself for $5 in his cabaret in Prince George, BC."

Morris didn't learn about the gambling losses until he received a call from David Maitland. It was a phone call he will never forget. "We haven't been paid for two weeks, Morris," David said. "What's going on?" Right away Morris knew something was very, very wrong. "Richard was really impeccable about paying the guys in the band," he explains. "Even if Richard was in LA or San Francisco or Dallas or whatever, the guys were always paid on time. Richard was a right-on guy. So, I jumped up and booted it over to the Landmark casino and everything had been cleaned out, all of the Pai Gow tables and everything. We lost a lot of money. I went running down to Los Angeles. Two of our homes there were already in escrow, while the sale was already closed for another. We had all these Cadillacs and they had all been sold off."

Brazilian Break

"When I came back to Vegas, I didn't have any money in the cage from all the shows. I lost it all because I trusted Richard. I never ever saw Richard again. I was, like, $10,000 in the red just in wages for the band. I really didn't know what to do. Then Delphine Nelsen, who was handling all of my calls and publicity at that time, called me up. She said, 'Morris I got a call from Caesars Palace and they got this guy from South America who wants to book you in Brazil.'

"I said, 'Delphy, here's what you got to do. You have him come down after the second show at Vegas World, which is about three o'clock in the morning. And if he has $10,000 cash with him, he can talk to me, and I'll consider Brazil.'

"She said okay, she would do that. I asked her what language they spoke down there, and she said, 'Portuguese.'"

Morris asked management people at Vegas World if they knew anybody who spoke Portuguese because he was going to need an interpreter so he could tell the Brazilian promoter exactly under what terms and conditions he would be willing to consider before signing any contracts. The closest translator that they knew about was in Salt Lake City, someone who had something to do with professional soccer contracts. So Delphine Nelsen made a call to Salt Lake City and the interpreter agreed to fly up to Nevada in time for the meeting with the Brazilian promoters.

If he has $10,000 cash with him, he can talk to me, and I'll consider Brazil.

"I drafted possibly the best contract I had ever drafted." Morris relates, "and Delphy typed it out so that we would have it ready for the 3:00 a.m. meeting. Ten thousand dollars upon signing the contract, plus ten thousand when leaving Las Vegas, a further then thousand when I arrive in San Paulo, and an additional ten thousand upon my leaving. I would be there for two weeks and perform every night, but there was to be a limit of 1,000 tickets sold per show."

Morris had made that rider on the contract because he had

The Brazilian tour was a lucky break that would bail out Morris from his debts.

been scammed before by promoters who hired him to play a show for a few hundred people and sold several thousand tickets. He really didn't want to perform to an audience of a hundred thousand people and be paid the same as if he had been singing to no more than 1,000.

The Brazilian tour was a lucky break that would bail out Morris from his debts. He was able to put the Coasters into the Galaxy Showroom in Vegas World to substitute for him while he was in South America. And when he arrived in San Paulo, his fears of another raw deal appeared to be needless. "They took pictures of all of our equipment the way it was set up in the showroom at Vegas World," Morris remembers. "And when we arrived down there, they had duplicated exactly the same stage setup that we had in Nevada."

When Morris arrived at San Paulo International Airport on the second day of June 1981, he was ushered into a Mercedes sedan at the airport and driven to his hotel by an imposing Italian security guy by the name of Cesar. "We were pulled over for speeding by this motorcycle cop," Morris recalls, "and Cesar asked me, 'Morris, have you got some money?' And I said, 'Sure, what do you need?' And he said, 'One US dollar.' And the patrolman took one dollar US and went on his way. He had just made a day's wages and he was happy to let us go on our way, too.

"Right after that, I made an appearance on Brazilian national television. And they asked me if I could actually play a guitar. So I picked up an acoustic guitar and I sang the first verse and chorus of *Love Me Tender . . .*"

This convincing reprise of Presley's on-camera performance from the movie of the same name convinced the Brazilian TV audience that they were looking at the real deal. This guy was as good as Elvis. He looked like Elvis. He talked like Elvis. And when he picked up that guitar and crooned just like Elvis, ticket sales accelerated. Greater San Paulo had a population of more than 20 million people. It was the fifth largest city in the world and boasted many opera houses and theaters. Morris played to packed houses wherever the promoters took him during the two-week tour.

"Everywhere we went," he recalls, "I remember audience responses were loud. The venues were mostly what they call soft-seaters — theaters and opera houses like the Orpheum Theatre in Vancouver, that kind of place. Real nice theaters to perform at, and they might have packed more than a 1,000 people into some of those rooms, but they were not soccer stadiums where they could sell a hundred thousand tickets. Then at sound check in this one venue we noticed that there were more like 10,000 seats, and when the people started coming in it looked like they had sold the venue out."

This was a clear breach of the contract that Morris had signed and he told the promoters that he wasn't going on unless they paid him an additional $5,000 US dollars. While they were negotiating, the fans were raising a ruckus and resorted to tactics that Morris and his band mates had not seen anywhere before in their travels.

"Some young guys," Morris relates, "climbed up onto the bass bins and tossed percussion grenades into the horn openings and blew them out. There were explosions. We were six or seven feet above that on a raised stage and no one was hurt. They didn't ruin all the bass bins and they didn't damage the midrange speakers or high range tweeters, but right away the promoters told us that they had sent someone to get some American money. They were going to pay us as fast as they could."

When the money arrived, Morris began his show. He had a wedge of bodyguards on stage while he sang. When he went anywhere near the front lip of the stage, they hung onto him so that fans reaching up or climbing up to get scarves that he tossed into the audience couldn't pull him down into their midst.

It was bizarre with these bodyguards walking with me on stage as I was singing.

"It was bizarre with these bodyguards walking with me on stage as I was singing," he recalls. "It was like we were all joined together at the hip. I was singing Eddie Arnold's song *Welcome To My World*, a nice and easy ballad to catch my breath, when all of a sudden the whole stadium erupted with screaming, hollering, and applause. I thought for a second that I might be singing

Brazil's secret national anthem, but as I looked behind me I saw that one of the bodyguards had tripped on a floor monitor and cold-cocked himself. He was lying there flat on his back. The audience was roaring and I just kept on with the show."

Venturing beyond the elegant 19th century buildings and sleek 20th century skyscrapers of the city, Morris learned that vast shantytown ghettos stretched as far as the eye could see and that conditions were even grimmer than the situations he had witnessed in Soweto and Bangkok. He immediately thought of the traffic cop who had been willing to accept a one US dollar bribe to look the other way and realized that millions upon millions of poor Brazilians were living in truly desperate circumstances. He had read newspaper stories about rats eating severely disabled street people that were so malnourished and feeble they could no longer get up and walk around. No one was coming to their aid. The most horrible story related was an incident of a dying, paralyzed woman whose female cavity had become a nest for baby rats. Other horrors he can't repeat because he becomes too upset to speak.

When the Brazilian tour had run its course, Morris returned to Nevada and resumed his shows at the Galaxy Showroom in Vegas World. He had covered his debts for the time being, but things would never be quite the same.

"I never saw Richard again," Morris laments. "It was tough. He had been my manager, my friend, my buddy, my confidant, my mentor, my partner in crime, and most of all he looked out for me. He took me to Paul Minichiello. He dressed me. He picked out my costumes for me. He did everything for me. When his mother died in Hong Kong, he came back and gave me a 24-karat gold chain necklace with a 3-inch gold medallion with a dragon on it worth about $8,000 from his mom's estate. Someone stole it out of my dressing at the Slipper. It was gone, and, now, like the medallion, he was gone. He always used to call me 'Mo.' He would say, 'Hey, Mo, let's go . . . ' and we kept on going and I thought we would never stop. But he was gone. He had vanished.

He would say, 'Hey, Mo, let's go . . . ' and we kept on going and I thought we would never stop.

He had lost face. For the first time I was truly on my own. I was in big trouble.

"I had been $10,000 down but Brazil bailed me out. After that Delphy looked after the day-to-day operation of the show, but we never saw Richard again. We lost three and a half million dollars at the Landmark, where Richard had that four-wall on the Pai Gow, and we both got taken to the cleaners."

After suffering the loss of his longtime partner, manager, and buddy, Morris found himself hanging out with Bob Stupak even more often than before. Stupak was always dreaming and scheming. "Before I left Vegas," Morris says, "he offered me some really outrageous propositions, but I couldn't handle it; I had to come home."

*Morris on the marquee at Vegas World, soon to
become the Stratosphere*

Vol. 1, Issue 47   July 3, 1981   Published every Friday by Galaxy Composition Inc.

Viva LAS VEGAS®

FREE TAKE ONE

Gaming News

Fifth Dimension
Return To
Las Vegas

Norm Crosby
& Blue Material

Morris:
The Elvis Legend
Continues

T.V. Notebook
Exclusive Interview
with Tom Smothers
Ladies Of The Evening

Complete
Entertainment Guide

Performing
Nightly At
Vegas World

Morris

Morris in the headlines again

Morris the clown

On the Road Again

You Can't Go Home Again

Gordie Walker was a Vancouver-born entertainer who got his start in the music business as a teenager playing in bands during the psychedelic sixties. After that, Gordie became a veteran of the bar band circuit in western Canada until he was diagnosed with cancer at the age of 60. Gordie was a victim of circumstance, a workplace induced alcoholism that was a result of working six nights a week for more than 45 years in bars, pubs, and skid row watering holes, where he was much loved for his upbeat personality and happy-go-lucky approach to life. Gordie had many career highlights, sharing stages with pals like Billy Cowsill, Dan Tapanila, and Danny Mack. He toured with Stompin' Tom Connors and had 45 rpm records out on Connors' Boot Records label. He was a kind-hearted, noble fellow and a good friend to Morris Bates over the years. Morris loved him like a brother in arms, but Gordie was also an opinionated, obstinate man.

The first time Gordie Walker met Morris Bates was in Alberta in 1974. As he recalls, "I first met Morris when I was living down the block from the Cromdale Hotel in Edmonton. I sat down at the bar and said 'hello' to the bartender. We were quite close at the time. I'm indigenous, one half Cree, the other half Scottish, and there was this guy Morris Bates up on stage with his band Injun Joe's Medicine Show. I

255

I was enjoying their show when this white guy walked in. He was the owner of the hotel and he said, 'What the f--- are those f---ing *Indians* doing onstage?'

was enjoying their show when this white guy walked in. He was the owner of the hotel and he said, 'What the f— are those f—ing *Indians* doing onstage?' The bartender said, 'The agency sent them . . .' and the white guy said, 'Get 'em off! Get 'em off!' And the bartender goes up and tells Injun Joe, who was Morris, what had just gone down.

"The show was over. It was finished. They had been fired and the bartender had told them to shut it down. I felt sorry for them, and I went up there and introduced myself, and told them that I had a rented house down the street there in Edmonton. I said, 'You guys are welcome to come and stay there, if you want to . . .'"

With no pay and no prospect of making money for two weeks until their next booking in another prairie town, Morris and his band and their girlfriends and wives were grateful to accept Gordie Walker's offer. Walker's generosity triggered a lifelong friendship. "Down the street we went," Walker relates, "with all the equipment, and I put them up for two weeks. We had a lot of fun together despite their being fired from the hotel. We would drink Double Jack. It was a cheap, fortified wine that they were selling in those days. Cherry Jack, Apple Jack, Berry Jack . . . And then they were off to their next gig. I was happy to see them happy."

The next time that Gordie saw Morris Bates was when Morris was performing on *The Merv Griffin Show* on Walker's television set back in Vancouver. As Gordie recalls, "All of a sudden there was Morris, and I said, 'that's my guy! He's done it! He's on *Merv Griffin!* You can't do better than that!' This was big for me. Here was a young Canadian from Vancouver and he was one of the three acts that performed Elvis songs on network television on the *Merv Griffin Show*. At the end of the show, Merv came over and thanked them, and that was that — but it was big for me. It made my day. My head went balloonistic. I'm a guy who has played with Roy Orbison, Jim Morrison, all sorts of guys when I was younger, but I think that tender moment was *the* moment of my life, a local guy that I knew singing on *Merv Griffin!*"

The next time that Gordie saw Morris in person, Walker was performing at the OK Corral on the downtown eastside in Vancouver and who should walk in but Morris Bates. The two men had not met face to face since the time that Walker had put Morris and his Injun Joe's Medicine Show band up in his rented house after they got fired by a racist hotel owner in Alberta.

As Walker recalls, "I'm playing the OK Corral and Morris comes in from Vegas. He's playing the Cave but not that night. He gets up on our stage in the OK Corral and sings that Ray Price song *For The Good Times*. After he's done he reaches over and hugs his good friend Peter Hamlin, who was sitting in on drums, and in the process they knocked over a cymbal stand. I thought, 'Hey, no big deal,' but my drummer, Andy McLean, got bent out of shape. When we were sitting down on our break, we saw Andy and Morris going at it, toe to toe. Wayne Gust and I go over to the altercation. And Morris is apologetic. He's trying to give Andy some money. He's sorry he upset the guy's equipment. He was being very gracious. And Andy hit Morris on his shoulder with his drumsticks. Morris says, 'You shouldn't have done that.' Now Andy is down on the floor and Morris is sitting on his chest. I turned to Wayne and I said, 'Andy's taking Tai Kwan Do, you know.' And Wayne says, 'I think he needs a new teacher.'

All of a sudden there was Morris, and I said, 'that's my guy! He's done it! He's on *Merv Griffin*! You can't do better than that!'

"Morris was in really good shape in those days. He was a tough guy. But he was very gracious, and when we stepped in he let the drummer up and that was that. End of story."

The next time that Gordie Walker met Morris, Gordie was playing the bar in the American Hotel on Main Street adjacent to the CN Railway Station. In 1979, it was one of the better-paying gigs in town, but it was a rough crowd and it took guts to play there. Gordie was a local hero, famous now among bar patrons throughout the city. Morris was playing to a different crowd, a mix of yuppies, tourists, nurses, firemen, and police department employees that comprised his West Coast fan base. When the word got out through the Morris Bates Fan Club newsletter that Morris was coming to town, young people would travel hundreds of miles from remote reserves to attend his shows and maybe get to come back stage and get his signature on a poster. However, fame and fortune also had downsides that Morris constantly dealt with, especially when he returned to Canada where fans adored him, but musicians that had not made it big in Hollywood or Nevada sometimes resented his success.

As Gordie Walker recalls, "Morris was playing the Cave and he came in after his show with this whole entourage." Walker had been elated when he saw Morris on *The Merv Griffin Show*, but he now had a totally different reaction to seeing Bates with his "Vegas entourage," which was, most likely, merely some band members, lighting guys, sound technicians, and their wives out on the town. As Walker recalls, "I remember thinking, 'Jesus, there's something wrong here. He's got all these followers. And I was angry. He brought 'em from Vegas. He paid the freight . . .'"

When the word got out through the Morris Bates Fan Club newsletter that Morris was coming to town, young people would travel hundreds of miles from remote reserves to attend his shows.

Morris told Walker that he had set aside some front row tickets for him for the show the next night at the Cave. Walker showed up the next night, but he was still bristling with his angry reaction to seeing his old buddy with a foreign entourage. He believed that Bates had become "arrogant" even though he was ushered in and shown to his seat in the front row of the number one nightclub in Vancouver. "My whole point was," he reiterates, "that *they* weren't his friends. I was angry as hell."

Morris may have felt a lot like Elvis must have felt at times when his Memphis Mafia accompanied him wherever he went. It was tough dealing with old friends who felt resentment because the star they had once known as one of their high-school pals or bar –room and pals had made it big in tinsel town or on the Vegas Strip. It was tough when you were resented because you traveled with a protective envelope of friends, relatives, band members, bodyguards, and a raggedy assortment of hangers-on dubbed a star's "entourage." In some countries where Morris and his musicians were scheduled to perform, an army of bodyguards was absolutely necessary.

After the show, which Walker admits was "flawless, awesome, and professional," the local bar musician went backstage where he was admitted to a dressing room. He claims he saw Morris grab an unauthorized fan by the collar and push him toward bouncers who threw the young fan out. And he saw red, vowing he would never forgive Morris. A year later, Gordie Walker was once again playing the American Hotel and who should walk in but Morris Bates to invite Gordie out to lunch.

"Gordie Walker and a lot of the local musicians resented me at that time," Morris says, "because I couldn't use them in my act. There were a lot of restrictions to get Canadian musicians into Vegas. And there are a lot of good players who can't play Elvis — they're great players but they can't play Elvis — and my show was choreographed, every note and every bar was arranged. You'd be amazed at how many hotshot musicians can mess up *Heartbreak Hotel.*

"I had a rule that guys who played for me could read music, read the arrangements for the show numbers, but a lot of those guys couldn't read music. They were still my friends, but I couldn't use them in my shows. A lot of Vancouver musicians at that time were into bands, but I wasn't a band. I had a show and running the show meant that Richard and I were running a business. There were a lot of logistics and we hired the best guys that we could find — the bottom line is that it is hard to be truthful and diplomatic at the same time."

A few years later, in the mid-nineties when Morris was leaving the office on Main Street where he was working and heading up the street to get into his pickup truck and go home, he ran into some people that were walking really fast, and he was curious. He wondered where they were going. "They were walking briskly by me," Morris recalls, "and I asked them where they were going in such a hurry. 'We're going to see Gordie Walker at the Marr!' they said, 'he's already fallen off the stage three times!' For the downtown eastside, Gordie was a beloved entertainer. He could sell

In a business where an entertainer's success is measured by liquor sales, Gordie Walker was a champion.

more beer in Vancouver's downtown eastside at places like the Marr Hotel than any other guy. In a business where an entertainer's success is measured by liquor sales, Gordie Walker was a champion."

Old Trails

Back in his home stomping grounds, Morris rehearsed a stripped down lineup of musicians in Vancouver in preparation for his first Canadian tour in five years. He had "learned the game of Las Vegas" the hard way, but he still had thousands of fans in western Canada, and they turned out enthusiastically to see the homeboy who had become a star in Vegas. There were many familiar faces along the way.

As drummer Scott Anderson recalls, "Sometime in the spring of 1982, I was in Fort St John on the last leg of the Elvis, Elvis, Elvis tour, and I got a call from Morris. He was calling from Vegas and he was putting together a band for a Canadian tour. Leroy Stephens was in that band; Wayne Gust was in that band, and a Bulgarian piano player by the name of Steven. Gisele Kaufmann was on lights and we had Larry Volen on sax and Bill Clark on trumpet."

"Coming back to Canada after all those years in Vegas made me feel assured and confident," Morris relates, "but I was not ready for the reality of being an Indian in Canada once again. It was my first time returning to Canada with my new girlfriend, Kimberlee, and my first Canadian road trip in years. I was excited to be working with my old friend, Dennis Compo, who was coordinating the tour. We left Vegas and met up with Wayne Gust in LA. Wayne would be playing guitar on the first leg of the tour. We drove up to Frisco and stayed the night and continued on to Vancouver, driving all day and night and arriving at the border crossing at about 5:00 a.m. in the morning. We cleared customs and made sure our visas were in order at immigration as we had a couple of Americans and a motor home coming in from Nevada.

"We had a couple of days before our opening at the International Plaza Hotel in North Vancouver, so we decided to check into a motel in downtown Vancouver. I'd heard great things about the showroom and the caliber of talent they were bringing in, and, on top of that, the Plaza was located on leased land from the Squamish Indian Band. I was definitely coming home. We were road-weary and totally burnt out when we pulled into the parking lot of the motel on Burrard Street and I got out and went into the lobby to get a room. Big surprise, the matronly but overly stern front desk lady assured me they had no rooms available. I looked out the window of the lobby at the vacancy sign that was blinking on and off. The parking lot was empty. But there was no room for me. My gold American Express card, ten thousand dollar's worth of gold jewelry, and my gold flaked late model Cadillac sitting outside the lobby was not enough to get me a room. The lady at the front desk assured me that if I did not vacate the premises she would call the police. 'There are plenty of rooms available on Granville or Hastings' Street,' she told me.

But I was not ready for the reality of being an Indian in Canada once again.

"I felt a sickening knot in the pit of my stomach as I walked back to the car and told Kim that they had no rooms. She said, 'Bullshit!' and stormed into the motel office. In about five minutes she peeked out of the motel office and waved a motel room key. The matronly lady at the front desk had rented her a room. Welcome home."

With veteran players on board for the Canadian tour, Morris no longer had to rehearse day and night for two weeks to whip his band into shape. As Scott Anderson remembers, it all came together pretty smoothly. "Right after Morris finished up at Vegas World, he came up here to Canada and we played the Plazazz Showroom in the International Plaza Hotel in North Vancouver. Pamela Martin from Channel 8 News and all of the media people came down to one of the gigs during our weeks at the Plaza."

Vancouver Province music critic Tom Harrison titled his full-page May 19, 1982 story: "Ladies still love the way Morris Bates does Elvis." Harrison reported that "all the women love Morris

All the women love Morris ... They clamber to the front of the stage at the Plaza Hotel to receive the scarves he lovingly drapes around their shoulders just like Elvis Presley used to do in Las Vegas.

... They clamber to the front of the stage at the Plaza Hotel to receive the scarves he lovingly drapes around their shoulders just like Elvis Presley used to do in Las Vegas. During *Hound Dog* a woman makes him a gift of a small plush puppy, and later on at the start of *(Let Me Be Your) Teddy Bear* another woman gives him a stuffed Panda, and everybody, men and women alike, rise and applaud Morris on his rendition of *My Way*."

"Morris really believes in what's he doing," Dennis Compo told Harrison after the show. "He really puts his soul into it."

"I take the songs and do the best I can with them," Morris confided. "I love doing it, and people love to see me doing it. God knows what I'll do when they stop coming."

Vancouver Sun critic Lee Bacchus was not as enthusiastic in his appraisal. The May 18th 1982 story he wrote for the entertainment section bore the bold headline: 'Missing: One Streak of Memphis Meanness.'

"I guess I left it at the US-Canada border," Morris says, "and the Plaza was about to get even more unnerving in the weeks that followed that opening night. I did smile when I read his critique where he wrote, 'Morris could sing circles around most Soul singers.' After all, I had sung shoulder to shoulder with legendary Memphis Soul singer, Wilson Pickett, in South Africa. But I didn't have too much time to spend reading my reviews in the daily newspapers — the old saying about death and taxes was about to rear its ugly head.

"On our return from Asia, Richard had worked out a deal with American Express to take care of a $25,000 credit card debt, but Richard wasn't with me this time, so it was me who fielded a call from the hotel manager informing me that Revenue Canada was downstairs armed with a 'garnishee order'. When I got down to the lobby, the two taxmen were peering into the showroom. I introduced myself and we shook hands and they got right to the point, asking me who owned all the music equipment. 'The musicians own their instruments and amps, and Long &

McQuade owns the sound system,' I told them. Then they asked me what the neon sign was worth. 'It isn't worth anything to anybody unless your name is *Morris*,' I snapped back at them. I was quickly becoming annoyed.

"We moved the conversation to the restaurant and they handed me the garnishee order. I read it and thought for a moment and said, 'You can't touch my money; this hotel is on Indian land.' Now *they* looked stunned. 'I'm a Status Indian,' I continued, 'and you know the law. Any Indian to make a living on an Indian Reserve is tax exempt.'

"This wasn't a normal reserve — a piece of land with just rocks and no water — there was a hotel, a Vegas style showroom, a shopping center and an office tower, but it was *indeed* an Indian Reservation. The taxmen said, 'You better get that Status Card, we want to see it.' I went up to my room and got my Status Card and showed it to them. Once again my Status Card had saved my butt. I felt reassured for the moment and sat down and worked out a deal with the taxmen, and gave them a series of postdated checks, assuring them that they could find me by simply opening up any entertainment section of any newspaper in Canada. Richard would have been proud of me."

You can't touch my money; this hotel is on Indian land.

Scott Anderson was happy to be back in the fold and looking forward to hitting the road once again with Morris Bates. As he recalls, "We headed out and played Calgary and Edmonton a bunch of times and went all the way to Manitoba. We did Canada for 49 weeks. To summarize, I would say that Morris put on that show night after night with pure willpower and grit, and the audiences got their money's worth!"

Morris remembers the first leg of the journey for all the wrong reasons. As he recalls, "I sent Scotty Anderson and our bass player Leroy Stephens on ahead to Calgary in my Caddy. Even though Scotty and Leroy often terrorized each other, they respected each other's talent. Together they were as solid a rhythm section as you could get. Wayne Gust was always conning me out of airfare in those days, claiming long road trips were an inconvenience to one or another of his many ailments. A few years before this, Wayne and I had experienced the Buddy Holly syndrome when the pilot of a small pontoon plane we were flying in from Kelowna to Nelson lost sight of the river he was following through the mountains and we spent some nervous minutes white knuckling our seats until he came out of a cloud bank and we began our descent onto Kootenay Lake.

It was a beautiful Sunday afternoon. And the pubs and liquor stores were closed. What could go wrong?

"I gave in and bought him a plane ticket, knowing he would reimburse me with his winnings from his first Lotto jackpot. So Wayne would fly along with Kim and I, while Scotty and Leroy drove to Calgary in my light brown and gold metal-flaked 4-door Brougham Caddy. That car had tinted windows, wire mags, and gangster white walls. It sat low and always looked out of place in Canada — a total heat score, plus it had Nevada license plates. They were grinning from ear to ear as I gave Scotty the keys and reminded him to be careful because it was a long haul for one driver and Leroy didn't drive. As I was giving them gas money and reading them the riot act, they stood there smiling like they just ate the canary. Scotty and Leroy both reassured me that they would treat my car with utmost care; they'd see me in Calgary, have a good flight. And as I glanced back over my shoulder, I could see that Scotty had his arm around Leroy's shoulder as they walked toward my car with the keys dangling casually off his finger. It was a beautiful Sunday afternoon. I trusted Scotty. Leroy was basically harmless. And the pubs and liquor stores were closed. What could go wrong?

"Kim and Wayne and I got to Calgary, checked into the Sandman Inn and spent the rest of the afternoon with the hotel chain's general manager Guy Fox and his wife, Marianne. They were always so gracious. We got along great — so well, in fact, that he would soon become my manager. Kim and I went out for the evening to a popular local eatery and ended up sitting in a booth next to Leslie Nielsen and his manager. While we were eating our dinner, we could hear Leslie and his manager trying to figure out how to jumpstart his career — they were really in a heated discussion. After listening to them all evening, I've not found Leslie to be funny or entertaining in any of his films. But he *was* in the movies and I wasn't. When Kim and I got back to our hotel room later that night the message light on the telephone was flashing. I phoned the front desk. The message was simple. 'Morris, your car has been impounded by the Lytton RCMP. We are hitching to Calgary.' It was from Scotty.

"There are no words to describe what happened next because that is exactly what happened – nothing. I just sat there. Communications systems back then were not like they are today where everybody has their personal cell phone. It was one step better than Morse code or the CPR Telegraph service. With only land-based telephones, and it somehow seems ancient to use that word 'telephone' today, you could only make a call to where the person was. If you didn't have a predetermined location or destination to meet or call, you were basically SOL. My musicians were hitchhiking through the Rocky Mountains. They might as well be, let me think, hitchhiking through *the Rocky Mountains* . . . I would just have to sit and wait. I left a message with the front desk clerk for the band members in the truck to give me a call when they checked in, no matter what time of day or night that might be, but I couldn't fall asleep and lay there watching the test pattern until about three in the morning, when the phone rang and I picked it up. It was Larry Volen, my sax player, and the most responsible member of the band. Larry told me that when the truck had left Vancouver Scotty and Leroy were behind them. They hadn't seen my Caddy since. They had kept to the speed limit the whole 660 miles and didn't think Scotty had passed the truck. By two o'clock Monday afternoon I was becoming seriously worried. Then Scotty phoned and told me that they had hitched a ride into Banff and would be in Calgary in a couple of hours and in time for sound check. He told me he'd explain the details to me later on.

"When they finally got to the Sandman Inn, Scotty told me that they had been caught speeding in the canyon and the RCMP

> My musicians were hitchhiking through the Rocky Mountains. They might as well be, let me think, hitchhiking through the Rocky Mountains . . . I would just have to sit and wait.

had confiscated my car. So they had made a sign that said 'Calgary, We Will Pay The Gas' and started hitchhiking. We hadn't known that in those days it was illegal for a Canadian to drive an American car in Canada without an American being in the car with them. Scotty, of course, is Canadian. The RCMP told me that I would have to pick my car up in person, and, of course, pay the fine for the speeding ticket and the impound fees. The Caddy sat in the Lytton impound lot all week. I had to fly out of Calgary on a Sunday morning on the only flight they had going to Kamloops and catch a Greyhound bus that took me west on the Trans Canada Highway to Lytton. When I got there, I had to explain to the constables on duty that the car was indeed mine and that the registration did match my name on my Indian Status Card, giving me the right to own an American car even though I was a Canadian Indian and had a Nevada driver's license. They were cool once I explained who I was, and that I realized they were just doing their job. I autographed some souvenir photos and posters, paid and autographed the speeding ticket, then drove all the way back to Calgary and arrived in time to get ready for my first show."

By the time that they moved on to the Mayfield Inn in Edmonton all was forgiven even if not forgotten, and the boys in the band were ready for some totally new and even more challenging adventures.

I autographed some souvenir photos and posters, paid and autographed the speeding ticket, then drove all the way back to Calgary.

"Steven the Bulgarian was a great guy and an excellent piano player," Morris recalls. "He could really play rock & roll piano. There was this one time that he bet all the guys in the band that he could drink a beer standing on his head. We were playing the Mayfield Inn in Edmonton and we were getting paid real good money, but the hotel manager was nervous about having rock & roll musicians hanging around his hotel. So when we had one night off, I talked with the guys before I went to have dinner with Kim. Before I left, I told Scotty that he was the bandleader, he was in charge, 'So, don't hang around the hotel and mess up!' At 8:00 a.m. the next morning, the front desk called and told me to be in the manager's office ASAP. When I got down there, the manager was all over me. Some of my guys had messed up some carpet in the lounge and one of them had puked all over one of the waitresses.

"I had a band meeting right there and then. I had all the guys in one room and I said, 'Okay, Scotty, what were you doing when Steve puked on the cocktail waitress?'

"And Scotty says, 'I was holding him by the feet.'

"Those guys were always pulling stuff like that, but that stunt could have cost us our jobs. I was getting ten grand for the week, and paying all of them real good money, and that stunt could have put all of us out of work."

We had a deal where you would have to buy a drink for a guy if he could remember where we had been for the last three weeks.

Musicians had to deal with boredom and fatigue on these relentless tours. Morris always had a vision, with will power and stamina to achieve his goals, but his band mates often found themselves victims of road burn and homesickness. "We were on the road for 49 weeks in a row," Anderson points out. "And when we were relaxing, we had a deal where you would have to buy a drink for a guy if he could remember where we had been for the last three weeks — there were definitely some brain cells being lost on some of those road trips, that's for sure."

Gisele Kaufmann remembers that the boys in the band often devised their own diversions in order to deal with the long distances they traveled across the flat Canadian prairies. "We would stop and get out of the bus," she recalls, "because everybody had to take a pee. And then the guys would find a target and have these rock throwing contests, and we would be there, like, forever . . . It was just guy stuff."

Gisele also credits Morris with being an inspiring entertainer to work with. "Morris was a great boss," she confides. "You never even looked at him as a boss. You respected him as an entertainer. He pissed you off sometimes. I have to say that. We had our moments. We had arguments about stupid, stupid . . . stupid stuff. Being on the road gets to you. These are the people you are around all the time and these things get to you. But it's like arguing with your big brother, and then you get over it — you say you're sorry, and you go on."

As the tour continued, the boys in the band found themselves playing more and more Sandman Inn showrooms. This had come about because Dennis Compo had booked Morris into a Sandman Inn in Calgary for the second engagement on the first leg of the tour and Morris had found a kindred soul in the hotel chain's general manager, Guy Fox. "Dennis Compo was booking our Canadian tour," Morris recalls, "and he set us up with Guy Fox and after a while Guy began acting as my manager. He booked all of the Sandman hotels. We played a lot of Sandman Inns, and he set up a lot of one-nighters in other venues and towns, too."

To promote Morris, Fox designed a new poster that read: "Direct from Las Vegas" and displayed quotes from Morris's appearances on *The Merv Griffin Show*, *The Dick Cavett Show*, and *20/20 with Geraldo Rivera*. "He paid me six thousand a week," Morris recalls, "and out of that he took a one thousand-dollar commission. He had a real beautiful home and he treated me like a son. He was a musician himself and he used to have the guys in the band over for barbecues. He was just a real nice man."

To promote Morris, Guy Fox designed a new poster that read: 'Direct from Las Vegas' and displayed quotes from Morris's appearances on *The Merv Griffin Show*, *The Dick Cavett Show*, and *20/20* with *Geraldo Rivera*.

Gisele Kaufmann remembers that: "Guy Fox was an entertainer himself. He was a German guy and he would sometimes get up and sing with the show. We were there for New Years Eve, and we got to know his wife, and he would get up and sing. He was like a straight Liberace, a real entertainer."

"We played the Calgary Sandman for two months straight," Morris continues, "which was a real treat in the middle of that long road trip, and we were able to get some sort of normal rhythm. It was a beautiful club and he treated us really well. We got fifty percent off all our food and drinks. I had a suite and the other guys were bunked two guys to a room. After I finished my shows I would go up to my room and the band would play until the end of the night.

"I remember that Leroy wouldn't drink much during the shows, but after the band was finished for the night, he would get into it pretty heavy. He was rooming with Scotty, and Scotty would buy food and put it in their mini-fridge in the room so that he would have something to eat late at night. Then Leroy would come in when Scotty had gone to sleep and eat all of Scotty's munchies.

"Scotty got pretty pissed off and one night he got under the bed and waited for Leroy to come in. So here comes Leroy drunker than a hoot owl and he goes straight for Scotty's food. Scotty grabbed both of Leroy's ankles and Leroy leapt up and fell on his face and Scotty is yelling at him, 'don't touch my food! Buy your own bleeping food!' It was just crazy.

> He only wore an Elvis costume for the seventies segment, putting on the white American Eagle suit because people loved it.

"Another time we were in a band house and Leroy was still eating Scotty's food. Scotty was always pretty skinny and he crawled up into one of those big old kitchen cupboards and shut the cupboard door. And Leroy opens up the door to the cupboard and there is Scotty, and he says, 'Hey Leroy, don't eat my food!' And Leroy damn near passed out on the floor that time. Every day of every week there was stuff going on all through that long Canadian tour."

Morris continued to modify his show, performing plenty of Elvis songs every night along with an evolving repertoire, though he only wore an Elvis costume for the seventies segment, putting on the white American Eagle suit because people loved it.

Union Plaza

After crisscrossing Canada with his stripped down show, Morris returned to the States. There were some personnel changes with Leroy Stephens, Larry Volen, and Gisele Kaufmann returning to Vancouver. "We played a couple of dates in the Midwest," Morris recalls, "and then we returned to Las Vegas."

It wasn't long before Morris was playing the Union Plaza in Glitter Gulch, where management had bought his show and was paying him good money. His tribute to Elvis had evolved, but it was his bread and butter, and even though he wanted to move on, people always clamored for him to sing those Elvis songs they loved so much.

"It was still as crazy as it always was in Vegas," Morris confides, "and I used to go up to Michael Silvey's place and chill out with Michael and his wife, Lori. Michael and Lori were totally in love with each other. I had to go somewhere to get away from the craziness. Michael was from Saskatchewan, but he had joined the U.S. Army and fought in Vietnam and done some R&R in Bangkok. He was president of a local motorcycle club, and we both loved to ride motorcycles. We had a lot in common and I felt safe when he was by my side. Nobody was going to mess with Michael. He was, like, my Red West. We went everywhere together. I guess he enjoyed being with a celebrity at times, but it was more than that — we were really close friends. Michael played bass guitar, and for a while he and Wayne Gust had a little bar band together that played lounge gigs there in North Vegas."

Morris was the best, I mean, some of the guys they had doing Elvis were not very good at all, they didn't look like Elvis and they couldn't sing.

"Michael and Morris were really close in those days, real tight buddies," Lora Silvey recalls, "and Morris always called me 'Lori'. Morris was the best, I mean, some of the guys they had doing Elvis were not very good at all, they didn't look like Elvis and they couldn't sing. But Morris was great. He had a lot of fans."

"Michael was the Nevada State Trapshooting Champion," Morris remembers. "We used to go trapshooting together. He'd shoot them; I'd shoot at them. He had a trophy case full of trophies he had won and a cabinet with all those beautiful guns that were in his collection, and years later he came up to Vancouver and visited with Wayne and me."

Morris was happy to be living in one place again, playing the Union Plaza. He played the Plaza twice, the second time for a full year with another four-wall contract, and ventured out of Vegas for lucrative one-night stands in Texas, Kansas and Tennessee.

"One year I didn't have to work much at all," he recalls, "but I liked it in Vegas and LA and I stayed there. I didn't come back to Canada. Then one night when I was out on the town, I went into the Nevada Palace and learned that Gary Baldwin was the guy in charge of the casino. I had worked for Gary at the Landmark and we got along pretty well. He was bringing in some real good acts to the lounge in the casino, and we cut a deal where I would go in there and be Morris Bates. I wouldn't dress up like Elvis at all. I still sang some Elvis songs, but I sang my own material and all of the other songs that I had always slipped into my tribute shows from time to time."

> We cut a deal where I would go in there and be Morris Bates. I wouldn't dress up like Elvis at all.

Playing a lounge gig in Vegas is a lot different than playing a showroom, but the bottom line is still the same — putting people in chairs — and at first Morris was able to pack the lounge. However, people complained that they had come to see Morris do his Elvis tribute. "I was singing all sorts of stuff," Morris explains, "but the fans just wanted to hear me singing Elvis songs. I had earned Gary's respect during our run at the Landmark, so when he cornered me after one of my sets and wanted to talk to me, I knew what was up when he said, 'Morris, you got a sec?'

"The Nevada Palace is located on Boulder Highway on the way to Hoover Dam, a fair distance from the Vegas Strip. When a guy from Utah had brought a group of about 20 people all the way out to the Nevada Palace Hotel & Casino and I didn't perform my Elvis show, you could hear him bitching all the way back in Utah. I knew it and could feel it. Morris Bates would have to take a back seat to the monster I had created – do what I had started out to do — make people happy and entertain my audiences. Morris in the white jumpsuit was back.

"Gary asked if I would do at least one Elvis show a night in costume to appease the people who had come especially to see me do Elvis. So I ended up playing one Elvis show for lounge money instead of the money I made doing my original Elvis show.

"I realized that by doing my Elvis show I had sort of done a deal with the devil, so to speak. That's what the audience always wanted and I was totally type-caste as an Elvis impersonator. It was ironic. The Silver Slipper had spent a million dollars advertising and creating 'Morris as Elvis'. At the Landmark, Richard and I had spent tens of thousands of dollars advertising 'Morris' on billboards. Now I was spending thousands of dollars to be 'Morris Bates' and not drawing the audiences, but *Morris* was packing the house.

"I finished out the contract, took some time off, and booked six weeks of engagements for November and December in the western United States. Our first stop was Hutchinson, Kansas. The owner of the club owned a plane and he used to fly to Vegas to catch our shows and was excited to have us perform at his club. I'd put an outrageous price tag on the show and he didn't even blink. The club held about 1500 people and was gorgeous, and I understood why he threw in all the extra perks and didn't blink. The engagement sold out.

"I'd changed a few band members since the gig at the Palace and was sorry to lose John Simmons. He was the original guitar player for the Righteous Brothers and kind of a local legend in Vegas and not only for just his guitar playing. John wouldn't travel, and as we looked for a replacement, the guitar slingers came out of the woodwork. A young slinger who'd paid his dues doing 16-hour shifts on guitar and pedal steel at the Silver Dollar Saloon was guitarist Jimmy Touk. He caught up to me one night and said he had heard I was looking or an axe man to travel. I asked if he knew anything about Elvis. He said he knew every Elvis song he ever sang and if he didn't his brother did; then paused for a second and said he didn't have a brother. As it turned out he didn't need one.

He was the original guitar player for the Righteous Brothers and kind of a local legend in Vegas and not only for just his guitar playing.

"The club was huge and the dance floor was up higher than the floor so it was a natural stage for my show. Kim sang backup along with this girl I'd hired through a Vegas booking agency to open my show for me as well as sing harmonies. She was a centerfold model for *Penthouse* magazine and she autographed a ton of them. During my show the soundman videoed me and showed me on these two big TV screens at each end of the club. It was unique to see myself performing in real time on TV. I had a lot of fun with that. We finished the tour and headed back to Vegas for Christmas.

"I was coming up the Strip and decided to see what was happening in my old haunt, the Silver Slipper. As I sat down some of the old regular staff said Hi and Sal the bartender brought me the same old same old and wished me a merry Christmas. 'Jeez, Morris,' he said, 'how long you been in Vegas now? About 10 years?' I thought for a second and said, 'no, not quite, but a long, long time.' I didn't even finish my drink. I went home and thought about it and decided to move to southern California.

I didn't even finish my drink. I went home and thought about it and decided to move to southern California.

The boys are back in town: Scott Anderson (drums), Larry Volen (sax), Leroy Stephens (bass), Bill Clark (trumpet), Wayne Gust (guitar), Steve the Bulgarian (keyboards).

Right: Gordie Walker

THE **ELVIS PRESLEY** STORY

Direct From LAS VEGAS

★ Starring ★

"One of America's Foremost Elvis Impressionists."
Merv Griffin Show
Las Vegas 1978

"Morris has the distinction of being able to perform Elvis's career in its entirety."
Geraldo Rivera 20/20
1978

"The longest running one man show to play Las Vega$ other than Wayne Newton."
Dick Cavett Show
1983

Management Blue Note Entertainment Services (403) 949-3922
Produced by R.D. ENTERPRISES

Actual Photo of Morris During Performance

Paying homage to the King at Graceland: Al, Hughie, Gil, and Morris

Vegas

RENO
TAHOE
ATLANTIC CITY

Los ANGELES
HERALD EXAMINER

Sunday, April 26 1981

Morris Has Outlasted All The King's Men

Savalas Off Telly, A Hit On Big Screen

Sammy Davis Goes To The Movies

Caesars' Omnimiax Is Alive

LV Scenery: Being Seen At The Scene

Ringo Starr's Latest 'Hazzard'

The Great Pretender

Settling Down

Morris Bates & the Cadillacs

By this time Morris had been doing his Elvis tribute show for 14 years and the thrill was gone. As he recalls, "the bright lights of Las Vegas had lost their luster. It seemed that life was passing me by and I was standing still. It was time to get out of Dodge."

When Morris decided to move to southern California, he spread out a map. Then he closed his eyes and put his finger on it, and told Kim that this is where they would live — at Lincoln and Magnolia in Anaheim. On weekends, he worked in a production show called America Sings that played conventions in venues like the Disneyland Hotel. He was performing 10-minute Elvis tributes for really good money, but he still wasn't getting any satisfaction.

"Finally," he says, "the magic was gone. Kim and I were having relationship problems and decided to have a sabbatical from each other. My career wasn't going anywhere, so I went back to Vancouver. I was feeling homesick, so I went home. I got a call that a local hotel in Williams Lake had gone bankrupt and was in receivership, being run by someone from the bank. I got hold of him and made a deal to play there as a house band until it was sold. The manager was a man by the name of Mervin (later to be known as 'Swervin' Mervin'), who had no experience at all in the

My career wasn't going any-where, so I went back to Vancouver. I was feeling homesick, so I went home.

hotel or entertainment business. I took the gig and we had a blast for six months." Morris called the new act Morris Bates & the Cadillacs.

"They had shut down the restaurant and all of the rooms," he recalls, "but they kept the Ranch Hotel Pub open, and we had the run of the place — we all had rooms of our own! Wayne was in the band. Leroy was in the band. Roger Satel was on guitar and Al Forsythe was on drums. We had to be on stage at nine and we quit at one, and we could do any-thing that we wanted." Taking full advantage of "Swervin' Mervin's" inexperience, the boys in the band became teenagers all over again.

"Mervin was so nice," Morris reminisces, "and we were pack-ing the club, so he was making money, and we were just having fun. We had wet T-shirt contests and we sold water bottles . . . I just wanted to get up there and play. I played electric guitar and I sang. I just wanted to have fun. I was still making a reasonable liv-ing doing something that I liked to do."

While Morris was at the Ranch Hotel, Kim flew up from Ana-heim, and he convinced her to sing backup vocals with the band. "She had sung with me in Kansas before this," he recalls, "and we had put together a good show so she sang with me again. She was with me for a month or so, but she had to return to LA because she had a four-year-old daughter, Danielle, that she needed to take care of."

After completing his six-month engagement at the Ranch Hotel, Morris hooked up with his old booking agent pal, Chris Siller, and hit the road. "Chris started out booking me as Morris Bates & the Cadillacs," Morris recalls, "but as the weeks turned into months we were getting more and more requests for me to do Elvis, and I was brought back into the fold once again per-forming two Elvis shows a night for very good money.

"Before Kim flew back to LA, we must have conceived our daughter, Brittany Lee, and when Kim came back up to Canada we decided that we were going to get married. Kim rejoined me in Edmonton at Klondike Days, where we were playing shows with Loretta Lynn's daughter, Cissy Lynn, who was booked as 'the daughter of a daughter of a coal-miner.' We played Red Deer and in Calgary I bought her a really nice diamond ring. Kim flew home again to Orange County, but Customs confiscated her engagement ring and she was really upset. Later my mom had to bring the ring to Vegas for the ceremony.

"Kim and I had decided we would get married in Vegas on December 27, 1987. We got the honeymoon suite at the Union Plaza. My best man was my brother BJ, but in Vegas they often have more than one guy stand up for you, so Michael Silvey was also there for me."Privacy has been something Morris has cherished during his 10-year stint in Nevada. When Morris and Kim exchanged marriage vows, all that local journalists could learn was that Morris had married a stunningly beautiful brunette who had won a Miss Orange County beauty pageant.

I was brought back into the fold once again performing two Elvis shows a night for very good money.

Morris and Kim's marriage marked the end of an era. It was Morris's first marriage and Kim's second. The newlyweds were headed for Canada, where they would eventually make their permanent home.

"I had taken my truck to Vegas so we could pick up our furniture, which was stored in Anaheim," he recalls. "I had a Ford diesel that had a special 100-gallon fuel tank installed for long hauls. We drove nonstop from Vegas to Anaheim and straight on through to Vancouver, unloaded the furniture, picked up my stage equipment and caught a ferry to Vancouver Island, all in one swipe. Kim and I officially started our honeymoon in Duncan, BC on New Year's Eve 1987. As soon as the Duncan engagement was over, we went back to Vancouver and I dropped Kim off at my mom's apartment.

"I knew how important it was to have Kim get an Indian Status Card so that I could have her put under my medical plan, which is covered by the Department of Indian Affairs. Being my wife, she would get legal Indian status, but I would still have to sponsor her for 10 years to get her Canadian citizenship. What the hell, we were in love. My first step was to register our marriage. So

The newlyweds were headed for Canada, where they would eventually make their permanent home.

I drove down to Hastings and Granville to the Department of Indian Affairs office, but couldn't find a parking spot until I was down on Cordova Street by the Army & Navy store. Even in those days Gastown was an infamous area of town, but I was in a hurry to get all my business done.

"By the time that I finally got all the legal work taken care of, it was getting dark, and, as I was walking toward my parked car, I could see that my driver's side window was smashed in. I started running full tilt. I had a lot of stuff in that car that I hadn't unpacked. The thief hadn't taken my eagle suit but had stolen my black, custom-made Gibson guitar. I have never really gotten attached to very many material objects, except for maybe my *Morris* ring, but who'd want that? I felt sick, and for the first time since I was a kid I felt scared. Who would do this to me? Didn't they know it was *my* guitar? I walked around the car for a few moments. I was stunned. I couldn't believe what had happened. As I calmed down, I got angry. I reached into the car and grabbed a few of my Elvis posters that had pictures of me with my ebony guitar and ran up Cordova Street all the way to the Vancouver Police Station. My hands were shaking so much that I could hardly fill out the incident report. All the time I was thinking, 'We're wasting time . . . why don't the cops take the poster and go find the person who stole my guitar?'

"I finished filling out the report and took off into the streets. It was dark outside and the underbelly of Main and Hastings was out in full force. I went through the bars on Hastings asking if anyone had seen anybody trying to sell a black guitar. 'It looks like this,' I said, showing the poster of me with my guitar, and telling anybody who cared enough to listen that there was a reward. I hit every bar and pawnshop in a sixteen block radius and came up with nothing. I never did find my guitar. If anyone reads this and knows where it is, there's still a reward.

I never did find my guitar. If anyone reads this and knows where it is, there's still a reward.

The Honeymoon Tour

"I never really considered performing to be work." Morris remarks. "For me the work was always between the shows. Most people work five days a week for fifty weeks, take their two weeks of vacation, and then travel and cram as much excitement as they possibly can endure into those precious 14 days. I was traveling from city to city, staying in the best hotels, and usually playing the most prestigious venues. The two hours on stage nightly was the best time of any given day. My days were free to explore the local tourist attractions and eat at good restaurants. I could sleep until noon and not feel guilty about not making my bed. If I had worked too strenuously the night before, I could just order room service.

"Our honeymoon was quite lengthy by most standards. It didn't seem necessary to run off to Hawaii or Vegas or Disneyland, not even Hong Kong, Africa, or England, as I had been to all of those places. Driving up through Spuzzum and the Fraser Canyon into the breathtaking Rocky Mountains, and on to Edmonton, the City of Champions, I was euphoric enjoying the beautiful panorama of western Canada.

"Kim sang backup all through that honeymoon tour. She didn't really start to show that she was pregnant until about two months before she gave birth to Brittany. She was still glowing when Chris Siller booked me for the longest single gig-to-gig driving road trip of my career. We drove from the town of High Level at the northernmost tip of Alberta to Northfork, Virginia on the eastern coast of the United States. We had a week to get there. No problem.

"As any hardworking musician knows when you are about to cross any international border, be prepared for cockamamie regulations preventing you from entering the country, and customs and immigration officials' 'I just don't like you' attitudes. So I was prepared — one Indian Status card, one BC driver's license, one Alberta driver's license, one Nevada driver's license,

One Indian Status card, one BC driver's license, one Alberta driver's license, one Nevada driver's license, one California driver's license, one passport with extra added pages, and one personal 'I've been everywhere, man' attitude.

one California driver's license, one passport with extra added pages, and one personal 'I've been everywhere, man' attitude.

"An hour before we reached the border I switched vehicles. I had my reasons for doing so. We would be crossing over into the USA at the Sweetgrass, Montana border crossing (Cree and Blackfoot territory), and I wanted to get my ducks all in line. I told Kim to drive across in the car with the Canadian guys and wait for me on the US side. I would follow with the truck and our American bass player Matt Eaglesson so that I could explain all the music equipment onboard. We would be picking up our sax player Gill Herman in Amarillo, Texas because he'd flown home for a couple of days to be with his family. I was cool when I drove up to US Customs and they asked our destination. I told them that we were on a tour of the southeastern US, which would start in Northfork, Virginia. I had most of the contracts in hand. The border guards wanted to look in the back of the equipment truck, which they did, then made some small talk about the music equipment, and, by the way, where were the rest of the guys? I said they were about an hour ahead of me. We would meet up in Great Falls, Montana. The immigration officer then asked to see my bass player's ID. Matt was from Seattle, which was no problem, then the guard asked me for mine. I handed over my Nevada driver's license and my status card. He asked for more, which I had plenty of. Next he asked me to explain all of the different driver's licenses. I told him that I had a residence in Southern California; I used to live in Vegas and still spent a lot of time in Nevada, but had spent most of this past year touring in Canada because I was using a Canadian booking agent.

"'Both of you boys,' he said, calmly, 'can cross the border, but that truck is stayin' in Canada.'

"I said, 'What?'

"He said, 'Your truck has got Alberta plates, it's a diesel and it doesn't meet California emission standards — it's not going into the US.'

"'We're not going to California,' I said, 'we're going to Virginia.'

"'You got cotton in your ears, boy?' he shouted. 'This truck is not going into the US.'

"I got real quiet for a few moments as he was walking away. Then he spun around and said, 'I know what you're thinking, boy. Don't try to cross at any other border crossing. You've been red-flagged and you'll lose your truck, your instruments and probably go to jail.'

"'What am I supposed to do?' I said.

"'Buy another truck, rent one, there's a Ford dealership up the road a bit, about 45 miles. They might be able to help.'

"I drove back to the Canadian side of the border and parked the truck in a border crossing parking lot. Matt and I walked across the border to see Kim and the guys at a restaurant motel complex in Sweetgrass. I told them they'd better get a room because they would be there at least until morning. Then I crossed back into Canada and went to the Ford dealership. They said they could redo the emission system in my truck, but it would take two or three days and cost $5,000. I just shook my head and wondered what I was going to do. Then I drove back to the border crossing to see if the immigration officer had gone home for the day. He hadn't. So I spoke with him again and while I was telling him how important it was to be in Northfork, Virginia, that my career was at stake, that I didn't want to get the reputation of a 'No Show Jones' and stuff like 'in this business, your word is bible . . .' I could tell that he was feeling my desperation. Finally, I sheepishly queried, 'Who is the captain or is there anyone that can possibly help me get this decision overruled or help me out of this predicament?' Without trying to insult him, I asked, 'Is there anyone else I can talk to?' He said that the chief immigration officer would be in at 8:00 a.m. I could speak with him at that time. Then he walked away. It wasn't exactly a 'warm and fuzzy' but it wasn't a flat 'no,' either. There was hope.

"At 8:00 the next morning I pulled my truck up to the border

Both of you boys can cross the border, but that truck is stayin' in Canada.

He had a spit-and-polish military bearing and without uttering a word of greeting he said, 'Where are you from, son?'

crossing and an officer waved me through and told me to park the truck in the immigration parking lot. I was on the American side, but there were still more hoops that I might have to jump through. I got out and saw an older immigration officer approaching me. He had a spit-and-polish military bearing and without uttering a word of greeting he said, 'Where are you from, son?'

"I thought for a moment, wondering if this was a trick question. He looked me right in the eye and said, 'Where's your mama live?' I was dumfounded but managed to say, '1220 Cardero Street in Vancouver, BC.'

"'You live with your mama?'

"I said, 'Yes,' in a plaintive voice that I scarcely recognized as being my own.

"'Well, you have a good trip now,' he said, and, as he was walking away he turned and said, 'I understand you sing a lot of Elvis's songs . . .'

"I said, 'Yes sir!'

"'My grandpa is from Tennessee,' he said, 'beautiful country. You take care now.'

"I was still dumbfounded, wondering what the **** was that all about. As it turned out all they had wanted me to acknowledge was that I had a Canadian address so they could confirm that I would be returning to Canada with my truck and not be selling it in the US and thus violating the US Customs & Immigration Act. As we headed for the bright city lights of Las Vegas, I felt foolish but relieved. We stayed in Vegas for a couple of days and Kimee flew to Southern California to be with her parents. Then we headed east toward Virginia.

Graceland

"We made Amarillo by morning, but my truck was having clutch problems, so we had to shift gears without using the clutch. Fortunately, we were on the interstate with a 100-gallon tank and we didn't have to stop and start a whole lot. We pulled into Memphis at about 4:00 a.m. in the morning and drove down Elvis Presley Boulevard to Graceland.

"There was a security guard sitting in a little guard shack underneath a sign that read ANYONE FOUND ASLEEP ON THE JOB WILL BE AUTOMATICALLY DIMISSED. I woke him up and he was very accommodating, offering us coffee and taking photos of us in front of the big Graceland sign outside the gate. Then he let us in and up onto the grounds as close to the front doorway as we could get without actually walking through the front door. In those days, Graceland wasn't the tourist Mecca that it is today. It was situated in a more shoddy section of town with a lot of used car lots and fast food outlets, and, of course, a lot of storefronts that specialized in Elvis memorabilia. My truck hobbled into Northfork grinding its last gears on the night before we opened.

"I was up at noon and grabbed all the newspapers. They had us in all the trades. I met with the hotel manager and he offered us anything we might need. He told me that opening night was sold out. We were going to have a good run. I hadn't played Vegas for a year and a half, but Northfork was ready for 'The Morris as Elvis Show, direct from Las Vegas.' When I learned that Northfork is home to one of the biggest military bases in the US, I decided to run over *G.I. Blues*.

We pulled into Memphis at about 4:00 a.m. in the morning and drove down Elvis Presley Boulevard to Graceland.

"In the summer of 1987 racism was very much alive and peeking out of every nook and cranny in the South. It wasn't in your face racism, but it was definitely bubbling under the surface. Usually I couldn't remember what I had for breakfast let alone what city we were in, but I do remember a call I got from a club owner as we were heading down to Florida to play a nightclub on the gulf coast. He wanted to know what exactly was the racial makeup of my band? This was the first racial band personnel issue I had faced since way back in '79 when Richard and I had been told that we couldn't bring our African American backup singers to Africa. This club owner sounded pretty serious, though, so I decided not to make light of what he was saying.

I told him that we were four Caucasians, a Tex-Mex from Texas, and myself, the star of the show. I was still thinking on my feet when I added, 'the guy doing the Elvis show, *Morris as Elvis* . . . I'm a . . . North American native person or a Native American First Nations guy. I'm a Canadian Indian, a reasonably fair-skinned Indian if I stay out of the sun kind of guy . . .'

"He seemed cool with the lineup and told me that there had been some positive response and they were looking forward to having the show come to their club. We'll see you when you get here kind of thing.

"Georgia is a tough state. You keep your P's and Q's together there or somebody will mess you up, real good. I always loved the song *Georgia*, but then I also remember what they did to Ray Charles. When I was young I remember singing 'Georgia, Georgia, the whole day through . . .' and this older gentleman said to me 'why don't you sing about Canada?' I really didn't have an answer for that. 'Alberta, Alberta, the whole day through . . . Maybe it could work. I knew *Muk Tuk Annie* by Jimmy Arthur Ordge, and I met Stompin' Tom Connors. Burton Cummings had a song called *Runnin' Back To Saskatoon*, a Canadian classic, but my mind was wandering as it does on road trips. I had been daydreaming in Georgia when we crossed the state line into Florida, and now six cop cruisers were coming after us with lights flashing and sirens wailing. It was *Smokey and the Bandit* all over again or one of those *Blues Brothers* movies, and they were after my truck. So we pulled over and they had us open up the truck to look inside and check out the musical equipment, then informed us that we were required to stop at the Truck Weigh-In Station to declare our load. All double-axel trucks over a certain gross weight had to check in — it was Florida state law. I explained that we had never had that situation and we'd been traveling all over the South. They reprimanded us and reminded me, 'You're in Florida now, boy, ignorance is no excuse for breakin' the law.' They also told us that they checked all commercial trucks as there was a bit of a drug problem there in Florida and you just

> It was *Smokey and the Bandit* all over again or one of those *Blues Brothers* movies.

can't be too careful. We said, 'Yes, sir!' and got the hell out of there as fast as we could. The nightclub in Florida was in a resort town with a beach crowd and young university student clientele. My band, it turned out, was more popular there than I was. I just did one show a night on weeknights and two shows on weekends, and my band handled the rest of the workload.

The first place I went into was a typical bar with neon beer signs and a jukebox playing and a few couples dancing. No one seemed to care or notice me and that was perfect.

"After my show, I had plenty of time to check out the local club scene. One night I saw the name of a New York based band that I had previously met in Saskatoon on a nightclub marquee. The way I remembered them was that they had a big band with a front singer, rhythm section, and four black guys in the horn section. It was a big group for a traveling club band. They had the place a-hoppin'. I got excited when I recognized the lead singer, but where, I wondered, was the horn section? During the singer's break we were both happy to see a familiar face, even though we had only hung out a few times together in Saskatchewan. I asked him where his horn section was, and he told me that they were up the street in a motel.

"'They don't allow black people on the premises here unless they are staff,' he said. I gave him a questioning look and he quipped, 'They make the rules, I don't . . .' I told him we were playing just up the street; I'd catch him later in the week. I checked out a couple of other clubs and then crossed a bridge that was sort of an unofficial border crossing to the black section of town. I didn't really know the difference but it wouldn't have mattered anyway. The first place I went into was a typical bar with neon beer signs and a jukebox playing and a few couples dancing. No one seemed to care or notice me and that was perfect. The bartender asked me if I wanted to buy a drink or a bottle.

"'What's the difference?' I asked him.

"'If you buy a bottle,' he told me, 'we just put your name on it and I keep it. Then you can just order a drink out of your bottle when you want one.'

"'Wow,' I thought, 'just like my Vegas slogan: *You don't have to buy a drink unless you want one.'*

"'That sounds all right,' I said. 'I'll bring a few of my guys around for a drink.' So I bought a bottle of Jack Daniels and the bartender poured me a drink. He got some tape and wrote 'Morris' on, stuck that on the bottle, and put it on the display shelf behind the bar along with the bottles belonging to the other patrons of his establishment. At the time I thought it was cool to walk into a bar and have your own special bottle of spirits with your name on it just sitting on a shelf and waiting for you when came in to have a drink. It was the eighties.

"As we toured the South and on up into West Virginia, Blue Ridge Mountain country, I was discovering Southerners had an especially warm spot in their hearts for Elvis. It also seemed the women had an even warmer spot. Kim was calling every other day and saying she was getting as big as a house and for me to be a good boy.

"While I was still on the road in the Deep South, Kim flew back up from LA to Vancouver with April, her girlfriend, who used to run lights for our show, and began looking for an apartment. Kim didn't know Vancouver. She was pregnant, trucking all over the place looking for a suitable residence, and dealing with people who would just yell out of their windows at her telling her that they didn't take kids or pets before they even got a chance to meet her. Finally, she found the main floor of a newly renovated house and set up a nursery."

After finishing his engagement in Roanoke, West Virginia, Morris and the boys in the band had a layover for a couple of days on a Memorial Day long weekend. During their layover, the band told Morris that they had been uncomfortable touring in the Deep South and felt even more trepidation about going into New York City for the next leg of the tour. They were homesick.

I wanted to play New York, but the band wanted to return to Canada, and I went along with them.

"I wanted to play New York," Morris recalls, "but the band wanted to return to Canada, and I went along with them. After fulfilling our two remaining US commitments in the South, I arranged to have Chris Siller book us back into Canada. By the time I got back to Vancouver from what was basically my last road tour with me doing my Elvis Presley Tribute show, Kim had made our newly rented house very homey and comfortable."

It was a great show, but I missed the birth of my daughter.

While he was in Vancouver awaiting the birth of his daughter, Morris got a call from his agent and accepted a good gig to fill in for someone who couldn't headline a Canada Day, July 1st show on Vancouver Island. "We loaded up the equipment and got on the ferry," he recalls, "and it was a great show, but I missed the birth of my daughter. She was born after midnight and the fireworks were going off on the island when I received a call. I was giving out cigars to the boys in the band and people in the club, but Kim never forgave me for that — for missing Brittany's birth.

"After that, I looked around for a job that would keep me in town." Morris Bates hung up all of his Elvis suits and accepted a solo engagement to play a posh new nightclub that had opened across the Fraser River from Vancouver International Airport. "I still sang lots of Elvis songs," he explains, "but I didn't wear my costumes, and I could do a wider variety of material. They had a real good Filipino band in La Botté that played dance music, and I took in my arrangements and they did my show with me. La Botté was a beautiful club — it had all the ambience of a smaller version of the Cave and they served an exquisite Italian cuisine. They paid me very well to do one show a night, and after I was finished working I could go home and be with my wife and newborn daughter." Despite these brief revivals of his career impersonating Elvis, the thrill was finally gone, though memories of those days and nights in Vegas are still bright in Morris's mind.

Viva Las Vegas

"Sitting with my back against the wall in the back corner of the showrooms of Las Vegas," Morris reminisces, "I absorbed the ambience created by the greatest entertainers of my generation in the entertainment capital of the world. On any given night

I first saw Willie Nelson at the tiny lounge in the Golden Nugget in Glitter Gulch. Richard sent me down there to check out Willie because we were being considered as an opening act for a 200-city tour.

you could witness good, bad, and outright embarrassing performances as the stars worked the Vegas audiences with their personal blend of shtick, comedy, and song and dance routines. Circus acts have also been part of the equation ever since the desert began filling up with hotels and casinos and Howard Hughes popularized cheap seats on domestic airlines. Because I was a performing at the Silver Slipper for the Summa Corporation family, I was extended the courtesy of the Castaways Casino, the Sands Hotel, the Frontier, and the Desert Inn. They were all under the Summa umbrella, but were also in direct competition with each other. Summa had also owned the Landmark before I went there to perform. I never paid for a show that I can recall. Richard always took care of the details. I just made sure to leave a healthy tip after enjoying a meal if was a supper show or just a couple of cocktails while holding hands and cuddling up in a booth as close to the stage as possible.

"I saw every performer I wanted to see while I was in Vegas. The ones I really liked I saw over and over. Some shows I just never got around to seeing, thinking in the back of my mind I'll catch them the next time they're in town. The major performers usually came in for a week at a time four times a year. Some performers, like B.B. King, live in Vegas but never perform there. Others retire there and just hang out. However, I seldom hung out with my fellow stars. My manager Richard had read me the riot act on many things, but the three bell alarm was 'sitting in with other acts.'

"The first shows I saw in Vegas were the lounge acts, which are free. You can sit in the casino and pull the slots and still watch the performers, whereas if you go into the lounge and sit down there is usually a two-drink minimum. The act I remember most clearly is The Goofers, playing next door in the Frontier Lounge. They were Louis Prima's original backup band. I first saw Willie Nelson at the tiny lounge in the Golden Nugget in Glitter Gulch. Richard sent me down there to check out Willie because we were being considered as an opening act for a 200-city tour if the Slipper didn't pick up our option. After seeing Willie's show, I was glad that the Slipper picked it up. I love Willie, but he had one outrageous bunch of dudes in his crew. The number one Willie rule is 'No Rules.'

"I saw his outlaw buddy Waylon Jennings at the Riviera. His broken-down tour bus in the casino parking lot kind of said it all. Waylon came on stage, sang a song, and then turned his back to the audience for the rest of his performance — one of the only shows I remember seeing where people were actually demanding their money back. He looked like he'd been rode hard and put away wet. The only redeeming thing about the Waylon Jennings Show was his wife, Jessi Colter.

"On one of my dark nights (the only night I didn't perform was Wednesday), I took my mom to see one of her favorites, Freddy Fender, at the Silverbird. I think he'd been hanging around with Waylon. After singing his opening song, *Jambalaya* by Hank Williams, he wobbled about, grabbed the mike, began to sing *Wasted Days and Wasted Nights*, and fell backwards into the drum kit. The curtain came down and his manager came out to say the audience could get a refund at the casino cage. I scooped my mom and headed for the exit as soon as Freddy hit the floor. We headed into the lounge to see a new friend, Gary Puckett of the now-defunct Union Gap. He has a really nice voice. The next morning I was coming up the Strip and I saw Freddy Fender and his manager jogging around the Silverbird parking lot. Unbelievable

When Lisa dressed up, she did look a lot like Priscilla Presley. Dolly didn't know what to think.

"Another dark night I took my mom to see another of her favorites, Liberace. Henny 'take my wife' Youngman was his opening act. Liberace was his usual over-the-top glittery self, his buddy driving him onto the Hilton showroom stage in an antique Rolls Royce. One of his routine punch lines came when he was seated at his piano. He would ask his audience if they liked his outlandish rings and flutter his fingers so everybody could see them before adding, 'You should; you paid for them . . .'

"Lisa was always telling me she wanted to see Dolly Parton. It was something about her being from Kentucky. She hardly asked much of me so we decided to go. When Lisa dressed up, she did look a lot like Priscilla Presley, and I do look like Elvis. We were seated up front, stage center, and Dolly didn't know what to think. She kept glancing at us all during her show. Upon leaving the showroom, I was asked to sign autographs, Lisa smiled a lot, and I was reminded why we didn't go out together much.

"When I had business friends come to Vegas I always took them to Siegfried & Roy. It was the most lavish and highly produced show on the Strip. I'd seen Siegfried stuff a tiger into a hat and pull Roy out; I was beginning to wonder about those two.

Englebert represented the perfected performer of his genre. He looked great.

Gordon Mills was the manager for both Tom Jones and Englebert Humperdinck. I was looking forward to seeing Tom Jones, but I didn't really enjoy him as much as I had thought I would. His show seemed forced, as if everyone was waiting for something to happen. Even when the ladies screamed, it seemed faked and the key throwing seemed rehearsed with shills (a gaming term meaning you're working for the house).

"I wouldn't have paid to see Englebert after being disappointed by Tom Jones' show, but because I didn't have to pay for it, I was in for a double treat. Englebert represented the perfected performer of his genre. He looked great. He was entertaining. He was funny. He was humble but not too humble. You felt oneness with his performance, and when he sang, he sang! If it is possible to sound better live than on record, he did. When he did his joke about his buddy, Tom Jones, he sang Tom Jones better than Tom Jones. After a couple of standing ovations I walked out of the showroom feeling like I was supposed to feel – drop a bundle on the tables and still feel I owed the casino money.

"Then there was master showman, singer, dancer, mime artist, musician, and jokester, Sammy Davis Jr. Sammy held court at Caesars Palace. I had performed on that stage during my *Merv Griffin Show* appearance, and I know that it is a huge stage. Sammy was a petite man, but on that big stage he was a giant of a performer. Frank Sinatra had installed the sound system in the showroom — it was the best money could buy. The voice that came out of that little body gave you goose bumps, so clear and so pure. When he performed *Mr. Bojangles*, he danced to his own prerecorded vocals. When he sang, 'Dance, Mr. Bojangles, dance . . .' his vaudeville slippers tapped his way into your heart.

Sammy was a petite man, but on that big stage he was a giant of a performer.

"Mr. Warmth, Don Rickles — all hockey pucks beware — was so strong that he had a comedian open for him. His rapid-fire delivery is mind-boggling. When you are just getting the first joke, you are already three jokes behind. He has blacks making fun of Jews making fun of Nazis making fun of Puerto Ricans making fun of Hindus making fun of Mexicans making fun of Indians making fun of white people, and, before he's done you forget who you were prejudiced against to begin with. He leaves his audiences with that special warm feeling that only he can provide. Rickles is the only performer who ever introduced Elvis to his showroom audience. He asked Elvis to stand up and take a bow, and then told him to sit down because he was making a fool of himself.

"When Glen Campbell appeared at the Frontier with Tanya Tucker, there were rumors of substance abuse circulating like crazy. By the time that Tanya had slit her wrists next door at the Frontier, I wasn't much interested in walking across the parking lot and slipping into a back booth to take in the Glen and Tanya show even if it was free. I did see Glen Campbell perform later on when the Riviera picked him up, and by that time he had got his good old boy charm back. He put on a terrific show. He was still a pro.

Rickles is the only performer who ever introduced Elvis to his showroom audience.

"When Sinatra came to Vegas, his presence was definitely felt; the whole town acquired a mess of folks with funny noses and 'make-you-an-offer-you-can't-refuse' attitudes. As only Don Rickles had the nerve to say, 'Frank, sit down, make yourself at home. Hit somebody.' Elvis may have been the King of Rock & Roll, but Vegas definitely belonged to the chairman of the board, Frank Sinatra. I had many opportunities to go but

As only Don Rickles had the nerve to say, 'Frank, sit down, make yourself at home. Hit somebody.'

never did see Dean Martin & his Golddiggers at the MGM. I didn't get to see his old nemesis Jerry Lewis, either, but I did ride in an elevator with him and his secretary at McCarran Airport when I was coming in from LA, and I saw him slight an autograph seeker. It seemed to me he always wanted to distance himself from *The Nutty Professor* image that had made him an international celebrity.

"You can tell who's worth seeing in Vegas just by being on the street on Las Vegas Boulevard when the showrooms empty out. The ticket brokers can make or break a show, especially a new show. Everyone cuts their own deals. You can walk up to the head *maitre de* and hand him a handful of black chips and you don't even need a ticket to the best seat in the house. You'd be amazed at how many people paid $20 plus to sit front and center for my $10 show. Richard kept the prices very reasonable so as not to mess with the brokers, but there was still plenty of grease to go around.

"Kenny Kerr's Boylesque Revue — the name says it all — six female impersonators including the star of the show, Kenny Kerr. We shared the bill and the dressing rooms with Kenny and crew. Kenny's impression of Barbra Streisand was a showstopper and comedian Little Lil's version of *Hurt* was priceless, but the real humor was backstage, where a 10-piece band, three female backup singers, and the cast of Boylesque shared four dressing rooms and a common area with one washroom with two stalls. We didn't know the difference between a bidet and a urinal.

"My first show was at 7:00 p.m., and we had to be backstage by 6:30 or it was a dollar a minute fine. Kenny Kerr and his 'sisters' were there at 6:00 p.m. primping for their 8:30 performance. Kenny is a gifted comedian with incredible timing and is rumored to have the best legs in show business. We never looked for fear of being turned into stone. Kenny was married to Roger, a cast member, but Kenny was the boss. The highlight of Kenny's show was his monologue as he would lovingly say to some guy from the heartland sitting with his wife, 'You want me, don't you . . .' You could see the guy changing different shades of red. When

Kenny was buying pantyhose, the clerks would always smile wondering 'why is a man buying pantyhose?' Then he'd throw them a curve and ask for a box of Tampons.

"Richard and I were invited to Kenny and Roger's first wedding anniversary. They had a nice home in the Vegas 'burbs fit for a star of his caliber. The party was packed with Vegas celebrities — Rip Taylor, Debbie Reynolds, Siegfried & Roy . . . The highlight of the afternoon was when Kenny and Roger sat in the middle of their living room kissing and cooing while marveling at all the wonderful gifts they so desperately needed. Oh, another cappuccino machine for two!

"I never saw Kenny Kerr dressed in drag except on stage, but at charitable functions or events where he was expected to appear in character he was dressed to the nines. As Kenny and Roger were pulling into their driveway after one of these soirees, a man came running out of their house. Kenny told Roger to dial 911, kicked off his high heels, yanked up his skirt and took after the thief like a shot. He flat-assed tackled the guy and brought him down, and held him until the police arrived. I assume the robber was seriously considering a career change as he was being held face down in the dirt by a woman. A very tough woman. The takedown made the local tabloids.

"Although rumors in Vegas are always rampant, I have a tendency to not believe anything I hear and only half of what I see. I went over to see Ray Charles at the Silverbird, which was always one of the best deals in town – a $10 show including two cocktails. I also saw Tina Turner at the same venue. I had met Tina at the Cave just after her breakup with Ike and she had her son running the sound. That rumor is true: she does have beautiful legs. No one expected the comeback Tina made in the mid-eighties or her sequential farewell tours that would jump-start another whole career. Both Tina and Ray Charles had respectable numbers but keep in mind Vegas is a gambling town. There were no numbers to be counted at the Sahara when Telly Savalas opened and closed on virtually the same night. Remember it's all about putting and keeping people in their chairs.

"The controlling influence in my bands was my guitar player. I used to be able to tell you who was on the other end of a guitar by hearing a single riff. One of my all time favorite guitarists was Sidro Garcia, a local hero, who was relatively unknown outside of Vegas. He and his ex-wife Beverlee Brown were the driving force behind his band, Sidro's Armada. Their show was a modern day version of Louis Prima and Keely Smith. When the spotlight focused on Sidro sitting center stage on a stool with his custom Fender Stratocaster, it was a showstopper, more than worth the price of the two-drink minimum. Sidro had refitted the tuning pegs of his guitar with banjo tuning pegs, which locked his guitar strings in tune. While even the best pro guitarists have trouble taking an out-of-tune guitar and tuning it up in 10 seconds, he could tune one while playing you a melody.

> I used to be able to tell you who was on the other end of a guitar by hearing a single riff.

"Roy Clark was a session guitar player, much like Glen Campbell and Jerry Reed were before discovering that their voices could sell records. I'd seen Roy at the Desert Inn and marveled at his guitar and banjo playing. His show was a mix of hit records and skits and comedy routines that he performed on his syndicated TV show *Hee Haw*. When Roy got serious, he pulled up a stool and gave guitar lessons with instrumentals like *Malaguena* and *Classical Gas*. He was unpretentiously funny. I don't know what motivated him to bring his guitar to a Sidro's Armada gig at the Hideaway Lounge at the far end of the Strip and sit in with Sidro. You could feel the excitement in the room as the dueling banjo player seemingly was going to give Sidro a lesson with dueling guitars. The stage was set, but in Sidro's controlled environment. Sidro had his pedals, and his special effects. He was in synch with his sound crew. As Roy plugged his guitar in, he was completely out of his. It started out cute but soon turned to a no-holds-barred riff-slinging competition, as most things do at 4:00 a.m. in Vegas. Sidro handed Roy his butt on a platter. I remembered what Richard had said about me sitting in with a band and having a potential train wreck. Roy stepped in front of one that night.

"I saw Willie Nelson again, this time at the Circus Maximus Showroom at Caesars Palace. He was hotter than the Nevada desert, but Willie could take the heat — he was from Texas. Willie was riding a wave of Williemania. Caesars has a reputation for booking the ridiculous to the outrageous, anything that's hot Caesars will take a chance, from Evil Knievel and his son jumping over the Caesars Palace fountain to 45-second boxing bouts. But Willie Nelson at Caesars? Las Vegas has a long memory, and it wasn't that long since Willie had been playing in Steve Wynn's little 200-seat hallway he called a lounge and Kenny Rogers was the house booker. Now Kenny was headlining at the Riviera and Willie was at Caesars.

"I went to the opening. It was pure pandemonium. Willie was not used to playing precise 90-minute shows. He started one of his endless medleys of his hits and ended up leaking over into the start of his second show. Caesars was not ready. They ran out of beer halfway through his first show. They didn't raise the curtain to start the show like most performers' shows; they just left it up the whole time. Willie had about 40 of his friends and family all sitting on stage, off to the side, but in plain view of the audience. Band members were just walking around the stage talking to each other. He had a big band — two drummers, two bass players, four or five guitar players, a steel player, a fiddle player and his sister Bobbie on piano. It was a country orchestra. The showroom had a festival feeling like everyone knew each other. They were hollering, 'Hi Bill, Hi Martha,' and waving to each other. Then someone in the audience would run and holler at someone on stage and he'd come down and give her a hug. As the houselights dimmed Willie walked out to center stage with no introduction, and people started to hoot and holler and clap. Willie smiled his mischievous smile for a split second looked dead into the audience and sang, 'Whiskey River take my mind . . .' The party was on.

"Did I mention I spent ten years in Vegas one night? A 99¢ breakfast can cost you $500."

Karaoke

When Morris Bates moved back to Vancouver after playing
Vegas and touring for the better part of two decades, he could
look back over his remarkable career and feel real pride that he
had done so well. All odds had been against him, stacked against
kids from northern reserves. But fame and fortune
fade quickly. He had lost one fortune and worked
doggedly to recoup his losses. He worked so long and
hard that he had exhausted his vocal chords.

He had lost one fortune and
worked doggedly to recoup his
losses. He worked so long and
hard that he had exhausted his
vocal chords.

Settling down in Vancouver, he also had more
time on his hands. He could see that eventually he
might want to retire altogether from performing, so
he began looking around to find something else interesting to do.
One of the first moves that Morris made was to use his experience in the music industry to get into the karaoke business that
was being introduced to North America. If karaoke took off like
Pac-Man, the Japanese arcade game, he might make a comfortable living.

"A lot of people," he explains, "if they win the lottery or come
into money will buy a restaurant or start a nightclub. They will
start up a business that may seem more glamorous, even though
they know nothing about it and won't do so well. Usually, after a
while, all their money is gone. The best advice you can get is to
stay with what you know. So I decided to get into the karaoke
business, which was big in Japan at that time but was just being
introduced in Canada and the States."

It was a hard sell at first, but Morris gradually coaxed people
up from audiences and the craze caught on. "I remember this one
elderly lady," he notes, "who came up to me in a bar in Blaine,
Washington, and asked me if I had Patsy Cline's *Crazy*. I reassured her that I did and asked her if she would like to sing it. The
concept was totally new and she didn't realize that she was
supposed to sing it. She blushed and wasn't really sure. But I reassured her and showed her how the words would be right there on

the screen for her. She sang *Crazy* and got a standing ovation from her friends and the whole bar. From then on I knew that karaoke was going to be a hit. I purchased four karaoke machines. It was an expensive setup. BJ came up with my 'UR the STAR' logo, and I was in the karaoke business."

Morris was one of the pioneers of the karaoke craze. "Both Kim and I were involved in the karaoke," he recalls. "We both had two machines and at the end of the night we weren't on the road, we both came home — we were a family. When we introduced it, karaoke became popular. It was great. I would sing a couple of songs and then someone would get up and sing a couple of songs. At first, it was a really hard sell, especially to convince club owners that you could get people to come up and sing to a TV and you would pack their clubs. But it took off and pretty soon and there were lineups to get into the venues, just like there had been when I was doing my Elvis shows.

"The woman who helped me get started remembered me from those days when I was doing my Elvis tribute. Her name was Janine Tidball. Her father owned the Blue Horizon Hotel, the Biltmore Hotel, and the Lougheed Hotel. She wasn't sure at first, so I asked her what was her slowest night, and she said, 'Wednesday.' So she put me in all three hotels on their slowest nights and it worked. I was booked up to seven nights a week. If it wasn't for my Elvis show notoriety it would of been a lot harder to sell the concept. Every club owner I approached was skeptical. I was so sure of myself that I used the same promo theme we had used in Vegas: 'If you don't like the show, you can get your money back.' It was the same concept with the exception: 'If I don't make you money, you don't have to pay me.'

"But as I was getting control of more venues every week I began to feel the heat from local musicians. Most hotel managers and club owners measure the success of their operations by one simple bottom line – selling alcohol — and, when times are tough, bands are replaced by duos and singles." Saturday afternoon jam sessions were another cost-cutting measure that had

From then on I knew that karaoke was going to be a hit. I purchased four karaoke machines.

become fashionable in the eighties. Karaoke was the ultimate cost saving tactic. With four karaoke machines on the go, Morris was putting a lot of local musicians out of work.

"I was never in any clique group," Morrris explains, "and I never hung out with all the jammers that go to all the jam sessions and play the same 12 songs and call it blues or jazz. It was the same music we were playing in the late sixties and early seventies. The standard approach was: 'play one verse and a chorus and jam for 15 minutes . . .' Hotshot soloists would show off their musical chops by cramming as many notes as they could into one musical bar. I just about got into a couple of fights with guys who were pissed because I had taken over some of their afternoon jams and some of the premier weekend gigs with my karaoke shows. But they were putting themselves out of business. They had forgotten why they were on stage, which is to entertain the customers who came though the door. Most bands were playing for themselves and forgetting about the audience. If you requested a song and they played it you probability wouldn't recognize it. Jam sessions were extremely nervy for novice performers trying to gain some experience. Your chances of the band knowing the song in your key was seldom and never; it was musicians playing for other musicians and the customers were paying the bill. But karaoke was a natural for a novice vocalist just trying to test the water and sing a song. Just as the reality and talent shows on TV are so popular, people just want to participate. UR the STAR was a perfect fit. With karaoke you had a band that knew thousands of songs, a key control, the lyrics in front of you, a subliminal melody and no attitude. Just follow the bouncing ball.

It was the same concept with the exception: 'If I don't make you money, you don't have to pay me.'

"I was always amazed at the caliber of talent out there. Some timid looking person you wouldn't recognize in a crowd of two would come up out of the audience and just nail a song like *MacArthur Park*. But after night after night of hearing endless vocal interpretations of *Roxanne* and other classics butchered, I was ready to head for an old-fashioned jam session. I'd dug another hole and the success was definitely taking its pound of flesh. Then Kim started to MC her own karaoke shows and we were both working seven nights a week. So we could enjoy some nights off, we hired MCs, who could sing, to sub for us. Kim hired some of her girlfriends to cover her machines and nights off.

"One night at the Biltmore Hotel, a guy came up and sang some Roy Orbison songs and he had some real potential. His name was John White and he was wearing a jean jacket with the word 'Hollywood' across the back in rhinestones. He was wearing dark sunglasses and said he 'just got in from LA' by way of Manitoba. He was a good singer and loved to sing Orbison songs, but he had trouble remembering the lyrics. So with the words popping up on the screen, karaoke was a snap. John introduced me to his friend Joel, also a singer, and John and Joel became my karaoke crew.

"Karaoke was in its infancy, and we had a hoot, enjoying a total monopoly for the first year, until karaoke became really big and everybody wanted it. John's wife, Maria, and their sons Chris, Brian, and Cody became like family, as did Joel's family. We were back in the nightclub business, except that there were no travel hassles, booking hassles, band hassles or personality hassles. Like Vegas, we were home every night."

Years later, when Morris ran into his first musical mentor, Joe Mock, he discovered that Joe had spent 10 years in Tokyo recording Elvis songs for karaoke records. "It was in the Roppongi district of Tokyo," Joe recalls, "and I recorded there for 10 years for Toshiba EMI Records. I sang all sorts of stuff. I did Gene Kelly's version of *Singin' in the Rain*, but mostly I recorded Elvis songs."

Some timid looking person you wouldn't recognize in a crowd of two would come up out of the audience and just nail a song like MacArthur Park.

Kim and Morris just married

Top: Morris's mafia. Bottom: Guests: Back row L to R: Michael Silvey, Lance Storkson, Morris, Kim, Shirley and Jim Gardner. Front row: Lora Silvey, Phyllis, Kim's daughter, Danielle

The new star, Brittany Lee Bates

Top: Brittany with grandpa Pascal.
Bottom: First guitar lessons for Brittany.

Let Me Be Your (Teddy Bear)

New Horizons

Promised Land

"In April of 1990 I turned 40 and my life began to change," Morris relates. "Elvis had died at 42. I wanted to make a difference to society, especially native society. I'm proud of my heritage, but I never got up on a soapbox to proclaim it."

In July 1990, a crisis developed in Quebec when the city of Oka issued a permit to a developer to expand a golf course onto land that the Mohawk nation claimed to be an ancient burial ground. When a barricade was erected by members of the Mohawk community of Kanesatake, the mayor of Oka, citing alleged criminal activity by the Mohawks manning the barricade, asked Quebec provincial police to intervene. When a SWAT team attacked with tear gas and stun grenades, a 15-minute gun battle ensued, and when the smoke had cleared one police officer was discovered to be critically wounded. As the summer protest ground on, the Mohawks of Kahnawake, just south of Montreal, shut down the Mercier Bridge over the Ottawa River and federal troops were mobilized.

At the same time in British Columbia, the long smoldering Gitxsan Wet'suwet'en land claim issue had been considered in court in May and June in Smithers and Vancouver, but trial judge Alan McEachern had not been receptive to tribal chiefs' presentation of oral history in their testimony.

In fact, he would soon rule that traditional Gitxsan life was "nasty, brutish and short."

Months before that decision was made, it became clear to tribal lawyers that money would have to be raised for an appeal. Litigation team leader Gordon Sebastian made a call to an old friend. Morris's old friend from Prince George College had become a prominent lawyer, now heading up the team representing the Gitxsan people in their treaty negotiations.

I told him, 'I don't understand politics. All I understand is music.' So I wrote the song Promised Land.

As Morris recalls, "I got a call from Gordon Sebastian and he wanted me to do something to help out. I told him, 'I don't understand politics. All I understand is music.' So I wrote the song *Promised Land* and they came up with some money to pay for making a CD and cassette release. I recorded and mixed it at a little studio near the Biltmore Hotel on Kingsway in Vancouver." The song featured an aboriginal chant and defiant, inspiring lyrics.

> We hear your words
> Your words are hollow
> You want to lead us
> We will not follow
> We make our stand . . .
> We're takin' back
> The promised land . . .

Morris remembers that his daughter, Brittany Lee Bates, loved the record and she would dance around the kitchen singing, "Hey, hi, hi, hey, hi, hi . . . hey, hi, hi, hey, hi, hi . . ." The song "was emotional," he admits, "but it was a political statement, about what was happening in Quebec on the Mohawk reserve and the actions that the Mohawks were willing to take when they blockaded the Mercier Street Bridge to support the Oka blockade. There were no treaty discussions going on, but real estate developers were planning to build a golf course on Mohawk land. Here in BC, Chief Justice Allan McEachern had turned the treaty process upside down. The only legal course of action that the Gitxsan people had after that was to appeal. But the cost of an appeal was $50,000. The Gitxsan didn't have $50,000."

Promised Land was released on the Git-Wet Records label in 1990. The CD and cassette release was made "on behalf of everyone from the Gitxsan Wet'suwet'en territory" and used to raise funds for "legal efforts to protect what is left of our territories."

"It was played all over Northern BC," Morris reports, "and it helped raised enough money to fight and win their appeal."

The defiant song championing aboriginal rights also found a sweet spot on radio dials in South America. "*Promised Land* was played on the radio in Brazil," Dennis Compo recalls. "The aboriginal people in Brazil locked onto it and started playing it. It became sort of their theme song down there."

No doubt, Morris aroused emotions with his protest song, but Gordon Sebastian and his legal colleagues also steered the resulting emotional response toward a positive result. The appeal was won in 1993, and on December 11, 1997 McEachern's decision was reversed. In a press release issued that day by the Gitxsan Treaty Office in Hazelton, Gordon Sebastian said, "Today the Supreme Court was 'nasty, brutish and short' to Judge McEachern's original decision. This changes everything regarding the land question. Any use of resources by outsiders on our traditional territories must now be justified on a case-by-case basis. The Supreme Court said aboriginal title covers more than just what we do that is integral to our culture — it means our rights are not frozen and have to include all modern uses of the land as well."

Promised Land was played on the radio in Brazil. The aboriginal people in Brazil locked onto it and started playing it. It became sort of their theme song down there.

As one court case was ending another was brewing, and before all was said and done, Morris would be broke and single. "My first three years of my marriage," he reveals, "would be the most stable I would ever experience as a family man in my life. Kim and I and Brittany were never totally alone — we were used to a lot of household traffic. April, Kim's friend, along with Gisele

I had no shortage of golf buddies. It was golf all day and karaoke all night.

Kauffman, had been there right from the moment Brittany was born and didn't see any need to change the situation. So April moved in with us. My Indian Status card gave me free access to the nearby executive golf course on the Musqueam Indian reserve so I had no shortage of golf buddies. It was golf all day and karaoke all night. As owners of technology's newest toys, our home became South Central. The marriage didn't last."

Campfire Stories

In April 1991, Morris Bates' father, Pascal, passed away. "As a young boy riding the range," Morris recalls, "my dad told me many stories sitting around the campfire. He said there are only two things in life: horses and women. The one with the most horses represents wealth and is looked upon as the most desirable by the opposite gender. To me, nothing has changed. Today, Corvettes and BMWs provide the horsepower and dating Hollywood starlets like Marilyn Monroe or Angelina Jolie is deemed a sign of success in Western culture. Wars have been fought over women and men have died seizing each other's wealth. Every society has its barometer for success, but it can all be traced back to horses and women. As a young man, I didn't think all that much about what my dad had said until President John F. Kennedy, the most powerful man in the world at the time, was assassinated, and his wife Jackie Kennedy married the richest man in the world and became Mrs. Onassis."

Another campfire story Pascal told illustrated the saying, "If you're in your territory looking at the ridge of a mountain through the early morning mist and see a wisp of smoke, whoever that campfire belongs to is not coming to pick blueberries." He also said that "when the poles reverse (meaning the north pole will become the south pole) the world will end, then civilization will start over again."

BJ made his father a gravestone. "The words that I carved on it," BJ recalls, "were: 'Pascal Bates born 1925, rode into the sunset April 9, 1991 — high, wide and handsome.'" With the death of the man who had inspired him to become anything that he wanted to be, the winds of change were blowing through Morris Bates' life.

"That year I went on my first real vacation. Kim dressed us all up in matching and color-coordinated outfits and we flew to Mission Viejo in Southern California for three weeks to be with her parents. Between Disneyland and Tijuana with Grandma, to Knott's Berry Farm and Magic Mountain, I finally went down to a local piano lounge one evening, got half snapped and sang all night for free.

"When I got back to Canada and collected all the money from the karaoke business my crew had done in my absence, it was the most money I'd ever made just sitting on my butt in sunny California. Just as the old saying goes, if it's too good to be true . . . I got a letter and learned I was being audited by Revenue Canada. I had invested what was to me quite substantially in a mismanaged mutual fund company based in Alberta called Principal Investment, owned and run by Don Cormie. I had lost over $60,000. When the air finally cleared, the company had been taken over by Metropolitan Life. I received a check for $750 and Revenue Canada was a-knockin'. As the Gitxsan Nation was fighting Canada and with me recording *Promised Land* my marriage was becoming strained, and as Kim and I were working full time and me fighting the taxmen everything seemed to come to a head. Finally, Revenue Canada and Kim both made me an offer – one was for bankruptcy and the other for divorce."

Native Youth Counselor

Morris Bates' concerns for the plight of northern kids from reserves who migrated to the large urban centers of Edmonton and Vancouver continued to grow. He had been able to help out land claims lawyers with his song *Promised Land*, but he couldn't see how his music could directly help northern children who

Native kids still become victims of the system of pushers and pimps established in the fifties by the sale of cheap heroin.

came to Vancouver and became victims of downtown eastside lifestyles.

Arriving in one of the larger Canadian cities, these kids soon discovered that there were limited opportunities for employment but plenty opportunities for drug abuse and prostitution. Native kids still become victims of the system of pushers and pimps established in the fifties by the sale of cheap heroin to junkies who lived on the fringes of Chinatown on the downtown eastside in so-called skid-row districts. Young aboriginal women become victims of spousal abuse. Young aboriginal men are often lured into breaking and entering and other petty crimes that lead to convictions or commission of more and more serious crimes until they are detained in correctional institutions. In some places, more than 40% of inmates are aboriginal, while only 2.5% make up the general population.

When Morris had a hard look at the reality that was facing young people in the nineties, he thanked his lucky stars — his loving parents and elders for the exceptional support he had received while he was growing up on the Sugar Cane Reserve and trying to get an education and find a way to make his way in the world.

Some things had improved since he was a kid, but others had deteriorated. Some children that had the support of their families were graduating from high school up north and continuing their education, becoming lawyers, architects, and social workers. Other young people could no longer count on getting logging jobs or work in sawmills, mines, or the fishing industry. By the early nineties, these resource-based industries were cutting back and shutting down their mills. Drug pushers and pimps had moved into the interior and were openly hawking their big city lifestyle in small town schools. By the mid-nineties, the use of crack cocaine, ecstasy, and crystal meth had reached epidemic proportions in northern BC mill towns, such as Prince George and Prince Rupert.

With his karaoke business percolating along pretty much on

its own, Morris contemplated a career change. "As part of our divorce settlement," Morris recalls, "Kim and I split up the karaoke business, but the novelty of doing karaoke was definitely losing its appeal. I wanted to do something more substantial with my life. I wanted to become a youth counselor, so I enrolled in the Native Youth Worker Training Program at the Native Education Centre in Vancouver. I thought that with all of my experience in the entertainment business and all of the life skills that I had acquired, I had a lot to offer young people who were looking for a direction in their lives."

Morris began attending classes in September and did his first youth worker practicum at the New Haven Correction Centre in South Burnaby and his second practicum at the Si Wilp Satxw Healing & Treatment Centre in Kitwanga. When he had almost finished this first-year program, he applied to take a course in criminology at the Native Education Centre in Vancouver. "They told me that in the summer I should decide what I wanted to do and volunteer at one of the organizations that might consider me for future employment. So I went down to the Vancouver Police & Native Liaison Society (VPNLS) office and filled out an application. They told me that as soon as I was finished my classes to report for work. That volunteer position turned into a part-time paid position and, by mid-summer, into a full-time paid position.

"On the first of August 1993, I received a call from Native Education telling me that I had been accepted into the criminology program, which started in September. I told them that I was working full time at the VPNLS, and they asked me to meet with one of their counselors as soon as possible. She explained to me that taking the criminology course would train me to apply for the position that I already had. The best advice was to continue working with the VPNLS and they would consider me again if I needed to reapply at a later date.

"I came up through the system really quickly," Morris says, "and by the time that the criminology students had begun their

> That volunteer position turned into a part-time paid position and, by mid-summer, into a full-time paid position.

classes, I was on their advisory committee." As a Native Liaison Worker, Morris sat on an advisory committee that carried out a cultural awareness program for new police recruits.

In November, Morris was sent to the Justice Institute of BC in New Westminster to be trained as a Specialized Victim Assistance Worker. During his first years as a Specialized Victim Assistance Officer, the justice system was changing. Instead of a having a reactive approach to justice, the system was moving toward restorative justice — a proactive approach, which included victim assistance and youth at-risk-programs. Morris would soon contribute to both programs and testify in front of The Standing Senate Committee on Aboriginal Peoples.

Morris would soon contribute to both programs and testify in front of The Standing Senate Committee on Aboriginal Peoples.

239 Main Street

When Morris began working as a Specialized Victim Assistance Worker in Vancouver's downtown eastside district, he reported for work each morning at the Vancouver Police & Native Liaison Society office at 239 Main Street. The office was located in the bowels of the city, three doors down from D.E.Y.A.S. (Downtown Eastside Youth Activities Society), better known as "the needle exchange," across the street from the Provincial Court Building, which houses the Remand Centre, kitty-corner from the Vancouver City Police station at 312 Main, and one block away from the infamous intersection of Main and Hastings.

The Carnegie Library, home of the busiest Community Centre in Canada and the nation's poorest per capita postal code, sits on the southwest corner of that intersection. At the other three corners are a bank, a resource centre, and the Owl Pharmacy, which gives a new meaning to "drug store" – it is one of the pharmacies that dispense methadone to addicted clients. Half a block west on East Hastings Street is the home of the controversial "In-site" project, originally called the "Safe Injection Site," an oxymoron of sorts, where addicts can shoot up illegal drugs in a controlled environment under the supervision of medical staff.

Approximately 40,000 residents of the downtown eastside residents are natives, living in what has been called the largest Indian reservation in Canada. To this population of drug addicts and displaced natives, add drug dealers, B&E convicts, car thieves, pimps, prostitutes, and welfare recipients, and you have the recipe for the volatile street-scene that gave rise to the most sensational serial-killer case in North American history. After being arrested on charges relating to missing downtown eastside women, the prime suspect, Robert "Willie" Pickton, boasted to an undercover police officer while in custody that he had picked up 49 of the prostitutes he claims to have murdered off these same downtown eastside streets. Many of the victims were aboriginal.

In response to the ongoing needs of downtown eastside residents, the Vancouver Police & Native Liaison Society was founded in 1991, two years before Morris Bates showed up seeking summer employment. Before his arrival, most of the employees, from the director on down, had been women. The Native Liaison Society office would be his workplace for the next 10 years.

In the beginning, the goal was to bridge the gap between the police and the native community. Building trust was a challenge, but Morris Bates turned out to be a perfect fit for the job. Already in his early forties, Morris had a maturity that reassured people who came in the front door looking for assistance. When he began to get results in his cases, the word spread on the street that Morris and the VPNLS could be trusted. The agency diversified its mandate to include a variety of essential services to the Native people in the area.

Approximately 40,000 residents of the downtown eastside residents are natives, living in what has been called the largest Indian reservation in Canada.

"239 Main was a truly unique office," Morris recalls. "It consisted of a director, two victim assistance workers, and two Vancouver PD constables. Anything that involved aboriginal people, justice, victims' rights, youth and elders' issues, housing, and a partridge in a pear tree usually ended up coming across our desks. There are 60 to 70 Native organizations and societies at any given time that vie for the precious few funding dollars that are allocated to the downtown eastside by the three levels of government."

Just which level of government has jurisdiction often becomes blurred as municipal, provincial, and federal authorities sort things out. "The City of Vancouver will tell you," Morris explains, "that they are responsible only for the native people in the Musqueam Indian Reserve, home to approximately 1,200 people, which, due to mixed relationships, means half of these are non-native. The provincial government stand is that all native people living on reservations are the responsibility of the federal government. The federal government disqualifies any mixed relationship natives from receiving benefits. Each government is turning a blind eye to the extreme poverty that urban natives endure. Very few resources are being allocated for them. There is no money for services, for education. They should have their own hospital."

Victim Assistance

As Morris explains his job, "A lot of people don't realize that if you are a victim of a crime, you are entitled to apply for victim's compensation. Our office handled the Victim Applications, and the Workmen's Compensation Board of British Columbia ran the program. All you needed in order to apply was to provide your name, address, and a police incident number. The process took about three months for the WCB to adjudicate and decide if a claimant qualified for compensation.

"Just walking around on the downtown eastside, minding your own business, you could become a victim of common assault, robbery, and just about any other violation of the Criminal Code of Canada. Victims were often beaten more severely when the perpetrator discovered they had no money. The WCB wouldn't compensate a claimant for loss of money or personal possessions, but I remember filling out a lot of applications where the victims had inflated their losses, claiming they were robbed of their welfare money and $300 leather jackets given to them by ex-girlfriends and so on.

"BC was one of the last provinces in Canada to compensate victims for pain and suffering. I never could understand what kind of scale the WCB used to adjudicate the claims that I sent in. I remember an elderly lady who was going into her hotel and a guy ran by and grabbed her purse. She hung on and was knocked down. She suffered a fractured collarbone. I processed her claim, and about three months later she came in all smiles and told me that she'd received $3,500 from Criminal Injuries Compensation and wanted to take me to lunch.

"In another incident that I remember a man was robbed and beaten with a baseball bat. I took pictures of his injuries and sent them in with his application. The beating had been so brutal that you couldn't recognize him in those photos. Three months later he received a check for $550. The bureaucracy was faceless and unfeeling and it reminded me of that old black and white TV cop show, *Dragnet*, where Sergeant Joe Friday would say, 'Just the facts, ma'am, just the facts.'

"One even more perplexing case that I processed for compensation was the situation of an elderly lady and her daughter who met up on Christmas Eve and began to walk home together. As they were walking along, the mother's dentures began bothering her and she took them out and put them in her coat pocket. The daughter was anxious to give her mother her Christmas present — a new coat, which the elderly woman immediately put on. As they resumed their walk, a man came jogging by and grabbed the elderly lady's purse and old coat, which she was carrying, and ran away into the night. The two women reported the robbery to the police and were given a police incident number. When they came to me, I filled out the proper paperwork and sent it in to the WCB. A few months later, they came back to the office and brought with them a letter that said she had been denied compensation for her stolen dentures. The mother looked gaunt, and I could see that she had

Just walking around on the downtown eastside, minding your own business, you could become a victim of common assault, robbery, and just about any other violation of the Criminal Code of Canada.

They told me flatly that it would be a waste of time to apply for an appeal because her teeth should have been in her head and not in her pocket.

lost a lot of weight, as she couldn't eat solid food. I phoned Criminal Injury Compensation and complained and requested an appeal. They told me flatly that it would be a waste of time to apply for an appeal because her teeth should have been in her head and not in her pocket.

"I was furious. I phoned Social Services and they told me that they replaced dentures every five years. It had been about five years since the elderly victim had received new dentures. They told me to wait while they found her file. They came back on line and said she was no longer on Social Services, that she was on Old Age Pension, and responsible for her own dentures. This lady was native and had a Status Card. So I phoned the Department of Indian Affairs, division of Native Health. I explained the situation. Their response was that she was indeed eligible for dentures every seven years, but that she'd only had her current dentures for five years. She would be eligible in another two more years.

"I was stunned. I was thinking that at this rate she would be dead in six months. I phoned her dentist and asked if I could come over and see him. He agreed. I went to visit him and wore my Police I.D. prominently. I talked with him and he understood the situation. Before I could ask, he said he'd make the dentures for her within the week. I said I'd do my best to see he was paid for his work. Then I phoned everybody and anybody who would listen to me about this denture situation. About a week later, I got a call from the Department of Indian Affairs. They said they'd pay for her teeth this one and only time, and it would be the last time that they would go against proper policy."

One of the most taxing court accompaniment cases that Morris handled at 239 Main Street was a particularly brutal double murder. He was assigned the task of accompanying the female victim's family members to court and helping them understand court proceedings. "A native girl and her Vietnamese cocaine dealer boyfriend had been brutally slain by a knife-wielding Native fisherman in what had been identified as a drug deal gone bad," Morris relates, "but it was complicated by the fact that both the female victim and the accused had been from the same reserve on Vancouver Island. Tensions were running high between the two families as they sat on opposite sides of the courtroom during this Supreme Court murder trial. When the judge ruled that a videotaped confession would not be admissible because the arresting officers had not read the accused his rights before obtaining the confession, I had to explain the decision to the victim's family and elders. I spoke with them and then asked the prosecuting attorney to come over and say a few words of reassurance to them, as well. He reassured them that he was still going to get a conviction even without the confession."

The graphic testimony of a forensics expert revealed that the confession was totally erroneous. The fisherman had confessed that he had been attacked by the drug dealer and had acted in self-defense. He had claimed that the knife-wielding boyfriend had stabbed the girl in the eye during the scuffle, but had also admitted that he had strangled her afterward. However, the forensic evidence clearly proved that the accused had not been acting in self-defense. He had attacked and killed both victims and the jury found him guilty. When the convicted murderer came up for sentencing, Morris had to console the murdered girl's family, which was difficult after the judge handed the convicted murderer a 12-year sentence for the murder of the girl and 10 years for the murder of the drug-dealer. Both sentences were to be served concurrently.

A native girl and her Vietnamese cocaine dealer boyfriend had been brutally slain by a knife-wielding Native fisherman.

"This is not justice," one of the murdered girl's relatives told Morris, "he killed her and got 12 years, and killed her boyfriend and got nothing!"

Zen Motorcycle Maintenance

"Two and a half years of court accompaniment and listening to the gruesome evidence had definitely taken a toll on my psyche," Morris relates, "and in the back of my head I knew I needed a break. I had driven my motorcycle to the sentence hearing so that I could be by myself after the hearing and not end up giving in to a request to give someone a lift home. As I left the courtroom and walked out onto the street I discovered it was snowing. There is nothing in the world that can bring you back to your senses faster than riding the streets of a metropolitan city like Vancouver on a motorcycle in a snowstorm. I made it about halfway home – to Burnaby at Clark and 12th — and in lieu of getting seriously injured in a traffic accident, decided to call it a day. I parked my bike under a tree on the street and called a friend. The next day the sun was shining, the snow was gone, and the birds were chirping.

"My buddy Brad was planning to ride his bike to Baja, Mexico, and he had been bugging me to go with him. I talked to my supervisor and she said, 'You've got sick days, overtime, and vacation time coming . . . Vancouver will still be here, and just as dysfunctional, when you return. So go get the court case out of your head.'

"I thought, 'Perfect!' I headed over to the DMV and got my motorcycle learner's license. I knew from previous experience that a driver's license was paramount I.D. for me to have when crossing international borders. Upon passing the written test, I was informed there was a probationary period plus a waiting list of three months to get a motorcycle driver's test. The motorcycle license was just a paper attachment to my already valid driver's license. The only difference was at the bottom of the motorcycle license was a single line that read: Restrictions: no freeway or nighttime driving and to be in the accompaniment of another motorcyclist. I took a pair of scissors and made quick

There is nothing in the world that can bring you back to your senses faster than riding the streets of a metropolitan city like Vancouver on a motorcycle in a snowstorm.

work of these restrictions . . . toot suite; Mexico, here I come!

"The motorcyclists I knew were either police officers or guys who couldn't cross the border with or without Indian Status cards. Brad was not one of them. He was a victim of a construction accident and was on a disability pension; his motorcycle was his only means of transportation. He knew his way around the mechanics of a motorbike, and brought a brand new meaning to the word 'frugal'. He boasted he could live quite comfortably in Mexico for six months on $1500 U.S. Somehow, I believed him. If my bygone ex-manager Richard Cheung could make buffalo squirm and some of my acquaintances could make one shit, Brad was in the diarrhea department. Every penny, let alone every nickel, counted. He was on a pension and Mexico is a nickel haven.

Anyone who has ridden a motorcycle or just driven down the Pacific Coast Highway from Washington through Oregon to California will unequivocally vouch for its sheer beauty.

"As we crossed the border my newly acquired motorcycle license passed immigration scrutiny and we were on our way, headed down Highway 101. Anyone who has ridden a motorcycle or just driven down the Pacific Coast Highway from Washington through Oregon to California will unequivocally vouch for its sheer beauty. Before leaving home, I had packed a tent, sleeping bag, raingear and all the other *Easy Rider* necessities, not realizing I would actually need them. Brad's idea of a night's rest after riding all day was to find a farmer's field with an indiscriminate haystack and pitch a tent behind it. I felt at least a State Park with outdoor washrooms and showers were more in line, but in late April they were not open for the summer season, and motels were completely out of the question for my nickel driven, peso bound, buddy. By the time we hit San Francisco rush hour and pulled into San Jose, it was dark and I was 'jumping ship,' heading for a bar and possibly a State Park. After a couple of cocktails, the waitress filled my thermos with coffee and directed us to what she believed was a State Park camping facility beside the ocean. With just the moonlight and the sound of the ocean waves to guide us, we pitched our tents on a bluff overlooking what we assumed was the Pacific Ocean.

"I had convinced Brad that with my Indian Status card I could camp anywhere I wanted, in any State or National Park, as long as I didn't camp there for more than three days and become a squatter. It was a constitutional right given to all Native North American Indians in accordance with the Jay Treaty of 1794 that acknowledged that Native North Americans didn't recognize the 49th parallel as the dividing line between indigenous Native cultures that have existed for thousands of years.

"The next sound I heard was some huffing and puffing and the rhythmic beat of footsteps outside my tent. Peering through the tent flaps, I could see a steady stream of joggers panting their way through their early morning ritual. And as I laid my head back down and started putting melody to the joggers' rhythmic beat, I heard sounds of screaming sirens above the rhythm of *Jailhouse Rock*. There were two squad cars, one a State Parks Board squad car with all the bells and whistles, and a San Jose Police Department squad car with a very aggressive female police officer for backup. This police officer was screaming this and that and saying we were in violation of camping in a city park – no vehicles were allowed there, and they could confiscate our bikes and charge both of us a $750 fine. As most Indians instinctively do, I humbly looked at my feet and apologized. I thought we were in a State Park. The two officers were vibrating about a foot off the ground by the time we packed up and they escorted us, flashing police lights and all, to the city limits.

There were two squad cars, one a State Parks Board squad car with all the bells and whistles, and a San Jose Police Department squad car with a very aggressive female police officer for backup.

"I asked Brad if I should have shown them my Indian Status card. He just glared at me and never spoke another word until we hit Barstow, California. After a while he calmed down and we split the cost of a motel room. The room had only one bed so we flipped for it. I won. Brad liked to camp so much the floor was a luxury, plus we had a washroom. We were styling . . . We chained our bikes up and hit the rack. Barstow is two and a half hours of straight desert driving to our next stop, Las Vegas. After a couple of days in Vegas we hit out for Laughlin on the

Nevada-Arizona border, then crossed into Mexico at a border town called Mexicali.

"There are no helmet laws in Arizona or Mexico. About two hours into Mexico I felt the *Easy Rider* syndrome setting in. I pulled over and took off my helmet. With my hair blowing in the wind, I was living the life. We camped on the East Coast of the Baja peninsula on the Gulf of Mexico for a few days and then cruised over to the Pacific Ocean side for a few more. Then I decided it was time for me to head for home.

"I didn't want to go up through Tijuana and LA, so we decided to cut over the mountains from Ensenada and cross at the border town of Tecate, the beer capital. It was sunset in Ensenada when we decided to head to Tecate, and, as I pulled off the highway exit ramp for Tecate, I hit an oil slick. My bike turned sideways and as I was skidding down the road I could see the sparks flying behind me. I kicked the road and managed to get my bike upright as I gained control on the dry pavement. In those few seconds, I made all kinds of deals with GOD. One being: Not to let me be busted up in a Mexican hospital. As He fulfilled His promise, I was shaking, hoping I could fulfill mine. I suggested to Brad we find a petrol station to fuel up for our trek over the mountains. He assured me with a smile that there was a petrol station midway with cheap gas.

"About an hour and a half later we pulled into this little Mexican mountain village. No petrol station. I was furious. For $2.00 we could have topped off our tanks in Ensenada. We were about an hour and change from Tecate, and Brad assured me he could make it. About 20 minutes up the mountain highway he pulled over and said, 'We have to go back to the village, I'm not going to make it.' I felt like that San Jose police officer! We headed back to the village and pulled up to the only building with lights on, the local store and hangout. There were about eight or 10 teenagers hanging out and they started smirking that my hombre friend spoke better Mexican than his brown-skinned amigo. As my US pesos started to speak, so did their English. They informed us the

I handed the *Federale* officer a five dollar bill. He took a gas can and 'found' a gallon of gas from a school bus up the street, and me and my frugal, nickel-saving senor buddy were on our way.

petrol station went out of business two years prior and they pointed us to the local police station down the road about one kilometer on the right — the house with the lights on. We survived the crater size potholes and found the Policia Federal station. It was an adobe hut with a cement and dirt floor. Inside were four or five Mexican Federales that looked like extras from John Wayne's movie, *The Alamo*. After numerous pomp and circumstance rituals I handed the *Federale* officer a five dollar bill. He took a gas can and 'found' a gallon of gas from a school bus up the street, and me and my frugal, nickel-saving *senor* buddy were on our way.

"The next morning we crossed over into the U.S. at Tecate. I was heading north to the San Bernardino Mountains and across the Mojave Desert to Canada. Brad was heading west to San Diego to have his bike checked over before heading back to Mexico, the South Coast of the Baja, and a six-month siesta. As the freeway separated, we gave each other a blast from our horns and never ran into each other for a year. It took me three days of hard riding through the worst rainstorms and flooding the western United States had experienced in decades. I reached the Canadian border and they waved me through immigration. I had nothing to declare except $2.75 and some rain-soaked plastic credit cards. Not even enough for a Canadian pint."

Years later, the convicted native fisherman became eligible for parole, and Morris drove bereaved family members to the parole board hearing in Mission. At the hearing, the convicted murderer failed to convince the parole board and family members that his remorse was genuine. This time Morris was asked to testify and told the parole board that he had heard this evidence presented three separate times and heard three separate versions. The man continued to serve his sentence.

Changing Lives

One of the most interesting people Morris met while working at 239 Main Street was a young lawyer who had just been admitted to the bar. Grace Li Xiu Woo's ancestry was European, but her name was Chinese because her French Canadian husband, a surrealist poet from Montreal, had legally changed his name to Yuan Woo.

"There was a legal aid strike going on at that time," Morris recalls, "but I was always on the lookout for a lawyer who was willing to help out on one of my victim's advocacy cases. One day, in walks Grace . . ."

"I think Morris was probably disappointed in me as a lawyer," Grace confesses. "I was never very good at advocating. I was so naïve."

"Grace didn't like the situation she was discovering on the downtown eastside," Morris says, "and she wasn't a good advocate, but she was willing to pitch in and help out."

"I only handled half a dozen or so cases through Morris," Grace explains. "Morris was there at the Native Liaison Society office to help people from the street, but he also helped me keep a bit of my sanity."

When a case that Grace was handling went horribly wrong and her client's ex-girlfriend allegedly committed suicide, Grace decided to go back to law school. Her decision was hastened by the sudden death of her husband. She credits Morris with helping her make that decision. Grace asked Morris to write a letter of recommendation for her, and she was accepted to do a master's degree in international law at the University of Quebec at Montreal. She specialized in indigenous law and completed her doctorate degree a few years later.

Morris was there at the Native Liaison Society office to help people from the street, but he also helped me keep a bit of my sanity.

"Grace is a law professor now," Morris says. "When I met her she had just graduated from law school and she wasn't mean enough to be a good trial lawyer. It was better for her to become

He was totally into the people on the downtown eastside. He was a total advocate.

involved in the academic world because there were, and still are, a lot of issues that need to be dealt with."

"Knowing Morris was a turning point in my life," Grace says. "He was the first native person with whom I really became friends and he certainly influenced my way of looking at things."

Despite their friendship, Grace was not fully aware of Morris Bates' first career. "When I knew him," she recalls, "I didn't know that he had been an Elvis impersonator, but he had mentioned meeting some kids on a beach and singing them some songs. But I didn't know he'd been big. I didn't know he'd been to Asia. He was totally into the people on the downtown eastside. He was a total advocate. You know, 'Can you help this person?' He had a really humanist approach."

Sometimes Morris surprised Grace, but never more than the time she told him about a job possibility she thought might interest his clients. As she recalls, "I read a story in *The Vancouver Courier* about how hard it was to find people to exercise race horses. I told Morris about it and the next thing you know he took the job himself. He said he needed the exercise."

"That job description advertised for a hot-walker at the Hastings Park racetrack on the PNE grounds," Morris recalls with a chuckle. "I knew my way around horses and I worked that job part-time for 10 years. I would go in at 5:00 a.m. in the morning and walk the horses and beat the commuter traffic, and then go to work in my office. The job carried on after I left the VPNLS until this stud colt knocked me up against a wall and fractured my toe. A few days after that, I stubbed that same toe and tripped and fell on it with my full weight and broke my ankle in three places. The doctor put seven pins in my ankle. I was flat on my back for three months. That was a lot more serious."

PROMISED LAND
MORRIS BATES

PROMISED LAND MORRIS BATES

GIT-WET RECORDS

On behalf of everyone from the GITKSAN WET'SUWET'EN territory THANK YOU for buying this recording.

Money raised by this effort will fund our legal activities to protect what is left of our territories.

FOR DONATIONS AND GENERAL INFO CONTACT:

Gitksan Wet'suwet'en Office
Suite 405 - 533 Granville Street
Vancouver, B.C. V6C 1Y6
(604) 682-1990

P.O. Box 229
Hazelton, B.C. V0J 1Y0
(604) 842-6511

With thanks to Jack Sebastian and Hagwilget Hall Ctee, B.J. Bates, Mike McDonald, the Office of Hereditary Chiefs, and Don Ryan.

Cover Design: Robert Sebastian

Executive Producers:
Morris Bates and Gordon Sebastian.

Morris takes a stand

Top: Morris's life-long friend, Gordon Sebastian, solicitor, Bottom right: Morris's colleagues, Vancouver Police constables Toby Hinton and Al Arsenault. Bottom: Morris's friend, Grace Li Xiu Woo

*The Carnegie Community Centre at Main & Hastings in the heart
of the downtown eastside ghetto, Canada's largest Indian reservation*

Stop overdose death and prevent infection. Be safe, take a break from the street, grab a coffee, and ask for help when you need it. All equipment is provided.

OPEN 10AM-3:30 AM

Ph: 604.687.SITE (7483)
139 E. Hastings St. V6A 1N5

Safe injection site

Top: Downtown eastside walk in dental clinic.
Bottom: Vancouver Native Health Society medical center

My Way

Reality Check

Scared Straight

The harsh realities Morris faced every morning outside the VPNLS office were an eye-opener, even for a kid from the Sugar Cane Reserve who had seen the corrugated tin-roof ghettos of Bangkok, Soweto, and Sao Paulo. In an effort to prevent native youth from falling into drug addiction, prostitution, crime, and even death, Morris developed an aversion program called Reality Check for Indigenous People, which aimed to scare kids away from this hell. "If I get to them first, there is a chance to help them," Morris explains. "That is the only way I can really do anything about the situation because after they get there, it's too late.

"Here's how the program got started. Someone phoned from one of the Indian bands up north and asked me to help them with a walkabout with their kids on the downtown eastside. That's how it happened. At first it was really informal. There was no program — I just it played by ear. I wanted to become a little more organized, so I asked veteran Vancouver Police Department constables Toby Hinton and Al Arsenault to make a presentation to my groups. Toby and Al were the driving force behind the award-winning documentary film *Through a Blue Lens*, a vivid presentation designed as a warning to anyone thinking about abusing drugs.

If I get to them first, there is a chance to help them.

335

"Toby and Al made really in-your-face, this-is-how-it-is-kids presentations to the teenagers in my Reality Check for Indigenous People program. They also accompanied me on some of the early walkabouts, but their uniforms became an unnerving presence to some of the street people and drug users."

"When I speak to them during my program," Morris continues, "I tell them about the changes that had been made to the Young Offenders Act when it was replaced by the Youth Criminal Justice Act. The age at which the presumption of an adult sentence applies was lowered from 19 years old to 14. I tell them that theft under $5,000 is a blanket charge that can also include theft of small amounts of merchandise, such as lipstick, chewing gum, and cosmetics. But if convicted you will have a police record and that can impact you for a lifetime. Possession of a tiny amount of a controlled substance, which is a federal offence, will stay on your criminal record and can impact your life forever."

In one alley, we've seen 10 or 12 people injecting themselves with drugs at the same time.

By 1995, word of Morris Bates' program was spreading. "It has a real impact on these kids, especially the girls," Port Alberni RCMP constable Ken Stevens told a reporter from *The Raven*, the Aboriginal Newspaper of BC and the Yukon. "They didn't realize how bad it was as far as prostitution, drugs, and alcohol go … In one alley, we've seen 10 or 12 people injecting themselves with drugs at the same time. We saw this one lady lying on the ground while a guy was injecting a needle in her neck. That was pretty scary. There were some tense moments there. It's a great program, especially if you're from an isolated town. You see what reality is in a place like that where you have nowhere to go. You can't help but step back and realize how much you have and how you take things for granted."

Scared Straight, a CBC-TV documentary, features a group of Tseshaht teenagers going through the R.✓.I.P. program with Morris Bates, Toby Hinton, and Al Arsenault. Parents throughout the province soon became interested in having their rural kids go through the program. More than a decade later, the Reality Check for Indigenous People is still popular. For his work as a native youth counselor, Morris was named winner of *The Province*, CKNW 980, and Global TV's *Operation* Phoenix Unsung Hero Award in May 2009.

Murder Mystery

Runaways and prostitutes commonly went missing from the downtown eastside, and Morris often found himself assisting concerned relatives who came to the 324 Main Street VPNLS office where the Liaison Society had been relocated inside the Vancouver Police Department building. "People would come into the office and tell me that their sister or mother or daughter had disappeared," Morris relates. "I would fill out a file and tell them that I would try and take it upstairs to missing persons. However, the way the system was set up, filing a missing persons report was difficult. In those days, the report had to be filed by next of kin in the jurisdiction where they were from, which meant that if they were from Quesnel, the report had to be filed in Quesnel. If a missing persons report was actually filed, the RCMP would have it on file but would not necessarily share the information with other jurisdictions. There was very little coordination or sharing of information between the various service providers. This would change over time. At that time, however, Social Services couldn't reveal whether or not a person had picked up their welfare check because of confidentiality issues. So the Vancouver City Police couldn't act on any of the requests that I was getting through the Native Liaison office because their hands were tied. It was a jurisdictional and confidentiality issue.

"By this point, the police department had begun to reform the missing persons department. They seconded a police constable to work in missing persons, which, before this, had been run by a civilian employee. The constable came to me and told me that she had just been promoted to constable/detective in missing persons, and Detective Ed Tempest had told her that she should

Morris was named winner of *The Province*, CKNW 980, and Global TV's *Operation* Phoenix Unsung Hero Award.

come down and introduce herself and spend some time with me. Ed Tempest was responsible for notifying the next of kin when one of the anonymous downtown eastside residents was discovered dead in an alley or a hotel room. His first task was to check fingerprint records and dental records in order to identify and then notify next of kin. There were so many missing persons that the new constable was overwhelmed, and she eventually transferred out of missing persons.

"We couldn't get any information on missing persons from Social Services. However, there were a lot of satellite offices that had been set up to allocate money to welfare recipients who could not be given their money on a monthly basis and had to be doled out money on a daily or weekly basis. We started receiving reports from these satellite offices that some of these women had not come in for their daily or weekly allocation of money. Social Services had begun to relax their confidentiality policies and begun to release information. I remember that one time one of the workers from a satellite office came over to the VPNLS office and told me personally that he was concerned because one of his clients had not picked up her check.

> There were so many missing persons that the new constable was overwhelmed, and she eventually transferred out of missing persons.

"Another odd thing was that some women were not picking up their methadone that was dispensed daily, but the pharmacies also had a confidentiality policy that didn't permit them to reveal information about whether or not one of the women had picked up their daily methadone prescription.

"The one case that sticks out in my mind is this young man who came into the office to report that his girlfriend was missing. When I tried to get some more information from him, he was reluctant to reveal anything substantial and told me that he would come back tomorrow. The next day, he came in and said that his girlfriend hadn't picked up her welfare check. I asked him, 'Who told you that?' He said, 'Social Services.'

"'That's a first,' I said to myself.

"I asked him if she was on the methadone program. He replied that she was, but the pharmacy would not give him any information. I turned to our liaison police constable and asked him if he would do me a favor and go down to the drug store and ask if she had picked up her daily allotment of methadone. I phoned the new missing persons detective. I had met him a couple of times and he seemed like he was bringing new energy to that department. He had made himself very available to us, and before the liaison constable got back from the pharmacy, the new detective had come down and was talking to me. The liaison constable walked through the door and told me that she hadn't picked up her script for three days.

"'I think we've got a problem here,' I told the missing persons detective. 'When a person doesn't pick up their free money and free drugs, I think there is something seriously wrong.' He looked at me and said, 'Morris, she's dead,' though he had no way yet to prove this. He was the first representative of the Vancouver Police Department to acknowledge to me or possibly to anyone else that there was indeed a serious missing persons problem. For the time being, her name was added to the alarming number of downtown eastside women who went missing and were feared dead in the 1997 to 2001 period. This woman's remains would be the first to be found during a multiple murder investigation at a pig farm in Port Coquitlam, where remains and DNA evidence of an additional 25 missing women would also be found.

Task Force

"Before they set up a missing persons task force, there were some bodies being found who were victims of drug overdoses and some were victims of foul play," Morris continues, "but there were a lot of missing women and we weren't finding very many dead bodies. The question was: Where were these women? Not much progress was made until they set up the task force. Then posters were printed up with pictures and names of missing downtown eastside women, and a $100,000 reward was offered for information leading to the conviction of the killer or killers. Vancouver

But there were a lot of missing women and we weren't finding very many dead bodies. The question was: Where were these women?

mayor Larry Campbell also promised that an inquiry would be made into the handling of the missing women's cases.

"When the reward was offered, the task force was flooded with information from people hoping to collect the reward. What came to light was that there had been quite a few perpetrators who had assaulted sex trade workers, but these attacks had gone unreported. Before this, the women had been reluctant to come forward and tell police officers that they had been sexually assaulted or unlawfully confined. There were a lot of horror stories. The task force was now listening to anybody and everybody who might have information or possibly had come in contact with the person or persons responsible for the missing women."

The public soon learned of this mystery and joined in the search for an answer, staging rallies in front of the police station. The driving force behind the demonstrations was the Downtown Eastside Women's Centre at 44 East Cordova. Because the public couldn't see anything being done about the situation, the pressure continued to build.

"As the task force sifted through the thousands of tips they were receiving," Morris continues, "by coincidence a woman reported to police that she had managed to escape from a man with a gun on a farm in Port Coquitlam. The RCMP took the allegation quite seriously. They went to the farm armed with a search warrant to investigate and made some gruesome discoveries. They immediately called the task force." The owner of the farm, Robert Pickton, was taken into custody and subsequently charged with a total of 26 counts of first-degree murder.

"Right away our office became the focal point and information center," Morris continues. "People from all over Canada wanted to know if their loved one's remains had been found on the pig farm. We were inundated and overwhelmed. The task force didn't release any information. They moved in their equipment and refused to release any information at all to the public. They were there for a year. They were saying that human

DNA remains were being found, but they couldn't immediately identify any of the victims. It takes six weeks to two months to match and process a DNA sample. In this case, the police had collected thousands of DNA samples. So there was no quick way around it.

"The task force did not have a support system of any kind in place for the relatives of the victims they were discovering. So they came to the Vancouver Police & Native Liaison Society because we were the only agency that had prior experience providing support services for the families of victims on the downtown eastside.

"The task force had been formed with members from the RCMP, the Vancouver City Police and the VPNLS. In the early stage of the task force, we were kept up to speed on the development of the investigation. Our first staff member to be seconded by the task force was one of our police liaison constables. He went to work for them fulltime. As the investigation progressed, our staff members were spending more and more time working for the task force.

We were the only agency that had prior experience providing support services for the families of victims on the downtown eastside.

"I spent the better part of a year between the VPNLS office at 324 Main and the Pickton pig farm on Burns Road in Port Coquitlam. With the limited funding of the Native Liaison Society, a dedicated board member, Eileen Lafferty, and a handful of volunteers and donations, a tent was set up directly across the road from the farm. The tent was put there to accommodate victim's families and help control local traffic and an endless stream of the curious 'I don't believe it happened here' sensation seekers."

This time spent in the tent consoling victim's relatives brought all of Morris Bates' training and previous experience into play. It was a challenging task to meet with these grief-stricken people who were not getting much information about the long and tedious excavations that were taking place across the road and beyond the yellow police tape barrier that prevented them from viewing the scene of the grisly killings, mutilations and disposal of their loved ones first hand. "Sitting there day after day," Morris admits, "was tough. First I felt sad. Then I felt angry. I was frustrated. A lot of the information that came out during the course of the forensic investigation was circulating as rumors years before the arrest and murder trial." Vancouver authorities don't concern themselves with what happens in communities like Coquitlam that lie outside their jurisdiction.

When civil lawsuits were launched claiming that police failed to properly investigate the case of fifty missing women and newspaper stories rife with key words such as "negligence" and "mishandling" were circulated, the Native Liaison Society became one of many casualties. "Due to staff shortages," Morris explains, "our second liaison constable was put back on patrol duty. The task force seconded our director and the other specialized victim assistance worker. The result was that I was only remaining staff person at the office. The Native Liaison Society was gradually being phased out, and the Attorney General's office, which funds victim's assistance programs, decided to not renew the funding contract. At this time, the Vancouver Police & Native Liaison Society ceased to exist."

Willie Pickton's murder trial began in January 2006 and dragged on for the next two years with the accused pleading not guilty to twenty-six charges of first-degree murder and the presiding judge reducing the number of cases that would be dealt with during the current trial from twenty-six to six. There was endless debate about the admissibility of evidence including taped statements that the accused had made to police officers, and boastful statements the accused was alleged to have made to associates and an undercover police officer. With an imposed media ban lifted, the daily court proceedings were suddenly of interest to international reporters who descended upon Vancouver like a plague of locusts devouring every living thing in their path. There were racy stories about Piggy's Palace, a nearby late night booze can that the accused and his brother had operated under the guise of a legal society, a dildo that had been used as a silencer, and excavated skulls that had been split in half and

> Willie Pickton's murder trial began in January 2006 and dragged on for the next two years with the accused pleading not guilty to twenty-six charges of first-degree murder.

contained severed feet and hands. Disgust breeds disgust, and the most bizarre and inappropriate reaction that the camera crews filmed were local kids running by and holding up *"Free Willy"* signs, which were their misguided attempts to justify the accused murderer's method of "cleaning up the downtown eastside."

When all was said and done Robert William "Willie" Pickton had been convicted of six counts of second-degree murder and sentenced to life in prison with the possibility of parole after twenty-five years. Both the defense and the crown have launched appeals.

The Senate Committee on Aboriginal Peoples

Ironically, in 2003, while the native liaison society was being disbanded and the murders of the missing women were being investigated, Morris Bates was invited to testify at hearings held by The Standing Senate Committee on Aboriginal Peoples. Once again, Morris had an audience, but seaking to the Senators in the spacious postmodern chambers of the Morris J. Wosk Centre for Dialogue was totally different from performing in the casino showrooms in Las Vegas. Morris admits he was nervous, but his responses were remarkably articulate as he chronicled the desperate reality that northern kids faced in the big city.

By this time, Morris had worked with more than 4,000 children through his Reality Check for Indigenous People program. He was fully qualified to describe the way it was on the downtown eastside. "The kids come to Vancouver," he told the senate committee, "they do not go to Edmonton. The girls who start up in Whitehorse go to Edmonton and Calgary, and as soon as it starts getting cold out there they come to Vancouver. Down here, if you walk down the street, there will be hundreds of people willing you to sell you a twenty-dollar flap of cocaine or heroin. Illegal drugs are very easily available in Vancouver. Kids cannot go buy cigarettes, but they can go buy crack cocaine."

"Once a girl has prostituted herself, her self-esteem is gone," he told the Senators. "She now is on the end of a needle or a crack pipe; she is now selling herself for money and she is probably only got a Grade eight or nine education. Once she can learn she can make five hundred dollars in two hours she does not want to go back to school and she does not want to think about earning eight dollars an hour."

"We are losing too many children to the streets; they are coming to Vancouver in droves from all over Canada. They are young adolescents at risk. We have the biggest drug problem in North America. Over 4.5 million needles a year are distributed by the needle exchange; that equates to about twelve thousand needles a day. The statistics say that thirty-five per cent of the people that get those needles are native. Drug use is causing many HIV and AIDS related deaths. We are only 2.7 percent of the population, yet we are just about twenty-four per cent of all the HIV cases in British Columbia. The 'VIDUS Project', the Vancouver Intravenous Drug Users Society, gave us those numbers.

"The native bands have been bringing their children to us so we can teach them about drug use. The problem is that too often the kids have already become caught up in drugs by the time they get to us.

"To tackle the problem I started talking to groups of kids once a month. In the beginning the groups were quite small. About three-and-a-half, four years ago, prior to this tape that you are about to see was made, I developed a new program. The program has grown, and has developed quite well.

"The program runs for about two-and-a-half hours, and is very intense. The kids sit in my office for about one hour and they see a video and then we discuss HIV, AIDS, and drug using. Then I take them on to the streets of Vancouver not five blocks from here where there is the most incredible drug culture in the world. That takes another 20 minutes. Then, we go back to the office and I ask them about what they saw on the street. That takes about 15 minutes. I also do a section about getting a criminal

I give each of them a little hematite stone to remind them that they have something tangible.

record and the Young Offenders Act.

"I give each of them a little hematite stone to remind them that they have something tangible. I tell them that, if they choose the life they saw on the street, they can throw that little rock as far as they can, because that is what they will be doing with their lives. Then I ask them if they think the people on the street are throwing their lives away?" To support this point, Morris screened a video clip of the CBC documentary *Scared Straight*, which the committee chairman called, "a very sobering video."

Morris clarified several issues during the proceedings. "I want to help them make an informed decision about the drug culture," he insisted, "how horrible it can be if they get caught into it. I am not scaring anybody. The producers put in the words 'scared straight'. The name of the program is 'Reality Check for Indigenous People'.

Morris also made a strong claim for the ongoing need for a native liaison society. "The native liaison has really bridged the gap between Aboriginal people and the police in the last ten years. Our office is really busy because we are the most unique organization in Canada; we have made a deal that we are a native organization in partnership with the Vancouver Police Department. We have established an incredible trust. When it started out I was only doing one group or two a month but now the program is so popular that I do that whole presentation myself inside with the kids."

I mean, there are just no native people walking up and down Robson Street.

When Morris was asked to talk about why when native youths "migrate" to urban centers they end up in "drug areas," he described the current situation. "As it happens all the native housing projects are in the Downtown Eastside. We have the Friendship Centre down in 1600 Block of Hastings, and we have Native Education up on Fifth and Main. There are six thousand accessible cheap rooms in the downtown block Eastside here. If you go down towards Fraser Street and you go down to Forty-ninth and Fraser the street signs down there are in Punjabi.

"People of their own culture like to be around their own people; it is very comfortable. I mean, there are just no native people walking up and down Robson Street, but if they are down there they have a really good chance they are going to run into somebody they know. I know it is a horrible situation but that is how it has sort of been. If you go to Richmond there is a large Asian community there; people would like to be around their own. Unfortunately, we have skid row in downtown eastside of Vancouver that the native people basically call home."

When asked to comment about the proposed downtown eastside injection site and harm reduction programs, Morris noted that he was opposed to this approach. "My program," he said, "is the only one of its type that does not agree with harm reduction. I tell the kids not to even go there. The harm reduction side is very powerful. They are thinking of having a shooting gallery where you can actually go in and shoot drugs and they are going to allow young people to go in there also. I mean, if you are fourteen years old they are going to allow you to go into the shooting gallery; I do not know how they can do this legally; last time I looked drugs were illegal.

Harm reduction provides needles for the kids. This gives the kids a confusing message.

"Harm reduction provides needles for the kids. This gives the kids a confusing message. They see the government giving needles away to people to use with illegal drugs. The kids are aware that HIV/AIDS is killing the native people

"The drug culture is embedded in the society down there. I took a group of kids out last night and there must have been a thousand people in those three blocks. The streets were packed. One kid wanted to know if we were really going to walk through the crowds. I said: 'Yeah.'

"I do not mind going on record; I do not care for it myself, but I am the only one that has this program. Everybody is sort of telling you that drugs, you can do them and facilitate them; I just do not go there with the kids. There are other people who they can get that kind of information from and I do not want to be one of them."

Morris also described how teenagers were selected as candidates for his program. "The RCMP or the school support workers bring the kids in to me. We deal with both native and non-native kids. Anybody can come and access the program. We have non-native girls from Abbotsford. I have never advertised; the phone just rings for the program. Once one school hears about it, another school calls me. I am asked to do presentations at various functions. I try to get the kids before the street gets them because once the street gets them, I cannot do anything about it. I can do something in that room with twelve or thirteen kids. Once they are out there with a needle hanging on their arm or at the other end of a crack pipe, there is nothing I can do."

> Once they are out there with a needle hanging on their arm or at the other end of a crack pipe, there is nothing I can do.

He also spoke about the lack of funding being funneled into his program and a general lack of funding for addressing any of the issues that were raised that day during the committee proceedings. "The federal government will finance a program for three years," he told the senators, "and after that time they stop funding the project. This is the cause of many failures. They did the same thing to us but we were fortunate that the Vancouver Police Department took us in and gave us offices rent-free. The Vancouver Police Department in essence picked up the federal slack so it was only Victim Services, our core funding for salaries, and the police department.

"I am sure you are aware of all the cutbacks that have come through the British Columbia government. I am up against a wall in that the program takes about two to two-and-a-half hours for me to do. I usually do it over my lunch hour because I bring the kids in at 11:00 a.m. and we do the hour inside. I am taking an hour away from the society as a specialized victim assistance worker so the victim assistance people are telling me that I am going to either have to cut the kids out or else get my own funding to extend the program. The job that I am paid to do is a victim assistance worker and I have been told that the mandate for victim assistance does not include crime prevention. I thought it did because I have been doing it for four years with their blessing.

"I work with the Vancouver Police Department and their

mandate is crime prevention. Either way I am doing it. I am with the police department and I am doing it for them. If victim assistance prefers not to have me do the program I can do it with the police department under the umbrella of crime prevention."

When asked what other duties his job entailed, Morris said, "We do a lot of court accompanying. We used to do a lot of criminal injury compensation forms. We are the only office in the Vancouver Police & Native Liaison Society so we cover the whole gamut of whatever comes through the door, but our core funding is from specialized victim assistance."

Fund my program. That is about all I can say.

When Senator Pat Carney asked, "What can we do to help you?" Morris said, "Fund my program. That is about all I can say. I do not know how much longer the victim assistance people are going to allow me to do this. I know the police department's got no problem, we are doing our mandate with them, but it is going to come down to probably having to look for some funding to do that program on my own, probably under the umbrella of the Vancouver Police & Native Liaison Society."

Speaking specifically about his program he said, "It is amazing to see the kids' response. When the kids finish the program they have to go home and write me a letter. I left you a bunch of those letters for you to read. I have also left the names of people who have used my resources: the RCMP, the schools and so on. There are quite a few. Four thousand young people have gone through the program. I did one on Monday, two on Tuesday, I am doing one this afternoon, two on Thursday, two on Friday, I am off on Saturday, and I am doing two on Sunday."

Senator Carney then read some of the comments from the letters that had been submitted. "Let me just put in some to give you the feeling of it," she said.

"Somebody wrote: *Thank you for the talk. It made me disgusted the way the alley stunk. I wanted to vomit. I know what drugs do to you. Drugs are bad for you. I am not doing drugs.*

"Obviously you are really getting your target audience. This is another one: *Yesterday what I saw was an eye- opener. It makes me think about the decisions I am making in my life. When you say that ninety-nine per cent of the junkies started by smoking bud, does that mean that ninety-nine out of a hundred people that smoke will become junkies? What I learned yesterday is how serious a problem drugs really are. After it all I felt disgusted at how they just do it anywhere.*

"You are obviously getting your message across."

"You are obviously getting your message across."

Morris went on to speak about lack of aboriginal representation on Canadian police forces. "I was invited to Ottawa," he told the senators, "and I represented our office for the national forum on policing in a multicultural society. There were fifteen aboriginal police there. We all sat down together and not one of those natives was a detective. Nobody is promoted past constable. There are all these issues, but at the very beginning it is those kids, and that is why I am here."

"When the society was first started they set up these little — it was called a `storefront project'. Mostly they set these little projects up to fail. Anyway, ours never failed because it was such a needed thing. I mean we have sixty-five thousand urban natives that we take care of. We also deal with the sex abuse stuff.

"We deal with spousal abuse, common assault, sexual assault, and historical sexual assault. We get those people from up north, because mostly when they have been sexually assaulted on their own reserve it is hard for them to go back to that reserve and they end up being ostracized and end up coming to Vancouver.

"A girl came to see me when I first started and she had been sexually abused — she had her first miscarriage when she was eleven years old. She didn't even know she was pregnant. The male members of her family had abused her. She went into counseling for three years just to get the statement out. The abuse happened when she was a little girl and she is in her fifties. A lot of stuff comes to our office because it can start there, but initially has to go back to where it happened. We get people from all over, not only British Columbia but from all over Canada that come and use that little office. It can be a very busy place."

When asked about native housing projects, Morris's testimony was equally revealing. "There is not very much of it in Vancouver. There is a very long waiting list. My mother is retired now, and she is living in native housing. She was on the list for about fifteen years. There are people who have been on it for six, seven, and eight years. That is a bad situation because the system itself is exposed to a form of nepotism. I have known people that have been on that list for six and seven years, and are still on it. I have known people that have worked in other native organizations and before you know it they have native housing. That is just sort of how it works. That is their business but there is just a real lack of affordable housing for native people.

Most of the kids cannot read the words, and yet, they are graduating these kids.

"If you want to see a real problem you should look at the school system. Up north the problem is severe. The schools get money for each child and cash that check in November. Soon after that, the child is kicked out of school. The highest rate of street-kids is native kids that have been kicked out of school for whatever reason. These native kids are not being given an education.

"I had a kid come to me one time to give me a report on some stolen car, and he could not spell his middle name and he was in Grade ten. When I get kids in for the program, I show them a flip chart and ask them to read it. Most of the kids cannot read the words, and yet, they are graduating these kids.

"As soon as the little box is marked that you are native, the school gets an extra nine thousand dollars, and that money goes in general revenue. If and when the kid makes a mistake and is expelled from the school, the school can take the money and do what it wants with it. That situation occurs a lot up north. I see a lot of northern kids in my program. Many of them are already in alternate education; they have been kicked out of mainstream education. The schools should be forced to keep those kids in school and give them an education.

"They put the native kids there and they have these little cultural programs, I mean, there is a little native girl that I know but she's got blonde hair and blue eyes and they have her going to computer classes and everything like that. Her little girlfriends are sent to play Barbie or go on a camping trip. They are not getting education to these kids and it is just pathetic.

"I had a police constable, he is non-native but his wife is native and he took the little box and crossed the 'X' because his wife had a status card. So when he crossed that little box that said that his family was native they took his son immediately out of mainstream education and put him in alternate education. He had to go back and fight like crazy to get his son back into mainstream education.

"You know, I mean, I get the part where kids are getting kicked out of school for drugs. I try to make sure they understand what it is to get a criminal record. I explain about theft under five thousand dollars. If you get caught with a joint it is supposed to be against the law and you are going to have possession of a controlled substance. It does not say whether it is two joints or a bag of cocaine, you can see it is possession of a controlled substance, and I want them to really understand that. The girls like to steal cosmetics. I just preach to them that it is theft under five thousand dollars; the charge does not say it was a five-dollar tube of lipstick.

"That is what I do. That is my wrap-up thing I do with the program. I take it off the drugs and go to that. They understand; if they get a criminal record they can basically kiss their butt good-bye — when you have a criminal record you cannot even get across the border. There are many consequences of getting a criminal record."

And when asked to describe resources for aboriginal people in Vancouver, Morris made even more revealing comments.

"There are basically no resources for aboriginal people in the city of Vancouver. Vancouver has come to the conclusion that there are no urban aboriginals here. The city is only responsible for one thousand natives on the Musqueam Indian Reserve. Only one-half live on the reserve. To the city of Vancouver there are only five hundred urban natives in

> If they get a criminal record they can basically kiss their butt good-bye — when you have a criminal record you cannot even get across the border.

Vancouver has come to the conclusion that there are no urban aboriginals here.

Vancouver and they live on the Musqueam Indian reserve. These other people who come from all over Canada do not exist to the city, so there are no resources for them. The city of Vancouver is not going to put any money into native programs or anything native because they believe they have only five hundred natives in Vancouver."

Before concluding his testimony, Morris pointed out several other issues.

"I think there are only ten detox beds in Vancouver for women. I might be off but there are not very many. They used to have a detox centre just down the street on Pender, but they shut that down. There is just one now, just across from the police department.

"The focus that I have is once those girls and those guys get up there and they are on the end of a needle they are basically done. I even tell them that those people out there I cannot do anything for them. But I can sit in this room and I can do something for ten or twelve kids, you know.

"Once they get out there, they are pretty much finished. I make them understand this is going to be their decision that they are going to make. I have letters from kids that did not make it. These kids have got to be educated and the reason I do the program is that hopefully that they will understand where their life can go if they take that funny little trail with those drugs.

"When I see what is happening down here with these kids it is just despicable. Some of these kids only have a grade eight or grade-nine education. I believe that the schools should be held accountable for educating those kids. I tell the kids that they have to stay in school. Nobody's going to get any place in this world with a grade-eight or grade-nine education in the year 2003 and so on. They have to have an education. That is what I really try to push in the program.

"I tell the kids to stay away from the drugs and go to school. I tell them not to listen to the harm reduction crap, sorry. It is difficult for these kids." He went on to fortify his view that harm reduction sends a wrong message to teenagers.

Near the end of Morris Bates' appearance, Senator Carney said, "I do want to say that in the letters from the children that you have counseled there is one paragraph that says it all. There is one paragraph that sums up the work that you are doing. This is a letter from a girl called Raven. I will not give her last name for reasons of privacy. She writes:

I will never forget this day; I learned things I didn't know before. It was on this day that I realized what kind of a job or career I want for myself and it was just by seeing how much help these people need and want. Thank you, Morris Bates, for caring and opening my eyes."

"Thank you, Morris Bates, for caring and opening my eyes."

The Vancouver Police & Native Liaison Society

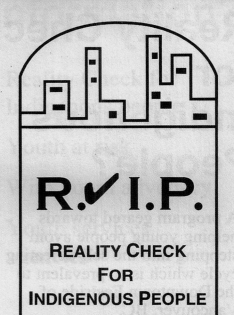

R.✓I.P.

REALITY CHECK
FOR
INDIGENOUS PEOPLE

...Making youth aware of the harsh realities of the 'street'...

324 Main Street
Vancouver BC, V6A 2T2
Phone: (604) 687-8411

The Pickton pig farm, site of at least six murders

Morris in the nation's capitol, lobbying Indian Affairs

Take a Chance on Life

Brilliant Career Move

"As the years have gone by, I have laid Elvis to rest," Morris laments, "but even today as I'm driving down the road, I unconsciously reach over and turn up the volume on my dashboard radio whenever I hear Elvis's voice. I will still watch for a few minutes before clicking away when one of his movies comes on TV, and listen attentively to any news-bytes about the Elvis mystique.

"That Tuesday afternoon on August 16, 1977, when someone knocked on my Anaheim motel room door and sobbingly told me 'Elvis is dead,' I, like the rest of the world sat down and took a deep breath," Morris recalls. 'People die, Elvis doesn't,' I thought. And while the world mourned and tears flowed, it was raining in southern California. To me, it seemed the whole world was crying. In the next few days as the world was coming to its senses, we were bombarded by media coverage of his most untimely death. His music was played relentlessly and around the clock, there were tributes, testimonials, and hur-ried timeline documentaries all identifying him as the undis-puted King of Rock & Roll.

"At the time, I read under the headline, 'Elvis Dead at 42: Brilliant Career Move.' I was furious. The audacity, the dis-respect, the ignorance, the total lack of sensitivity. What

'People die, Elvis doesn't,' I thought. To me, it seemed the whole world was crying.

359

lowdown headline-hunting journalist would write an article like that? But now I think that journalist may have been right in a perverse way. You only have to go to any record mart or weekend swap meet to see the impact that his 21-year professional career has had on our society 32 years after his death. No one has asked for a refund for their tickets to Elvis's sold out 'show that he never gave' in Portland, Maine. Last year Elvis was the top grossing entertainer of the year. Would Elvis's reputation be as strong as it is today if he hadn't died in 1977? Would people still be buying his records? Or would there be empty seats at his shows? Would they want to see him performing with a pocket full of Viagra and a karaoke teleprompter to help him remember the lyrics to his hits? Would they wait in anticipation to see if he would stumble on stage? Would they dress up like Elvis and attend countless Elvis festivals now held throughout North America? That secret is buried in the Meditation Garden in Graceland in Memphis, Tennessee, with the Eternal Flame For Elvis (EFFE) burning brightly."

Elvis Festivals

"The old cliché goes that things happen in threes," Morris reflects. "First was the passing of Ed McMann, followed by Farah Fawcett and Michal Jackson the last week of June 2009. McMann was Johnny Carson's sidekick from *The Tonight Show*, which was staged at the Sahara Hotel in Las Vegas from time to time. There wasn't the same excitement that his late night TV show exuded, but it was a bit more risqué with a lot of inside celebrity humor. Apparently, there had been a long-running feud between Wayne Newton and Johnny Carson that eventually turned into a lawsuit. It seemed Johnny considered Wayne to be an Elvis impersonator of sorts and therefore wouldn't book him on *The Tonight Show*. Wayne won a cease and desist order to stop Johnny from making him the butt of his jokes. There was more action with Ed McMann and his cronies at the casino crap table than in the showroom.

"I was just settling in with my memories of Ed McMann's booming voice hollering instructions to the tumbling dice when I heard the news that *Charlie's Angels* star Farrah Fawcett had passed away. She had been praying for a miracle but had lost her battle with cancer. Later that day the whole world was shocked to hear that Michael Jackson was dead at 50. I don't know what surprised me more — his untimely demise or his marriage to Elvis Presley's daughter, Lisa Marie Presley. Once again Ed McMann played second banana and Farrah Fawcett may have gotten best supporting actress kudos, but it was the King of Pop who stole the show.

"In this mournful nostalgic mood, I headed out to the Eighth Annual Penticton Pacific Northwest Elvis Festival. I'd never been to an Elvis festival before and had no idea what to expect. I was in Las Vegas appearing at the Silver Slipper in 1978 but didn't bother to go to Colonel Tom Parker's first Elvis Convention at the Hilton Hotel's Convention Center. He charged $25 just to go in to buy Elvis memorabilia. Vegas was totally 'Elvisized' that year, but that was 31 years ago. Boy, I was starting to feel old.

"As I drove north from Rock Creek to Penticton in my partner Eileen's smart car with the roof down, I slipped in a CD of my show that was recorded at the Cave in 1979 and started to prepare myself to be re-Elvisized. I was wondering if people would be walking around like zombies with dyed black hair, mutton sideburns, dark sunglasses, and white jumpsuits, sneering at each other with a lot of 'Thank-you very much, Thank-you very much' one-liners. There were about 30 Elvis tribute artists (now known as ETAs) competing in the professional and amateur categories, and, I think, I noticed that there were also two women competing. Mayor Dan Ashton even dons an Elvis suit for local parades.

"I got to the afternoon performance a bit late and only saw about ten of the ETAs and knew only one. There were no backup musicians. They were all performing to pre-recorded backing

There had been a long-running feud between Wayne Newton and Johnny Carson that eventually turned into a lawsuit.

tracks, equivalent to karaoke, but the audience was very responsive to each and every act, giving the atmosphere a comfortable feeling that everyone was there for one reason — their love and adoration of Elvis Presley and his music.

"What amazed me as I watched the ETAs perform was the material that they selected. They seemed to choose songs from B-sides of singles or obscure songs from obscure albums. The song that stuck out for me was *Walk A Mile In My Shoes* by Joe South, which I hadn't heard in years. The wind was blowing briskly across Okanagan Lake and some of the performers were jokingly suggesting the wind might blow them and their capes away. A couple of others were concerned about their hairpieces.

The song that stuck out for me was *Walk A Mile In My Shoes* by Joe South, which I hadn't heard in years.

"One of the ETAs sat down at the park bench beside me, and I casually asked him how the competition process worked. He explained the afternoon winners go on to the evening competition and then to the Sunday final. There was one show at the Convention Centre with the Elvis Ultimate Show Band, where two previous competition winners performed at 8:00 p.m., but that show was sold out and had been for some time. He was in a leather outfit similar to the one Elvis wore in the '68 *NBC Special* and I remembered what Merv Griffin had said to me during that taping at Caesars Place. 'Aren't you hot in that leather?'

When they announced the 10 finalists, the ETA took off to go backstage. The audience applauded and hollered for their favorite, and the Elvis impersonators were hugging and high-fiving each other for making the cut when the MC announced the singing of the finale, *Viva Las Vegas*. He handed the mike to one of the Elvis competition finalists to sing the first verse. Then he handed the mike to the next performer in line to sing the second verse. But disaster struck when the third performer got the mike and started to sing the third verse instead of going into the bridge of the song. By the time they realized they were singing the verse over the music of the bridge, the song had turned into a train wreck. All the Elvis impersonators were wiggling and gyrating to the beat of the music, but they finally got it together for the *Viva Las Vegas* ending.

While I was driving around Penticton, it brought back a lot of memories of the times I had performed here as a headliner for the Penticton Peach Festival in '74 or '75, long before I went to Vegas. My memories were just a blur, but I remembered it was outdoors at nighttime, that there were about 6,000 people at the show, and it was mayhem. Well it's 35 years later and I'm thinking of scalping a ticket, if there's any to be had, to see a performance similar to the one I gave here all those years ago.

"I drove by the convention center and at 6:30 there was already a lineup waiting to get in. I decided to try once more thinking I must know somebody. I pulled up behind the convention center and I noticed two guys who looked like they were working security. I went to a 7-11 store and changed into a pair of slacks, put a vest over my T-shirt, grabbed some soft drinks and a sandwich, and drove right up to the back door of the center. I got out of my car, put my goodies in my backpack, and headed straight for the door. As I got to the door I said to one of the guys, 'They don't let you smoke inside?' He said, 'No sir,' as he swung open the door and let me inside.

"I smiled to myself, thinking, 'I've still got it!' I was backstage and looking at what was to appear as quite a production. I could see someone adjusting some equipment, and I hollered, 'Hello,' and to my complete and utter surprise it was my old bass player, Leroy Stephens. Leroy was as surprised to see me as I was to see him, and, as we were saying our hellos, the production manager of the show, Brian, came on stage and Lee introduced me to him. He said he knew who I was. Just then I got another real surprise — coming up the stairs was none other than DJ Fontana, Elvis's original drummer, whom I hadn't seen in 31 years since he was playing with Ricky Saucedo at the Stardust Hotel & Casino in Las Vegas and I was at the Silver Slipper. DJ looked great, and Lee was beaming as DJ informed me they would be doing the 50's segment of the Elvis Ultimate

All the Elvis impersonators were wiggling and gyrating to the beat of the music, but they finally got it together for the *Viva Las Vegas* ending.

Show Band production. Leroy Stephens and DJ Fontana would be laying it down for the first part of the show. I congratulated DJ on his Induction into The Rock & Roll Hall of Fame along with Scotty Moore and Bill Black, and, then, as the rest of the musicians were arriving, I said to Leroy, 'Give me your pass, you're in the band.' He smiled from ear to ear and reminded me to give it back as he might need it later.

"I hadn't felt this much excitement in the air since I'd finished up my engagement at the Landmark Hotel in Las Vegas. The people were ready and waiting to be entertained by the magic that was Elvis Presley. The air seemed to be electric. Then Brian, the production manager, came over to me and said, 'Morris, bring back any memories?' I smiled and said, 'You have no idea.' Both of the previous contest-winning performers turned in excellent performances. I don't mean that there weren't a few hiccups, but all in all they had definitely done their homework. The young man doing the fifties and sixties segment stayed in the third person persona so as to not try to become Elvis. He has an excellent voice, but on his rendition of Elvis's version of *Surrender*, his voice totally cracked, he apologized to his audience and said he'd like to try it again. On his second take his voice crapped out again, but the audience loved him for trying, as they were Elvis fans. He'll learn, as I did after 3,224 straight performances, to make more use of his backup singers. Shawn Klush, the second Elvis performer, stayed in character though his whole performance of Elvis's show *Aloha from Hawaii* that he performed in its entirety. Excellent show! Someone should check his DNA. I was proud to be associated with the legions of Elvis fans around the world.

"That evening did bring back a flood of memories as I'm sure it did for everyone else. When I think back and wonder if I had not proceeded with my Elvis Tribute Show would I have lived the life I have lived? Would I have traveled the world and embraced it with the same zealous innocence? Would I have gained the insight into the same humanitarian views I dearly hold? I don't

Excellent show! Someone should check his DNA. I was proud to be associated with the legions of Elvis fans around the world.

really know, probably not. Has it made me a better man? I think so. I think everything happens for a reason and I am proud to have been an Elvis Impressionist for all those glorious years. I'm glad I followed my father's advice and took a chance on this life.

Hematite Stones

Morris Bates still loves music as much as he did before he retired from the stage, and, on rare occasions, he still performs. When he was invited a few years ago to stage a Christmas show at the Alkali Lake Reserve near Williams Lake, he decided to put a band together and rehearse them in the basement of his Maple Ridge home. He was coming full circle, back to the Cariboo country where he had been raised.

Morris was inspired by Elvis Presley to take a chance on life. His father, Pascal, taught Morris that he could do anything he put his mind to, and, even though the odds were heavily stacked against a Shuswap Indian kid from the Williams Lake Indian Band making it in the music business, let alone becoming one of the highest paid entertainers in Las Vegas, Morris overcame all obstacles and realized his dream. His five consecutive years on the Strip and his ten-year stint in the entertainment capital of the world, where he packed showrooms night after night, qualify Morris as the number one Elvis Impersonator of all time. However, it is his second career working with the Vancouver Police & Native Liaison Society as a youth counselor and victim assistance officer that makes his story unusual in the annals of show business biographies.

Morris overcame all obstacles and realized his dream.

"The transition I went through," Morris remarks, "from the time I first got into the music business until today has been an overwhelming experience. I witnessed the brutal in-your-face racism of South Africa, the beauty, discipline, and culture of Southeast Asia, extremes between wealth and poverty in South America. We still live in a world where people refer to each other in racial slurs and belittling acronyms that are meant to demean and dehumanize each other. However, the times they

'We still have our rocks!' they told me. They were just *'punkins'* and they all had their hematite stones.

are still a-changing. I grew up as a status Indian, a ward of the federal government, and graduated to being aboriginal, indigenous, and now — First Nations. I never believed that I would see the day the people of the United States of America would elect their first African American President, nor could I predict the optimism that this would bring to the whole world. The changes I have witnessed in my life have been unbelievably overwhelming."

Morris Bates continues to stage his Reality Check for Indigenous People program from time to time on the downtown eastside streets of Vancouver. His work as a native youth counselor is still in demand. One December afternoon, when Morris was shopping for Christmas presents in a London Drugs store in East Vancouver, he was greeted by five young people — they remembered Morris from the time that they had attended one of his Reality Check programs and he had given them a special piece of hematite.

"They were really excited," Morris recalls, "but at first I didn't know who they were. They recognized *me* and they were saying, 'Hi Morris, Merry Christmas!'"

"I said, 'Hello,' and they reached into their pockets almost simultaneously and pulled out their hematite stones. 'We still have our rocks!' they told me. They were just *'punkins'* and they all had their hematite stones. It was unreal. I gave away more than 8,000 of those rocks . . ." These kids were inspired by Morris Bates to take a chance on life. They are destined to beat the odds against them.

Morris in the ghetto

Top: Pascal Bates and his dog Badger — May they rest in peace. Bottom: Phyllis Bates — The best den mother ever

Above: Morris backstage with his proud mother. Bottom: DJ Fontana, Elvis Presley's drummer, meets Morris backstage at the Penticton Pacific Northwest Elvis Festival

Top: The late Alma Cunningham, Morris Bates' foremost fan and archivist. Bottom: Eileen Lafferty at the Commodore Ballroom: "Elvis lives in my basement."

References

Adhikari, Richard. "He's Elvis not just onstage." *Singapore New Nation*, November 14, 1977.

Anonymous. "Bachelors Three Open New Cabaret." *Williams Lake Tribune*, December 31, 1969.

Anonymous. "Bachelors Three Bow In." *Williams Lake Tribune*, January 2, 1970.

Anonymous. "Bates wins MVP, all-star, too." *Williams Lake Tribune*, March 22, 1969.

Anonymous. "Bates: the Pelvis is more streamlined." *MacLeans Magazine*, May 1982.

Anonymous. "Cultures Clash and Blend in Friendship." *Williams Lake Tribune*, March 4, 1970.

Anonymous. "Delgamuukw Decision Announced." Press release from Gitxsan Treaty Office, December 5, 1997.

Anonymous. "Elvis look-a-like is here." *Kuala Lampur Times*, November 1977.

Anonymous. "From Sugar Cane to Memphis with Morris 'Elvis' Bates."
Williams Lake Tribune, June 26, 1974.

Anonymous. "Just Like Elvis." *Waikiki Beach Press*, December 29, 1977.

Anonymous. "King Elvis On Stage." *Surabaya Times*, November 1977.

Anonymous. "It's a secret but Morris is a Smash." *Las Vegas Star*, June, 1978.

Anonymous. "Look-a-like Lisa fears for the future." *Durban Daily News*, July 31, 1979.

Anonymous. "Morris and Family." *Williams Lake Tribune*, December 28, 1976.

Anonymous. "Morris Bates the man who would be king." *Vancouver Sun*, August 1977.

Anonymous. "Morris back at the Slipper." *Backstage*, April 19, 1979.

Anonymous. "Morris Fits the Slipper." *Las Vegas Mirror*, April 28, 1978.

Anonymous. "Morris sets Brazil Tour." *Las Vegas Mirror*, May 15, 1981.

Anonymous. "Morris show salutes Elvis." *Las Vegas Review Journal (cover story)*, July 31, 1981.

Anonymous. "Morris: The Cat Who Lasted." *Los Angeles Herald Examiner (entertainment section cover story)*, April 6, 1981.

Anonymous. "Morris: The Legend Continues." *Viva Las Vegas (cover story)*, July 3, 1981.

Anonymous. "Morris well received by home fans." *Williams Lake Tribune*, July 5, 1979.

Anonymous. "Silver Slipper: Elvis Look-a-like Enjoys Success!" *Las Vegas Star*, December 1979.

Anonymous. "The Elvis Presley Story at the Landmark." *Las Vegas What's Happening Now (cover story)*, 1980.

Anonmyous. "The King is Back: Morris as Elvis." *Las Vegas Mirror*, April 28, 1978.

Bacchas, Lee. "Missing: one streak of Memphis meanness." *Vancouver Sun*, May 18, 1982.

Berk, Lynn. "Morris isn't Elvis but that's all right Mama." *Backstage*, October 1979.

Berry, Mick. "Don't miss 'Elvis'." *The Capetown Argus*, July 27, 1979.

Bowman, Pierre. "It's Elvis, Almost . . ." *Honolulu Star Bulletin*, December 30, 1977.

Brunt, Johnathan. "Elvis Sightings." *Spokane Spokesman Review*, August 20, 2007.

Cameron, Stevie. "The Big Fix." *Elm Street (Canada's Magazine of Substance & Style)*, April 2003.

Carrigg, David. "Hanging it up after 27 years. Vancouver cop patrolled downtown eastside since early 1990s." *Vancouver Province*, May 1, 2006.

Chapman, Aaron. "History of the Penthouse Nightclub." *Vancouver Courier*, February 6, 2008.

Coleman, Carl. "Elvis: a bit more than a memory." *The Cape Times*, July 1979.

Conway, Norma. "An Evening with Morris Bates." *Williams Lake Tribune*, June 3, 1976.

Cunningham, Alma. "Morris Fan Club Notes: Calling All Fans." *Williams Lake Tribune*, August 31, 1978.

Delaney, Larry. "Evan Kemp Obituary." *Country Music News*, March 3, 2008.

Denver, Bobby. "His majesty the king." *Music Maker*, July 20, 1979.

Dinoff, J.L. "Elvis Impersonators keep memory alive." *Las Vegas Review Journal*, July 16, 1978.

Duff, Cilla. "And the King was a cabbage." *Johannesburg Citizen*, July 9, 1979.

Edgar, Patti. "Trying to break the cycle of natives and the law." *Vancouver Sun*, May 17, 2003.

George, Chief Dan. "Lament for Confederation." Posted at *www.ammsa.com/buffalospirit/2003/footprints-dangeorge.html*.

Gregory, Sandra, producer. *Elvis Lives*, a BBC-TV documentary featuring Morris Bates, August, 1980.

Guyman, Suzie. "Morris Bates Has Best of Both Worlds as he pays tribute to Elvis Presley." *This Is Las Vegas (cover story)*, September 18, 1981.

Harada, Wayne. "Le Boom Boom club set for New Year's." *Honolulu Advertiser*, December 27, 1977.

Harada, Wayne. "Three Visions of Elvis." *Honolulu Advertiser*, January11, 1978.

Harrison, Tom. "Ladies Still Love The Way Morris Bates Does Elvis. *Vancouver Province*, May 19, 1982.

Hoffman, Neil. "Morris as Elvis: Thrilling his audiences at Vegas World." *Viva Las Vegas*, January 9, 1981.

Holloway, Marilynne. "Pelvis Power." *The Cape Times*, July 23, 1979.

Horning, Glynis. "Elvis look-a-like." *The Mercury*, August 3, 1979.

Jones, Gwynneth. "Morris Bates, the Cariboo's own Elvis." *Photo Museum of Cariboo Chilcotin Collection*.

Levett-Harding, Leslie. "Trying To Bridge That Gap: John De Kock," *The Cape Town Argus*, July 25, 1979.

MacIntosh, Susan. "A Tribute To Morris." *Yorkton News*, April 17, 1977.

Mackie, John. "Surviving on the strip: the Penthouse reaches 60." *Vancouver Sun*, September 29, 2007.

Mackie, John. "The Penthouse Cabaret on Seymour." *Vancouver Sun*, November 1, 2007.

McKeown, Kevin. "Morris wows screaming Elvis fans." *The Columbian*, March 13, 1979.

Montgomery, John. "Elvis show comes to South Africa." *Sunday Express*, July 8. 1979.

Moore, Scotty. Quote by DJ Fontana at *scottymoore.net/vegas56/html*

Morris Bates' testimony to the Standing Senate Committee on Aboriginal Peoples, March 19, 2003.

Palmer, Vaughn. "Will the real Elvis . . ." *Vancouver Sun*, 1977.

Paterson, M. "50's Revisited." *Spotlight*, June 1977.

Petten, Cheryl. "Footprints: Chief Dan George." *Windspeaker* web site writer at the Aboriginal Multi Media Society's web site: *www.ammsa.com*.

Read, Jeani. "Elvis impersonation one of the best around." *Vancouver Province*, January 23, 1978.

Shackelly, Darryl. "Prison circle or tales of abuse." *Vancouver Sun*, May 17, 2003.

Sin, Lena. "Elvis holds class at the heartbreak hotel." *Vancouver Province*, May 8, 2009.

Starling, Merry Lynn. "Morris uses memories, talent to do Elvis show." *Las Vegas Review Journal (cover story)*, July 31, 1981.

Stupak, Bob. "Yes, You Can Win!" Galaxy Publishing, Las Vegas, Nevada, 1992.

Wasserman, Jack. *"News To Me* daily column," *Vancouver Sun*, circa 1976.

Watson, Dave. "Vancouver Easter Be-In." *Georgia Straight*, May 8, 1977.

Wiggins, David. "Scared Straight in East Vancouver." *The Raven, the Aboriginal Newspaper of BC and the Yukon*, May 1999.

Wilson, Tony & Betty Jo Grande. "Morris as Elvis: a mans view, a woman's view." *Vegarama*, April 1979.

Wiwchar, David. "From a dream to success in one year." *The Raven, the Aboriginal Newspaper of BC and the Yukon*, 1999.

Woods, Sylvia. "Youth Editor Meets Morris." *UBCIC News*, April 1979.

If I Can Dream

Acknowledgments

Research for this book began with an archive of newspaper clippings and memorabilia fan club president Alma Cunningham had amassed and Morris discovered by serendipity. "When Alma passed away," Morris explains, "no one knew how to get hold of me. Someone contacted my cousin Gloria in Williams Lake and she hauled away two truckloads of boxes, taking them from Quesnel back to her home. I never did realize all the work Alma did for me. She was a promo machine from Hell. She had a fan club list that was unreal and from all over the world — from places I hadn't even played; she sent them birthday cards, Christmas cards, scarves, you name it. Over the years, quite a few people told me I should do a book. I toyed with the idea but never got around to it until I ran into my old drummer buddy Stephen Gibbons-Barrett and his book-writing pal, Jim Brown."

This archive was complemented by interviews with band members Scott Anderson and David Maitland. After Morris retired, Scott went on to play with Lisa Brokop and Jann Arden, while David toured with Vegas acts before returning to Portland. Nowadays, they are both producing sessions for aspiring young acts.

I also had the good fortune to meet Phyllis Bates, Morris's mother. Phyllis is a remarkably vital woman in her eighties, a fully independent resident of a native housing complex in East Vancouver. Morris's brother, BJ, called one night and provided some brotherly love. Lyle and Grace Bobb talked about their involvement in the extended family of Morris Bates' fans who became lifetime friends while attending his shows in Canada, Nevada, and Hawaii. Fellow musician Gordie Walker contributed a unique interview concerning his friendship with Morris. Grace Woo spoke of the days when she had befriended Morris while working on the downtown eastside.

In late June 2008, Lora Silvey phoned to tell me that her husband, Michael Silvey, had passed away. Michael was a friend and unofficial bodyguard to Morris during his celebrity days in Vegas. That same weekend, Gisele Yates (nee Kaufmann) called to tell Morris's story from a woman's point of view in charge of his light show. When Morris was working with the Native Liaison Society in Vancouver in the nineties, Gisele had been a civilian employee with Prince George detachment of the RCMP, but has since returned to Vegas and is now married to former bandmember Kenny Nelsen. Morris Bates' former manager Dennis Compo cleared up some of the aspects of Morris's career that had still been blurry when we were in our third draft. "Dennis was a fun guy to be around," Morris acknowledges. "We will always be friends." They are but a few of the many people who comprise Morris Bates' extended family.

My lifelong friendship with Stephen Gibbons-Barrett was crucial in understanding Morris's accomplishments and personality. Stephen played in Morris's band in the early years but left to resume his painting career as an abstract artist. Our project began in March 2008 when Morris and Stephen discovered that they were living less than two blocks from each other in the Fraser Valley.

But it was Morris himself who befriended me, trusted me, and revealed to me the challenges he met in his careers as an Elvis impersonator and a native youth counselor, and when Morris found a power spot on the banks of the Fraser River and began to contribute handwritten stories, our manuscript really began to hum on all cylinders. Morris is a great storyteller. His road and stage stories bring this book to life in ways reportage cannot. He still loves to entertain, even between the covers of a book. He is also an inspired counselor. When I attended one of his Reality Check for Indigenous People programs with northern youth and their elders, it was remarkable how he had successfully adapted his show business persona to motivating young people to take a chance on life.

Photography Credits

Marilyn Anderson
Morris Bates
Rebecca Blake
Blue Note Entertainment
Thomas R. Butler
CA Compo Cheung & Associates
D. Chercover
Franco Citarella
Jim Coenen
Alma Cunningham
Linda George
Stephen Gibbons-Barrett
Julia Graff
Terrence Haywood

Arlene Henderson
Tim Malito
Clarence Meisney
Jon Murray
Rose Nollette
Marie Nowak
James O'Mara
RD Enterprises
Denis Seguin
Dorothy Sneed
Southern Sun Hotels SA
Mrs. Spence Sutton
Dorothy Sneed
Lloyd Thomas